Trials and Triumphs

Trials and Triumphs

A Colorado Portrait of the Great Depression,
With FSA Photographs

Stephen J. Leonard

UNIVERSITY PRESS OF COLORADO

Published by the University Press of Colorado, P.O. Box 849, Niwot, Colorado 80544

The University Press of Colorado is a cooperative publishing enterprise supported, in part, by Adams State College, Colorado State University, Fort Louis College, Mesa State College, Metropolitan State College of Denver, University of Colorado, University of Northern Colorado, University of Southern Colorado, and Western State College of Colorado.

ISBN: 0-87081-311-0

Jacket photos: Arthur Rothstein, FSA, Library of Congress; Marion Post Wolcott, FSA, Library of Congress)

The paper used in this publication meets the minimum requirements of the American National Standard for Information Sciences—Permanence of Paper for Printed Library Materials. ANSI Z39.48–1984

∞

10 9 8 7 6 5 4 3 2 1

*To my parents, grandparents, and other relations, most of whom
survived the 1930s in Colorado:*

Josephine Halley Heimrich
Patrick Heimrich
Christian Krakow
George Krakow
Katherine Halley Krakow
Barbara Leonard
Mary Richards Leonard
Violet Krakow Leonard
William K. Leonard
Mary Krakow Murray
Anna Richards
Edward Richards
Ruth Richards

Contents

Preface

An ostrich named Alexander tried to kill Clyde Hill late in the night of Sunday, January 20, 1935. It was cold — 10 degrees below zero. Hill, the director of Denver's zoo, had entered the bird's enclosure to make certain that it had taken shelter. In the gloom Hill trudged toward what he thought was a large rock. Belatedly he realized it was Alexander. "With a squawk and a vicious kick," the bird attacked. Hill fled to a nearby hillock. Alexander laid siege. Three times Hill tried to escape. Three times he was driven back, to wait, to freeze. "I never saw so many stars in my life," Hill told the *Rocky Mountain News,* "as I sat there on top of that mountain, my teeth chattering like a trap drum." Finally Hill remembered his flashlight. By shining it in Alexander's eyes, he confused the big bird. Hill ran for the fence and scaled it. The ostrich bit the fence wire. "Tomorrow," said Hill, "we're going to fight it out with pistols."[1]

Hill's midnight misadventure gave newspaper readers cause to chuckle. They could also empathize. By 1935 Colorado, like the rest of the country, had been long besieged by the Great Depression, a monster uglier and more persistent than any ostrich. By 1935 Franklin Roosevelt's New Deal had taken more than three stabs at curing the economic breakdown; none had done the trick. If Hill could outwit an ostrich, why could not the nation escape the Depression?

The stock-market crash of 1929 did not trigger an immediate breakdown in Colorado, although miners soon suffered from reduced industrial spending. Plagued by low farm prices in 1931, Colorado recognized that it would not remain isolated from the national collapse. By 1932, as businesses and banks failed, some impoverished Coloradans marched off to Washington, D.C., to join other veterans demanding that bonuses promised them for World War I service be paid early. Others formed self-help cooperatives; a few turned to communism. In early 1934 an unruly group marched on the state Capitol, where, according to one account, they ousted the legislators and held "the first Communist meeting to be held under the dome of any state Capitol in the United States." But most swam in the political mainstream, electing the progressive Edward Prentiss Costigan to the U.S. Senate in 1930 and embracing Franklin D. Roosevelt in 1932.[2]

FDR's New Deal offered hope. The Federal Emergency Relief Administration once supported nearly a quarter of the state's people; the Civilian Conservation Corps put young men to work on thousands of outdoor projects including the building of Denver's Red Rocks Amphitheater. The Works Progress Administration at its peak employed more than 40,000 Coloradans. By backing the Colorado–Big Thompson project and the John Martin Dam, the federal government attempted to check drought and dust.

Through luck and skill Colorado grabbed far more than its share of the federal pie. By using Uncle Sam's money, the state built an infrastructure that undergirded its economic boom during and after World War II.

Having gotten back more than two dollars for each dollar they sent to Washington, D.C., Coloradans might have been expected to say thanks. Some did, many did not. A few supported the New Deal out of principle, some out of necessity. "I need to eat," said George Carlson, a landscape architect, when he asked John A. Carroll, one of Denver's leading Democrats, for a job. Many were ambivalent or mildly critical. Even the pro-Roosevelt *Lamar Daily News* complained, "For almost three years now many of our people have been practically maintained by various relief agencies. . . . We are still a proud people. We do not want a continuation of the dole, nor of work that is merely wasted work." Others were outright hostile. Edwin C. Johnson, Colorado's Democratic governor (1933–1937), declared in 1944, "As I see it, the New Deal has been the worst fraud ever perpetrated on the American people."[3]

The debates fueled by Roosevelt's economic experiments guaranteed lively politics. With the state's Republicans in eclipse between 1930 and 1938, liberals and conservatives fought within the Democratic party, the main event being the contest between U.S. senator Edward Costigan, an ardent New Dealer, and Edwin Johnson, known as "Big Ed." He was, said historian Robert G. Athearn, one of the "politically hairy chested." Tarzan, as always, won. Costigan's health broke in 1936, and Johnson took his Senate seat.[4]

Republicans reasserted themselves by 1938, although conservative Democrats such as Johnson, Alva B. Adams, and Lawrence Lewis survived for a time. By 1944 the state's political landscape looked much the same as it had 20 years earlier. In 1924 Colorado's newly elected governor, Clarence J. Morley, was a Republican, as were five of its six members of Congress. In 1944 its newly elected governor John C. Vivian was a Republican, as were five of its six members of Congress. From a superficial political standpoint those 20 years in Colorado's history look flatter than North Dakota.

In reality the era was far from featureless. Hard times brought drama as well as pain. Farmers faced three Ds: depression, drought, and dust, plus floods and grasshopper plagues. Migrant farm workers, many of them Hispanic, found their low standard of living further lowered. Johnson's blockade of the state in 1936 against the entry of "alien and indigent labor" was hailed by some as a way of cutting down on "Mexicans," a designation many non-Hispanic Coloradans applied both to U.S.-born Hispanos and to recent arrivals from Mexico.

The decade saw much ordinary unpleasantness: the bungled hanging of Eddie Ives (1930), the Towner bus tragedy (1931) in which five children froze to death, the kidnaping of Charles Boettcher II (1933), the death of Baby Doe Tabor (1935), the Green Mountain Dam strike (1939). The ledger also had a plus side: the creation of a modern highway network, the construction of hundreds of public buildings, the initiation of state old-age pensions, the installation of up-to-date sewage treatment systems, the advent of fast trains, the development of a fledgling ski industry, the football wizardry of Byron "Whizzer" White, the poetry of Thomas Hornsby Ferril.

When the Farm Security Administration dispatched photographers Arthur Rothstein, Russell Lee, Marion Post Wolcott, and John Vachon into Colorado in the late 1930s and early 1940s, they took upbeat pictures — hardly suggestive of a depressed people. War in Europe coupled with U.S. defense spending finally drove the Depression away. After it had fled, Coloradans chose to talk more of their victories than of their defeats. Being pinned down by an ostrich was no fun, but it was bearable if, in the end, one managed to climb the fence.

In *The Mythic West* (1986) Robert Athearn wrote of Westerners during the Depression:

> They chose to go on, gnawing at the hand that fed them, while alternating between vituperation and lamentations over the sad role of the enslaved. Defenders of these politically schizophrenic people explained that such attitudes arose from a defensiveness that was generated by the misfortunes of a normally hard-working, honest, independent people. In part, that was a rationalization of their disinclination to acknowledge any political debts to an administration that had bailed them out of deep trouble.[5]

Schizophrenia has led to amnesia. Today the New Deal is largely forgotten in Colorado. Perhaps, at the distance of more than half a century, it is possible to look back with some objectivity, to admit that both the liberals and the conservatives were right some of the time.

From trial came triumph. If gratitude was not one of Coloradans' priorities, at least survival was.

Stephen J. Leonard

Trials and Triumphs

ONE

The Year of Discontent: 1932

There is a possibility of destruction in various places in city [Denver],
attacks upon warehouses, plants, etc.

Agent 57 Report
January 22, 1931[1]

The devil baby, a horned and hoofed demon with a tail, supposedly
born in Denver in June 1932, could, it was whispered, talk at birth. A
peddler reputedly made the monster by bewitching an expectant mother
who refused to buy a good-luck charm. Nurses at Denver General Hospital
denied that they were holding the cursed child in a cage, charging visitors
25¢ a peek. Mothers-to-be showed up anyway, demanding to see the
creature. Priests in north Denver calmed pregnant parishioners while
doctors tried to quash the tale. Suspecting that greedy street-vendors
concocted the story to drum up business, Walter B. Lowry, Denver's acting
mayor, vowed to punish rumormongers: "Any person who is found to be
responsible for any part of this vicious thing will go to jail."[2]

Agent 57, a spy working for Colorado's National Guard, also believed
in devils. His Satans were adults bearing names — Haydee U. Zeitlin,
Dorothy Eil, William Dietrich, Michael Shantzek, Solomon J. Greenberg —
and belonging to organizations — the International Labor Defense League,
the Trades Union Unity League, the Agricultural Worker's Industrial
League, the International Workers of the World, the Communist party.
During 1931 and 1932 they rallied the unemployed, encouraged Hispanic
farm workers to strike, urged blacks to swim at an all-white beach in
Denver's Washington Park.

Attacking governments from Denver to Washington, D.C., they demanded relief and threatened to fight rather than starve. Greenberg and
Shantzek even passed out anti-war literature at Fort Logan's Citizens
Military Training Camp — pacificists called it the Citizens Monkey Training Camp — in violation of Colorado's anti-sedition law. The adjutant
general said that Greenberg was hurt as he tried to escape from an angry
group of military trainees. Or was he brutally beaten as he claimed? Agent
57 did not ponder such puzzles: "This question has ceased to be child's
play but has become a real menace."[3]

Mammon, that greedy devil, prowled in 1932, tempting bankers to
recoup their stock-market losses by dipping into other people's money.
With his accounts at Colorado Springs's City Savings Building and Loan
an estimated $1.2 million short, Walter C. Davis fled the state. Arrested in
New York, he hanged himself, a choice he apparently judged preferable to
facing thousands of angry depositors back home, some of whom had

talked of kidnaping his daughter to insure his return. Pueblo bankers suffered similar hostility when the Railway Savings and Building Association went broke, leaving 23,000 account holders unable to withdraw their money.[4]

Fiends even took animal form. Watered fowl, "two decidedly dead and ancient chickens," appeared in Denver's West Side Court, mute and soggy witnesses in the state's case against merchant Charles Jamison. He was charged with pumping the birds full of water to increase their weight and his profits. Eighty shaggy, horned, and bearded goats plagued Mrs. John Whisnand, a poor widow trying to sell her home in Colorado Springs. No one would buy it when they saw her neighbor's goats, so she wrote to Lieutenant Governor Edwin C. Johnson: "The stench is terrible. . . . when it begins to thaw and gets a little warmer I don't know what we will do." Unable to help her, Johnson responded in platitudes: "It seems as though trouble comes in bunches. They say that when it rains, it pours."[5]

Beginning in late 1929, trouble came in bunches: the stock-market crash, bank failures, drought, unemployment, unrest. Devils cropped up everywhere, some, like the goats and bankers, real; some, like the Communists, overblown; some, like the devil baby, unreal. Mired in the worst economic breakdown of the twentieth century, Coloradans looked for answers, imagined phantoms, and hunted witches.

Scapegoats were easy to find. In 1928 William H. "Billy" Adams had been elected Colorado's governor by an overwhelming majority, and Herbert Clark Hoover had swept the state in his bid for the presidency. Then *The Denver Post* lauded Adams for his wisdom and praised Hoover as the "Great Engineer." Yet, four years later the *Post* declared that Adams, "after nearly half a century of office holding and feeding at the public trough," should be put to pasture because of his "total lack of executive ability, his petty politics and the rank incompetency of his political appointees."[6]

Adams fell partly because he did not deliver the efficient, honest government he promised. Hoover's partisans once proclaimed Hoover a genius capable of controlling the juggernaut of the nation's government, economy, and society. Deified in 1928, he was damned in 1932. For many Coloradans the gulf between prosperity and depression was bounded by his presidency. As they lost the paradise of the 1920s, illusion though much of it was, many of them pinned a tail on Billy Adams and drew horns on Herbert Hoover. "He promised us chicken in every pot," Anna Carlson of Denver remembered. "All we got were the feathers."[7]

TWO

Farewell to the 1920s

He is the most interesting and best informed man in America to meet at close range and anybody who thinks or says that Herbert Clark Hoover is not a real, honest-to-goodness companionable fellow of the real western type is wet all over.

The Denver Post
November 4, 1928

Herbert Hoover's campaign train pulled into Pueblo's Union Station 10 minutes late at 6:30 P.M., November 3, 1928. "I never enter the borders of Colorado without a feeling of mental expansion," he told the crowd of 15,000 as he praised the state's "rarefied and bracing atmosphere." Blaming Democrats for the economic slump after World War I, he credited Republicans with restoring prosperity. He promised to keep good times rolling by maintaining high tariffs to protect the sugar beets Coloradans grew, the cattle they raised, the lead and zinc they mined. The band played, the crowd cheered, the train departed on time at 7:30 P.M. carrying the presidential candidate in his private car, "Sunset," homeward to vote in California.[1]

Grand Junction slept as the nine-car special slipped through before dawn on November 4. As much as western Colorado's Republicans missed shaking hands with their standard-bearer, they knew he did not need to hustle votes in Montrose, Durango, or Steamboat Springs. Folks in those towns sometimes elected homespun Democrats such as Governor William H. "Billy" Adams, an Alamosa rancher, or Congressman Edward T." I never play politics" Taylor, a Glenwood Springs lawyer. Generally, however, they voted Republican because they distrusted eastern, big city Democrats—the kind living in Denver and in faraway places such as New York City.[2]

Alfred E. Smith, the Democratic presidential nominee, was born and bred in New York City. He seemed to favor protective tariffs; so did Hoover. He said he cared about farmers; so did Hoover. Hoover backed Prohibition; Smith maddened temperance militants by arguing that their dry crusade had fizzled. Judging Smith all wet on Prohibition and wishy-washy on other issues, many voters also disliked his eastern ways, his Manhattan machine politics, his accent, his Irish ancestry, and his Catholicism.

The Ku Klux Klan, master of the state's Republican party in the mid 1920s, had lost most of its clout by 1928, but anti-Catholicism still possessed some voters. Yet, had Smith been a Baptist, Coloradans still would have chosen Hoover, a well-groomed and well-regarded advocate

Alfred E. Smith (1873–1944) at Denver's Union Station in late September 1928. Next to the hat-waving Smith is Governor William H. "Billy" Adams (1861–1954); next to Adams is George A. Collins (1877–1946), a leading Denver Democrat who managed Smith's western tour. (Colorado Historical Society)

of a status quo most thought worth preserving. The state's most widely read newspaper, *The Denver Post,* praised Hoover: "Never was there a more charming man." The *Colorado Springs Gazette* lauded his "education, experience, and training." In Trinidad, the Las Animas County seat, the *Chronicle-News* touted him as a friend to the coal industry, although it admitted local miners backed Smith.[3]

Miners helped Smith carry Las Animas and adjacent Huerfano County. Three other southern counties, Conejos and Costilla, swayed by Hispanic Catholics, and Mineral, so small it hardly mattered, also favored the "Happy Warrior." The rest of the state gave Hoover a landslide 253,872-to-133,131 victory. In La Junta a Smith partisan settled her unwise election bet by pushing a peanut around the courthouse square with a crooked toothpick attached to a yardstick — a 55-minute chore. Her discomfort was mild compared to that of the Democratic party. Republicans won three of Colorado's four seats in the U.S. House of Representatives, leaving Edward Taylor of Glenwood Springs the lone Democratic survivor. Colorado's General Assembly remained Republican, and the Grand Old Party almost made a grand slam in filling state executive offices. Only the jackpot of the governorship eluded them.[4]

William Adams, commonly known as Billy Adams, survived the Republican onslaught. A conservative Democrat first elected governor on an anti-Klan ticket in 1926, he campaigned quietly in 1928, spending pre-election days rounding up his cattle — a ploy that appealed to the voters' distrust of politicians. His personal triumph did little for the Democratic party, split between liberals, who favored government regulation of big business, and conservatives, who did not. Lee Taylor Casey of the *Rocky Mountain News* predicted that as long as good times lasted, "the Republican party in all probability will remain in power whether it behaves itself especially well or not."[5]

Good times eluded much of Colorado in the 1920s as the prosperity sparked by World War I gave way to post-war recession and stagnation. Between 1920 and 1930 the state grew by 10 percent to reach 1,035,791, an increase lower than the national growth rate — the first time since the 1860s that Colorado had fallen behind the rest of the country. Denver, the state's most populous city, with 287,861 residents, ranked twenty-ninth nationally. Pueblo took second place in Colorado, with 50,096, trailed by Colorado Springs, with 33,237. Greeley, with only 12,203, claimed the number-four slot, followed by Trinidad (11,732), Fort Collins (11,489), Boulder (11,223), and Grand Junction (10,247). Roughly half the state's citizens lived on farms or in towns with fewer than 5,000 people.

As the decade ended, it appeared the whimpering twenties would go out with at least a muted roar. The state's 1928 assessed valuation exceeded $1.5 billion, $12 million more than in 1927. One million more sheep grazed in its pastures or fattened in its feedlots in 1928 than a year earlier, and one million more trout swam in its hatcheries. Automobile registrations, heralds of Coloradans' love of cars, rose by 13,000 between 1927 and 1928 to a total of 259,948. To supply motorists with gasoline, the state's oil wells yielded a record 2.75 million barrels in 1928. Early in 1929, Denver financier Claude K. Boettcher predicted "a lengthy period of continued good times."[6]

Boettcher had reason for his cheer. Agriculture, manufacturing, and mining provided economic diversity Colorado had lacked in its formative years when mining had dominated. Once the domain of gold and silver kings, the state celebrated new heroes after 1900, including Claude Boettcher's father, Charles, who helped build the sugar-beet industry. At the January 1929 San Luis Valley Stock Show held in Monte Vista, promoters put up tents to house overflow exhibits and braced themselves to feed big eaters at the hog-growers' banquet. The show's success foreshadowed

First elected to the U.S. House of Representatives in 1909, Edward T. Taylor (1858–1941) served until his death. "They make 'em tough out in the Rockies," he told his congressional colleagues. (Colorado Historical Society)

a bountiful year for local farmers, whose dogged devotion to potatoes, particularly Brown Beauties, yielded five million bushels in 1929. Among potato potentates that year, L. E. Schutte of Monte Vista won special status by growing more than 30 tons on one acre, making him the U.S. spud king.[7]

Sugar-beet growers also prospered. Their harvest, more valuable than any other Colorado crop save hay, fetched in excess of $18 million — almost a third of the nation's sugar-beet total. In 1929 nearly one in every five cauliflowers grown in the United States, one in six cantaloupes, goodly crops of lettuce, cabbage, celery, cucumbers, onions, peaches, pears, and an imponderable number of beans poured from Colorado's cornucopia to fill wagons, freight cars, and local fairs. Kremmling's 1929 Middle Park Fair boasted a 10-pound rutabaga. Montrose's Western Slope Fair gave farmers a taste of the future by providing airplane rides. In Pueblo the state fair drew an estimated 50,000 to break previous attendance records.[8]

Pueblo's Colorado Fuel and Iron Company (CF&I), the nation's largest steel plant west of Chicago, posted a profitable 1929, prompting directors to budget $1 million for 42 additional coke ovens. Boosters cited the rising value of manufactured products in the 1920s as proof of industrial prowess, but data from 1925 showed the state ranked thirty-third nationally, with much of its industry — the making of sugar, pickles, ketchup, and butter, the slaughtering of pigs, sheep, and cattle — dependent on agriculture and ranching. If agriculture faltered, so would manufacturing, and so would Colorado.[9]

Mining, after agriculture and manufacturing the third mainstay of the economy, did not fare as well. Throughout the 1920s the output of most

metals and of coal fell. Plagued by deteriorating rail service and without good highways to bring tourists, tattered bonanza towns staggered toward oblivion. In 1930, Aspen counted only 705 residents, Cripple Creek, 1,427. Near Leadville, Elizabeth Tabor, popularly known as Baby Doe, the impoverished widow of silver king Horace A. W. Tabor, held on to her shack at the Matchless mine while the town of 3,771 watched its citizens move away or die.

Optimists could overlook the negatives by concentrating on the progress they had made. Durango's city manager William H. Wigglesworth recalled seeing the first stagecoach to reach that southwestern Colorado community, the first train to serve it, the first automobile to chug along its streets, the first airplane to soar in its skies. Many people over 50 in 1929 remembered the advent of electric lights and telephones. Those over 40 had witnessed the coming of automobiles, motion pictures, X rays, and airplanes. By mid-1929 some residents of Pueblo, Colorado Springs, and Denver were cooking and heating with clean-burning natural gas, thanks

Colorado Fuel and Iron Company's giant works in Pueblo produced 600,000 tons of steel in 1929–1930. (Pueblo Library District)

to the 1928 completion of a pipeline from Amarillo, Texas. No commercial radio stations broadcast in the state in 1919; by late 1928 there were 17, including 8 in or near Denver, 3 in Pueblo, and 1 each in Colorado Springs, Fort Morgan, Greeley, Gunnison, and Yuma.[10]

Partisans of the good old days sometimes wondered if all the changes were for the best. The *Julesburg Grit-Advocate* reflected on a bygone era when it reported in 1928 that an errant buffalo herd had blocked a railroad train near Sterling. The *Steamboat Pilot* bemoaned the replacement of the city's gray workhorses with a tractor. Guardians of goodness in Boulder and Monte Vista opposed showing movies on Sunday. And the citizens of Buena Vista, one suspects, respected the old-fashioned directness of Howard K. Frey, the Chaffee County treasurer, who, when advised to get a lawyer to defend him against embezzlement charges, responded, "No, by God, I am guilty, guilty as hell."[11]

Frey's means of enrichment were unorthodox; his fondness for money was not. Many hoped to get rich, and a few did. Nearly 150 Coloradans made more than $30,000 in 1926, a princely sum in an era when potatoes sold for 3¢ a pound, dilapidated Fords for $20, and a snug bungalow in south Denver for $5,750. That year one Coloradan reported an income greater than $1 million; two made between $500,000 and $750,000. The *Rocky Mountain News* speculated that U.S. Senator Lawrence C. Phipps, once a partner of the steel magnate Andrew Carnegie, held the number-one slot, with the heirs of Pueblo banker Mahlon Thatcher and Denver oilman Verner Z. Reed taking second and third places. Colorado Springs may have taken umbrage at the *News* assessment, for the Pikes Peak town claimed Spencer Penrose, whose copper holdings sometimes brought him an annual income of $1 million.[12]

Even if the guesses were correct, income was only one measure of wealth. Charles and Claude Boettcher often plowed profits back into their ventures. What was Louise S. Hill, the doyenne of Denver society, worth? Her great mansion on Capitol Hill and her trips to Europe hinted that she still clung to part of the fortune made by her father-in-law, the smelter king Nathaniel P. Hill. Rumor also shouted that Frederick G. Bonfils, publisher of *The Denver Post*, had stacked up money to match the Rockies.

"Hoover Victory Means Boom to Denver as Stocks Climb," proclaimed the *Rocky Mountain News* in 1928, and it reported a "Huge Total in Dividends Will Be Paid in the City." To toast great times, Denver socialites staged a "Hard Times Party," a fete in which the upper crust dressed like the lower class in hopes of winning a $500 costume prize. The spoof probably sat poorly with 220 striking employees of the Michael Heller Tailoring Company in Denver who were struggling to live on an average salary of $5 a week. Hispanic migrant workers picking sugar beets north of Denver, making, when they had work, around $3 for a 10-hour day, also knew the reality of poverty.[13]

Neither the poor nor the rich worried about high taxes. The state levied no income tax, and the federal government in 1929 collected only

$3.5 million in income tax from individual Coloradans, less than 5 percent of whom filed returns. Property taxes provided the bulk of local revenue, much of it for schools.[14]

State gasoline taxes, which rose from 1¢ a gallon in 1919, when they were first imposed, to 4¢ in 1929, yielded more than $5 million in the latter year to build and maintain highways, a sum easily swallowed by the state's harsh climate, rough terrain, and overall vastness. A few cities boasted asphalted streets, but only Grand Junction, among towns larger than 5,000, reported more than a quarter of its streets hard-surfaced. With the exception of a few hundred miles of highway, mainly along the Front Range, pavement vanished at city limits, condemning motorists to rough rides along rutted roads. Railroads, although effectively linking Front Range cities, served western Colorado less well. Nearly 700 miles of track separated Grand Junction from Craig, although the towns were only 115 air miles apart, and people wishing to travel from Grand Junction to Denver faced a 424-mile train trip.[15]

Spencer Penrose (1865–1939) made money from Cripple Creek gold and Utah copper. He spent part of it on Colorado Springs's Broadmoor Hotel and the Cheyenne Mountain Zoo. (Local History Collection, Pikes Peak Library District)

Denver's Cullen-Thompson Motor Company, a Chrysler dealership at Tenth Avenue and Broadway, reflected the opulence of the 1920s. (Colorado Historical Society)

Coloradans were willing to pay for highways. Prisons were different. The Cañon City penitentiary jammed 1,037 men and 24 women into buildings designed to house 558. Lucky convicts got single cells four feet wide; others doubled in four-foot-six-inch cells. Discipline by torture and no hope of mercy — Governor Adams granted neither pardons nor paroles — left inmates angry and violent. The prison exploded during the afternoon of October 3, 1929, when Danny Daniels and four confederates seized 11 guards, threatening to kill them if warden Eugene F. Crawford did not provide a getaway car. When Crawford refused, Daniels murdered seven of his hostages, including hangman Jack Elles. Although chaplain Patrick O'Neil, a Benedictine priest, failed to dislodge the crazed men with a dynamite blast, Daniels, seeing no hope of escape, shot his companions and then killed himself.[16]

The insurrection, which left 12 dead and parts of the penitentiary in ruins, commanded newspaper headlines in early October. By mid-month, editors had shifted their attention to the Lamar trial of three members of the Fleagle gang, bank robbers and murderers. In Durango the *Herald-*

Democrat focused on happier news, the October 13 festivities opening the town's municipal airport, an event mildly marred by the crash, without fatalities, of a stunt-flying Douglas plane. Denver also dedicated its municipal airport in October. Fifty thousand watched Governor Adams light the buildings and runways on the evening of October 18. Tens of thousands came the next day to see the largest aircraft to visit the city — an 11-passenger Boeing biplane. To demonstrate precision flying, pilots competed in destroying balloons. To show army air power, bomber crews dropped explosives on a giant cardboard village, destroying it quickly.[17]

As dreams of flying machines inebriated Denverites in October, simultaneous reports of a nosedive on Wall Street sobered them. During the 1920s high-flying speculators borrowed to buy stocks, using their shares as collateral to borrow more. As long as the "Hoover Market" shot up, investors avoided repaying their margin loans because their assets exceeded their debts. When prices declined, lenders demanded their money and popped the speculative balloons. Rising through August of 1929, the market slowly deflated in September, leading to a substantial shrinkage on October 3, up to then the year's worst decline. Prices briefly rose. Then on Friday, October 18, 1929, the day Denver turned on its airport lights, the market plunged. Monday, October 21, was no better; Tuesday saw a rally, but on Wednesday the rout worsened, and Thursday trading erased more than $1 billion in value. On Tuesday, October 29, panic selling and record volume torpedoed the market, resulting in a $16 billion loss. Cities Service, a utility holding company widely held in Colorado, where it controlled the Public Service Company, dropped $18 a share on October 28 and $5 more the next day, when it closed at $22.50, nearly $46 less than its pre-crash high. CF&I, a $68 stock on August 7, stood at $35.25 on October 29.[18]

"Small Traders Are Wiped Out in Stock Crash," the *Rocky Mountain News* reported. Distraught investors in Colorado Springs besieged brokers with telephone calls or rushed to their offices. Denver speculators jammed brokerages on Seventeenth Street, the self-proclaimed "Wall Street of the West," to watch clerks chalk up disaster on big blackboards. E. Warren Willard of Boettcher and Company recalled the pandemonium as Claude Boettcher's friends who had borrowed money to buy stock begged, "Don't sell me out, don't sell me out!" Boettcher turned the dirty work over to his partner, James Q. Newton. "Jim Newton said, 'The best thing we can do for you, . . . we're going to sell you out right now.' " Responding quickly to the crisis, Willard ordered Boettcher's salesmen to start tracing securities. "It took two years for some people to find out where their securities were, but we protected all of them."[19]

Ordinary people read of Seventeenth Street's woes and marveled at Senator Lawrence Phipps's reputed loss of $4 million. But Phipps's fickle fortune meant little to most of them. They had no idle dollars to risk, they received no dividends from U.S. Steel, and their only financial tie to Cities Service came when they paid their electric bill. Echoing the thinking of non-investors, the Grand Junction *Daily Sentinel* suggested the debacle

Dedicated in 1929, Denver's Munici- pal Airport, renamed Stapleton in 1944, was a small-scale operation in 1934. (Colorado Historical Society)

would "teach people a lesson. . . . The smug complacency that has charac- terized some local wise-acres, who believed that they would just keep riding to glory on a certain speculative stock or two, has been nothing short of amusing."[20]

The Trinidad *Chronicle-News* blamed the debacle on speed: "Folks everywhere and in all ways are traveling too fast." The *Durango Herald- Democrat,* thankful that folks in the San Juan basin did not fancy playboy speculations, maintained that "no bread and meat fundamentals have been touched." Denver's dailies also minimized the crash, stressing what they said was a sound underlying economy. Far from the conventional wisdom of the capital city, Charles H. Leckenby's *Steamboat Pilot* saw the breakdown more clearly: "It gave a shock to business which will be felt in every corner of the land."[21]

The *Pilot* knew Colorado depended on its exports. Leadville's zinc and molybdenum miners, Routt County's ranchers, Denver's meat packers,

Eaton's sugar processors, and Pueblo's steel workers produced for a national market. Little of the state's agricultural bounty and only a small fraction of its mineral output stayed at home. If demand for sugar or silver slackened, if prices for potatoes or lead fell, Colorado would suffer.

The crash alone did not cause the Depression. The shock simply worsened economic ills that were poorly understood then and that, despite the musings of economists, have not yet been adequately explained. Few people even partially understood the complexities of banking, the dangers of speculation, the pitfalls of an unregulated securities industry, the intricacies of international trade. Senator Phipps believed in high tariffs, and most Coloradans agreed. They did not see that protective tariffs raised prices for consumers and that trade barriers kept other countries from selling in the United States, depriving them of the money they needed to purchase U.S. exports. Nor could Colorado count on the domestic market to absorb the bounty of its farms, factories, and mines. Rich men like Spencer Penrose and Lawrence Phipps could afford lots of potatoes, but

Petertown, a community of "junkers" who roamed Denver's alleys looking for discarded treasures, demonstrated that the "roaring twenties" did not roar for everyone. Divided into two clusters of shacks, one at Sixteenth Avenue and Bryant Street, the other at Nineteenth and Bryant (location of above home in 1927), the bachelor enclave, founded in 1873, continued to flourish in the 1930s. (Colorado Historical Society)

neither could choke down spuds by the million. Seamstresses making $5 a week and prison guards earning $105 a month could have eaten as much, or more, than Phipps or Penrose. They just did not have the money to do so. Like a jerry-built house, the economy tottered.

Ignorant of the impending hurricane, Coloradans went about their business late in 1929. Cañon City celebrated the completion of the Royal Gorge Bridge. Boosters in Pueblo pointed to the Whitman Hotel and the Railway Savings building to prove theirs was a wide-awake city. Shoppers in La Junta enjoyed their new Montgomery Ward store. Would-be movie stars in Colorado Springs awaited the arrival of Alexander Film Company's studios, which planned to relocate from Hollywood.[22]

The *Montrose Daily Press* delighted in Western Slope Motorways's new bus, "perhaps the classiest thing in its line that has ever shown up here," a 15-passenger, blue-and-orange Cadillac with wicker seats, curtained windows, and hydraulic brakes so powerful they nearly threw a passenger through the windshield. With the "Great Engineer," Herbert Hoover, in the White House, with frugal Billy Adams in the governor's chair, most Coloradans confidently looked forward to the 1930s, unaware that the crash had put the brakes on the economy.[23]

Good-Bye to Good Times: 1930–1932

Left a widow without means, I have raised and educated a fine clean boy of nineteen without asking help of any one until now. Within the last three years — a bank failure — a motor accident — long severe illness of my son, and this thing called depression. Now we are really quite hungry.

> Jenette Beresford to Charles Boettcher, May 12, 1932[1]

New Year's merrymakers in Colorado Springs greeted 1930 at a Broadmoor Hotel dinner-dance, while atop nearby Pikes Peak the AdAmAn Club set off fireworks, a tradition dimmed that night by clouds shrouding the mountain. The *Pueblo Chieftain* remembered 1929 as a "near record" year and predicted that 1930 would be even better. Claude Boettcher celebrated New Year's Eve at home in Denver with 75 guests. After giving the women expensive party favors — stylish hats and ivory-clad mirrors — he doused the lights at midnight so all could watch artificial silver rain sprinkle on his mansion grounds — a glittering harbinger, they no doubt hoped, of a prosperous decade.[2]

For a while it seemed that Colorado would escape the brunt of the ill economic winds raking the East, and, in a dry summer, searing the Midwest. Tourists, many fleeing Kansas and Nebraska heat, headed for the cool Rockies in 1930, with more than a quarter million visiting Colorado's premier attraction, Rocky Mountain National Park. Most came by auto or by train, but improved air service made it easier for a few to fly. In 1929 only the Western Air Express regularly served the state, taking mail and passengers between Cheyenne, Denver, Colorado Springs, and Pueblo. During 1930 Denver installed night-lights at its new landing field, and 20 other towns dedicated airports; by the end of the year three companies gave Coloradans connections to distant places such as Kansas City and Dallas.[3]

Stay-at-home Denverites watched their $4.5 million City and County Building take shape and sidewalk-supervised construction of the marble-faced federal customshouse at Nineteenth and California. For their entertainment there were new theaters: the Mayan on South Broadway and the Paramount, a $1.25-million Art Deco fantasy on Sixteenth Street. North of the city, Continental Oil's refinery got cracking, as did another million-dollar venture, the Ralston Purina Mills at Forty-sixth Avenue and York Street. In Pueblo, Colorado Fuel and Iron won a Chilean rail contract for

Three generations of Boettchers in 1920. Left is Claude K. (1875–1957), center is Charles I (1852–1948), right is Charles II (1901–1963). E. Warren Willard, a family friend, recalled that Charles and Claude were so close that "Charlie [Charles II] never really got close to them." (Denver Public Library, Western History Department)

$250,000. North of Fort Morgan a lucky strike brought in a 400-barrel-per-day oil well.[4]

A little good news did not fool astute observers. Plunging metals prices — silver, above $1 an ounce in 1920, below 40¢ in 1930; copper down by a third in a year, and lead by a half — told Coloradans that they, too, would suffer from the national slowdown.[5]

Leadville, once Colorado's Golconda, quickly felt the impact. Fearful that the Colorado and Southern Railroad (C&S) would stop serving the Cloud City, officials asked Denver in January 1930 to use South Park granite for its City and County Building so C&S could get the freight revenue. Denver refused. Five men died in a cave-in at the Climax mine

in June, a tragedy blamed on the molybdenum company. Unable to survive as a theater, Leadville's Princess degenerated into an indoor miniature-golf course while the Clarendon Hotel courted an ignoble future as a garage. Other white elephants fell to wreckers — the Armory, the St. James Hotel, the Harris Block. Clouds momentarily lifted in late July as Baby Doe Tabor and her brother Philip McCourt reopened the Matchless mine, but soon their workers quit and sued for back pay. On the meager plus side of the ledger, the town posted the advent of talking pictures, the first titled, *Chasing Rainbows.*[6]

Many mountain towns had futilely pursued an elusive rainbow since the mid-1890s — the hope that silver would be favorably linked to gold as a standard of value. In Breckenridge the *Summit County Journal* championed silver: "The paper bills are short lived; they carry germs and disease." In Denver, Frank Cannon, head of the National Bimetallic Association, and the octogenarian former senator Charles S. Thomas made silver a religion. "There are some things," Thomas insisted, "which

Elizabeth "Baby Doe" Tabor (1854–1935) at Matchless mine. Baby Doe hung on to the Matchless, perhaps out of sentiment, perhaps because she had no better place to go. (Colorado Historical Society)

do not admit of compromise. The law of gravity, mathematics, and bimetallism are among them." Leadville liked such rhetoric. So did Aspen, which, with its silver mines shut by late 1930, asked the state to hire idle miners for road work.[7]

Hard-rock miners were not alone in their distress. Coal companies, hobbled by slackening industrial demand and competition from natural gas, slashed thousands of jobs in the 1920s and continued cutting in 1930. In the heart of southern Colorado's coal fields the Trinidad *Chronicle-News* minimized Las Animas County's ills by celebrating the area's 50,000 acres of pinto beans. Bean consumption, the paper proclaimed, soared in hard times because beans were cheap and so tasty that U.S. senators ate bean soup.[8]

Beans could not save Trinidad, where, by September 1930, residents and transients were begging the Red Cross for help. The *Chronicle-News* reported on the dispossessed, including "weary and bedraggled young girls and middle-aged and even elderly women. . . . some carry light packs, others heavy packs, some carry suit cases or grips." Tumbling off freight cars, sometimes hitchhiking, occasionally coming by car, the "box car tourists" and "gasoline hoboes" asked for "gasoline and oil and clothing and food and other things." In a candid moment the *Chronicle-News* admitted in November 1930, "These are not normal times."[9]

Farmers, temporarily spared the drought that killed corn and wheat in the Midwest, had a mixed year in 1930. Wheat and potato growers saw prices rise. Sugar-beet producers pulled up lumpy vegetables worth $10 million more in 1930 than in 1929. Yet, farmers' total cash income declined 14 percent. Colorado's companies, many dependent on agriculture and mining, also staggered. Some 3,000 corporations reported profits to the Internal Revenue Service in 1930, but their nets were 40 percent lower than in 1929. Thousands of unprofitable firms, including many food processors, registered losses of more than $28 million.

The *Julesburg Grit-Advocate* in October 1930 assured its readers, "Times have been better here than in practically any other section of the nation." That was true largely because times were so bad elsewhere. Some midwestern states saw the value of their farm products cut in half; nationally the decline was 30 percent. Manufacturing slowed; unemployment rose. In Washington, D.C., Herbert Hoover preached confidence and government economy. In Denver, Billy Adams cited the same scripture. Seemingly without solutions, they soon found themselves challenged by men and women offering answers.[10]

Edward Prentiss Costigan, a gentle Galahad, was ready to do battle. Fifty-six years old in 1930, he looked back on a distinguished reform career. A quarter century earlier he had fought the corporation-backed, political machine of Denver's mayor Robert W. Speer. As leader of the state's Progressive Republicans, Costigan unsuccessfully ran for governor in 1912 and 1914, suffering in the latter campaign for his defense of striking coal miners. Having endorsed Woodrow Wilson for president in 1916, he

Mabel (1873–1951) and Edward (1874–1939) Costigan at their Denver home (1642 Detroit Street), which they shared with Josephine Roche. (Photo by Harry Rhoads, Denver Public Library, Western History Department)

merited a political plum — appointment to the U.S. Tariff Commission. Anxious to give consumers the benefit of low tariffs, he warred with other commissioners, most of whom supported high tariffs. Blasting protectionists, "a united tariff band . . . reckless on occasions of facts and the law," he resigned in 1928 and returned to Colorado to become counsel for the Rocky Mountain Fuel Company.[11]

Josephine A. Roche, daughter of the founder of Rocky Mountain Fuel, took charge of the company, the state's second largest coal producer, in 1928. With degrees from Vassar and Columbia, and with wide experience in social work including a stint as a probation officer for Benjamin Barr Lindsey, Denver's juvenile judge, Roche differed from other mine owners.

They disliked paying high wages; Roche rewarded her workers. They hated unions; Roche encouraged miners to unionize, and she made John R. Lawson, a United Mine Workers organizer, vice president of Rocky Mountain Fuel. "Capital and labor," she declared, "have equal rights." When Oscar Chapman, another of Lindsey's former probation officers, pressured Costigan to run for the U.S. Senate in 1930, Roche enthusiastically seconded the nomination as did Mabel Cory, Costigan's activist wife.[12]

Costigan's friends sensed victory in 1930 partly because Republican senator Lawrence C. Phipps decided to retire that year, a move *Time* attributed to his awareness of "rising hostility" in Colorado. He hoped to bequeath his senatorship to William V. Hodges, but Hodges was beaten in the Republican primary by George H. Shaw, like Hodges a well-heeled attorney. Costigan faced a Democratic primary, his most formidable opponent being Morrison Shafroth, son of John F. Shafroth, once the state's governor and once a U.S. senator.[13]

The Shafroth halo did not stop Denver's young Democrats — including Chapman, John A. Carroll, and Charles F. Brannan — who captured the city's Democratic party for Costigan. He also counted on support from labor leaders, including former Colorado congressman Edward Keating, editor of *Labor*, a rail union newspaper, who with his union brothers carpeted the state with Costigan propaganda. From Leadville one of Shafroth's backers reported, "Literature, compared only to Montgomery Ward catalogues in volume has verily flooded the county."[14]

Costigan trounced Shafroth in September and smashed Shaw in November to become the first Democrat from Colorado elected to a full term in the U.S. Senate since 1912. He thanked Keating for the triumph, saluting him as "Dear King-Maker," and he recognized the value of his Young Turks in Denver, many of whom would reap rewards for their service. His victory also rested on Republican disunity, on Shaw's inept remark that farmers could get along with wheat at 50¢ a bushel, and on the faltering state economy. By November 1930, Coloradans worried increasingly about the low prices of coal, lead, and silver and about unemployment — the issue Costigan put first in his platform. Two years before Franklin Delano Roosevelt popularized the term, Costigan promised voters "a new deal."[15]

He pled for federal aid to the unemployed in his first major Senate speech, a masterful oration spanning four days, which Washington columnist Robert G. Allen judged "one of the most beautiful and telling I have ever heard." The Senate, less moved, rejected Costigan's call for grants to states for relief. Lawmakers also scotched his plan to make small federal loans to needy citizens. Instead, Congress in 1932 approved Herbert Hoover's Reconstruction Finance Corporation (RFC) to lend millions to corporations and banks, an approach Costigan castigated as "billions for big business, but no mercy for mankind."[16]

Difficult for miners and disappointing to farmers, 1930 was neverthe-less a tolerable year for many Coloradans, who, though they retreated from Hooverism by electing Costigan, still tilted toward conservatism by giving Billy Adams a third term and re-electing three incumbent Republican congressmen — William R. Eaton, Charles B. Timberlake, and Guy U. Hardy — as well as the conservative Democrat, Edward T. Taylor. The state had escaped the drought and had not endured as much industrial distress as the rest of the nation primarily because it had less industry than other parts of the country.

Not until 1931 did Colorado seriously suffer from the Depression; by 1932 it was deeply mired in the morass. *The Denver Post* daily reminded its readers, " 'Tis a privilege to live in Colorado." The *Steamboat Pilot* bragged, "Northwestern Colorado — The Most Prosperous Section of the United States — Still Is The Land of Opportunity — Tell Your Friends about It." Such blatant Babbitry reminded the attorney Thurman Arnold of "a prayer meeting held to bolster up the wavering faith of a congregation sorely troubled by doubt." It may have gulled the gullible, but the facts belied it.[17]

The value of Colorado's industrial products slid from more than $306 million in 1929 to less than $184 million in 1931. Farmers, hit by drought, crop failures, and low prices, earned under $82 million in 1932, a paltry sum compared to the nearly $213 million they had gotten in 1929. The giant sugar processor Great Western Sugar Company lost almost $500,000 in 1931; in 1932 its deficit exceeded $1 million. Less reputable entrepreneurs also found themselves squeezed. Investigating bootleggers in mid-1932, the *Rocky Mountain News* reported that retailers were "engaged in ruthless price cutting" leading to "prices at the lowest levels since prohibition came into effect. . . . the depression has hit the bootleg business worse than any other business."[18]

Some numbers went up, pointing to an economy going down. People used more butter and less margarine as the price of butter fell. And as their finances worsened, they killed themselves more readily, raising the num-ber of suicides from 168 in 1929 to 257 in 1932, one of the dramatic exits that year being made by Alfred Johnson, a sawmill worker who, depressed by the Depression, disposed of himself by dynamite.[19]

The Colorado State Federation of Labor reported in December 1930 that up to 90 percent of its members were working three days or fewer per week and that 50 percent "or more are not working even part time." In Denver, the Federation guessed, 20,000 were idle. In Colorado Springs, Mayor George Birdsall woke up to local unemployment in mid-January 1931 when 500 men marched on city hall to demand relief. Estimates made in mid-1932 put the number of unemployed Coloradans at 65,000, more than 16 percent of the state's workers.[20]

Unemployment was only part of the trouble. To cut costs, businesses cut salaries. Finding that it would have to reduce its overhead or go broke, the Broadmoor Hotel in 1931 asked the Colorado Industrial Commission

When Colorado Springs abandoned its street railway system in 1932, Pueblo bought the old cars. (Local History Collection, Pikes Peak Library District)

for permission to lower wages, a pill it sweetened for some by reducing low-paid workers less than high-paid managers. Belt-tightening failed, and the hotel went bankrupt in August 1932.[21]

A reorganized Broadmoor survived; other businesses died. Creede's newspaper, the *Creede Candle,* went out late in 1931. Grand Junction's buses stopped running. Colorado Springs's Interurban Railway Company's trolley cars ceased operating on May 1, 1932, replaced the next day by 18 buses. Station KVOR broadcast the ceremony as Mayor Birdsall launched the small white fleet by splashing one bus with Manitou mineral water. "Colorado Springs, situated at an altitude of 6,036 feet, will have the distinction of having the highest bus system in America," boasted Stanley P. Steward of the White Motor Company. The hype did not impress Kenneth MacKenzie, who had ridden the city's first electric car in 1890. "Little did I think then that a $2,000,000 business like this would come to nothing."[22]

Colorado Fuel and Iron (CF&I), its sales plummeting, reduced coal miners' pay from $6.52 a day to $5.25 in August 1931. A month later it chopped wages by 10 percent in its Pueblo mill to 44¢ an hour, a blow to nearly 2,500 workers, most of whom had been idle for several months. CF&I also lowered coal prices, a move that squeezed Josephine Roche's Rocky Mountain Fuel Company, which needed to maintain prices in order to pay its unionized workers pre-Depression wages. To rescue their Robin Hood, miners lent Roche half their salaries.[23]

Willing to sacrifice her fortune, Roche could be generous for a time. Fort Collins residents, voting in April 1932 to continue subsidizing their street rail system, also demonstrated an altruistic spirit. Others thought cutbacks the only solution. Arthur Roeder, president of CF&I, seeing his competitors lowering wages, concluded that "we will have to do one thing or the other — either follow suit or go out of business." At the American Beet Sugar Company, President Sidney W. Sinsheimer fired workers and pared salaries to reduce outlay by 20 percent between 1930 and 1931. That was not good enough for 80-year-old Charles Boettcher, who controlled the company. "It has kept me awake at nights," Boettcher wrote Sinsheimer. "Put the knife in deep and do this thing up in good shape. . . . Let your general manager, general superintendent, chief engineer and all other engineers, two attorneys, and various other people take a vacation without pay."[24]

Not counted among the unemployed, many farmers might as well have been. The bountiful rains of 1930, which allowed most growers to ride out the first year of the Depression, did not return in 1931 and 1932. As Denver drained Cheesman Reservoir, the deep-water Lake Michigan whitefish stocked there died. Dry-land farmers were no better suited for a drought. "Dried up," the *Colorado Springs Gazette* explained in July 1932,

Colorado coal production, which stood at nearly 10 million tons in 1929, dipped to 7.2 million tons in 1937. Yet, despite competition from natural gas, coal was still widely used for home heating, as this 1937 picture taken at Sixteenth and Blake in Denver indicates. (Colorado Historical Society)

"is a new agricultural term in the local vocabulary" by which farmers mean fields that are "clear gone, without crop, grass or soil; brown when they should be green." The term aptly described much of eastern Colorado, where parched, unirrigated land yielded nothing, or next to nothing: "little sprouts of corn which . . . could almost be pulverized between the palms." Children looked for rain in vain, running to their parents when they spied even a small "pancake" cloud. To find pasture for their starving cattle, the Alexander Brothers drove a large herd south from Las Animas into Baca County, creating a scene "reminiscent of the old west."[25]

Farmers with water discovered that their apparent good fortune meant little. Hog Day 1932 brought the usual hoopla to Monte Vista: a tug-of-war between men and a tractor, a $10 prize to the man fastest at loading 28 sacks of potatoes on a truck. Speedy spud handling, normally a virtue in the San Luis Valley, which produced more than 10,000 carloads of tubers in 1930, was less important in 1931 when shrinking demand reduced the harvest to one-fourth its 1930 level. Growers hoped to recover the next year: "One crop is sufficient to bring the miracle about." But 1932 brought no miracle. Prices slid below 25¢ a hundred-weight; growers cut pickers' wages to 3¢ a bag. Demanding 50¢ per hundred pounds, growers let their crop rot, rather than harvest it.[26]

Palisade orchard owners faced low peach prices and high transport costs in 1931, forcing them to suspend picking. They encouraged Coloradans to "eat more peaches," and when railroads lowered freight rates, they resumed shipping. To prop up prices, they agreed not to sell low-grade fruit to independent truckers who, it was feared, would undercut the market. In a similar vein Arkansas Valley cantaloupe growers blamed local Japanese farmers for selling inferior produce. Sniff the melon, growers urged customers. "If it smells like a cantaloupe instead of a gourd — then it is a good melon."[27]

Checking on stories of distress, investigators found starvation and "comparative nakedness" in eastern El Paso County in the summer of 1932. Little girls wore only flour-sack slips. One mother, having refashioned her own clothes for her six daughters, dressed herself in flour sacks and wrapped her worn-out shoes in string. Farmers without a corn crop in 1932 lacked food for their animals and the cobs they usually used for fuel. Albert Evans, a Red Cross official, reported, "Thousands of farmers are actually seeing their livestock starve." In August, Charles A. Lory, president of Fort Collins's State Agricultural College, backed a drive to collect food for the destitute. Forced to seek aid, one old man broke down in tears. "I've been farming out there for 18 years and never supposed I would have to ask for help. I have always been able to make a living."[28]

Destitute farmers and unemployed workers could not pay property taxes. Assessors reduced the state's overall value by nearly 20 percent between 1929 and 1931 to levels not seen since 1913. With their constituents demanding deeper cuts, politicians economized. The state saved money and temporarily relieved overcrowding at the penitentiary in 1931 by releasing several hundred felons at once, a move that came to naught because the number of new convicts increased by more than 200 that year. Finding the prison as packed in 1932 as it had been in the riot year of 1929, Episcopal bishop Irving P. Johnson urged Governor Adams to appoint a parole board to allow for the orderly release of inmates.[29]

Local governments also pinched pennies. Fred Neal of Baca County suggested eliminating road work: "We traveled over the prairies once, and we can do it again." Holyoke fired one of its three firemen, dismissed its band director, and slashed salaries in 1932 to almost half of what they were in early 1931. Boulder cut salaries of its 12-man fire department in June 1932, giving firefighters $114.75 a month. It also reduced police pay by 15 percent, leaving the chief with $153.75 and patrolmen with $114.75 per month. In Durango, La Plata County taxpayers asked that the county court deputy be fired. Bent County workers took a 10-percent cut in 1931 and another in 1932.[30]

Sheriff Lee Templeton saved Adams County the cost of court trials by persuading most of his prisoners to plead guilty. Monte Vista closed its library. Estes Park hoped to replenish its coffers by taxing the local YMCA camp, and Denver hauled the privately supported University of Denver into court in a futile attempt to make it pay taxes. Leadville simply went broke; by mid-1932 it could not pay its employees.[31]

The Colorado State Taxpayer's League opposed "the election of immature minds to the state legislature." Alamosa's League asked for a year's moratorium on tax sales. Taxpayers sued Costilla County treasurer Fred Trujillo to keep him from selling delinquent property. Such auctions usually yielded little because land prices had crashed. Joe M. Wood, the state's public examiner, recommended in 1932 "that four-fifths of Costilla county be given back to Old Mexico because it wouldn't bring anything at a tax sale."[32]

Taxpayers insisted that schools trim salaries and lay off teachers. Cash-poor districts paid with warrants, IOUs backed by future tax collections. Lucky teachers in Craig got face value for the paper; those in Steamboat Springs took a 5-percent discount. By the autumn of 1932, Montrose teachers could not persuade banks to honor their warrants at all.[33]

Few Coloradans attended college. The University of Colorado, the state's largest university, registered 3,070 in 1933, and Fort Lewis College near Durango made do with fewer than 100 students. When the Colorado Agricultural College in Fort Collins reduced salaries by 10 percent early in 1932, the Jefferson County Taypayer's Association applauded and urged other schools to do likewise. In Breckenridge the *Summit County Journal* attacked "so-called institutions of higher learning" as "the most arrogant, insistent and persistent tax eaters in the whole state."[34]

Trustees at Colorado State Teachers College in Greeley authorized President George W. Frasier to adjust pay monthly. He reduced some salaries by 15 percent, cut building hours to save on fuel, limited telephone service, and stopped spraying the lawns, a frugality he feared would allow the bugs to grow fat and the dandelions to flourish. Recouping diminished state subsidies by raising tuition seemed unwise to administrators, who feared increases might force some students to drop out. In a bold move the Board of Agriculture in August 1932 abolished the $15-per-semester tuition at the Agricultural College in Fort Collins and at Durango's Fort Lewis College. Both schools cut lab fees. Fort Lewis lowered room and board charges to $5 a month and lent textbooks for free. To teach Adams State College students manners, President Ira Richardson gave teas during the 1930s; tea was cheap. At CU (University of Colorado), Minnie Norlin, wife of President George Norlin, maintained "a wardrobe of party dresses" that she "lent to girls who would otherwise hesitate to attend college functions."[35]

Private institutions struggled. At Denver's Regis College the Reverend Joseph Ryan, S.J., head of the accounting department, raised ducks and chickens to help feed his fellow Jesuits. The suicide of Colorado Woman's College (CWC) treasurer Ernest H. Braukman produced $25,000 in life insurance, which the school used to pay debts, but it could not make $100 monthly payments on its pipe organ, which it returned to the manufacturer. University of Denver (DU) administrators coerced faculty into donating $78,000 in salaries to the school; those who refused were told to resign. By building a library and through other gifts, DU's angel, Mary D. Reed, shored up the university. Businessman William E. Porter provided similar help to CWC by donating $20,000 to complete a dormitory.[36]

Yet the wealthy suffered, some slipping from affluence, others finding their portfolios severely reduced. Statisticians guessed that there were only 29 millionaires in Colorado in 1932, down from 181 in 1929. Louise Hill complained to her son Nathaniel: "The stock market is so depressing, there is nothing to do or say. I would not think of going to Europe, of course, in the first place, there is no one in Paris, I hear. I don't intend to buy any clothes — just wear my old ones — so there is not much use in my going to Europe, is there?" Hill bravely swallowed her nasty financial medicine. "I suppose that, on account of so many dividend cuts and omissions, I will be obliged to stay in Colorado altogether. That would not be a very bad punishment, for all my best friends are here."[37]

Unlike the average Coloradan, who between 1929 and 1933 suffered a decline in annual per capita income from a none-too-comfortable $889 to a meager $628, Hill had financial cushions including "25-30 gallons of marvelous old whiskey," which she found in the wine closet of her mansion at 969 Sherman. "Could get $50 a gallon for it — but won't sell." She enjoyed another happy surprise as she faced life in Denver, where "nothing exciting ever happens." Prices fell, making her money worth more. A pound of steak that cost her cook 50¢ in 1929 could be bought for 33¢ in 1932. First-class postage went up in 1932 to 3¢ an ounce, but navy beans, although likely not a staple in Hill's diet, could be had for 5¢ a pound, 9¢

cheaper than in 1929. A gas price war in early 1931 allowed her chauffeur to tank up at 14¢ a gallon.[38]

Distressed that her son, Crawford, sent telegrams rather than night letters, she nagged him by quoting John D. Rockefeller, Sr. "Take care of the dimes — they make dollars; the dollars take care of themselves." Frustrated when her dollars refused to tend to themselves, she asked Frederick G. Bonfils, publisher of *The Denver Post*, for advice. "He always insists, of course, upon my buying bonds. I tell him that is because he has such a big income, he cannot spend it."[39]

Government bonds, at least, were safe. By late 1931, the value of New York Stock Exchange shares had declined 60 percent from their pre-crash highs, making fools and paupers of some who had plunged back into the market in 1930. Property values skidded; banks went bankrupt.

From Colorado Springs to Craig, from Denver to Del Norte, savings and loans as well as banks failed during 1931 and 1932. Often they were victims of the times: loans sweet in 1929 soured in the early 1930s. Sometimes, as in the failure of the First National Bank of Aurora, whose president T. Frank Gilligan admitted eight years of falsifications, their demise revealed chronic skullduggery. During the troubled summer of 1932, police searched for Walter C. Davis, president of Colorado Springs's City Savings and Loan, suspected of absconding with more than $1 million. Smaller fish were already in jail: Edward C. Sharer, manager of the Dollar Building and Loan, and Fred N. Bentall of the Home Savings Building and Loan. Sharer said he was "afraid of nothing. My conscience is clear." Bentall, a church deacon, traced his long fall back to 1910, when he "started juggling funds. . . . Since then things have been going from bad to worse."[40]

Two thousand irate depositors at a mass meeting in Colorado Springs blamed Governor Adams and demanded that Eli M. Gross, Colorado's Building and Loan commissioner, be arrested for neglecting his duties. Anger at Railway Savings officers was still so intense in Pueblo two years after the thrift failed that their embezzlement trial was moved to Eads, where it took a jury two hours to convict three of them.[41]

In an era before federal deposit insurance, optimists could only hope that sale of defunct banks' assets would partially repay depositors. Grant McFerson, the state's bank commissioner, gave good news in July 1932 to creditors of the State Savings Bank in Colorado Springs, which died in December 1931 after its president shot himself. They were to receive 40¢ on the dollar. A similar windfall befell Crested Butte bank account holders who read of the death of embezzler Charles Ross late in 1932. His $75,000 in life insurance, it appeared, would help cover the bank's debts.[42]

Not everyone was as lucky. Two years after the Phillips County State Bank went broke in 1932, depositors had recovered only 15 percent of their money. The Bank of Fountain listed assets it valued at $50,000 when it failed in mid-1930; an auction in June 1932 brought only $1,460. Loans once valued at more than $33,000 yielded $600, ranch land $1 an acre; the

With her family gone, Louise Hill (1860–1955) rattled around in her Capitol Hill mansion at Tenth Avenue and Sherman Street in Denver. Unable to use her main dining room for a luncheon in 1939 because it was being painted, she was forced to seat her 19 guests in the small dining room. (Denver Public Library, Western History Department)

On leaving the U.S. Senate, Lawrence C. Phipps, Sr. (1862–1958) sold his Washington, D.C. mansion, "Single Oak," and returned to Denver, where in 1933 he spent $310,000 to build Belcaro, a 54-room, 33,123-square-foot Georgian masterpiece at 3400 Belcaro Drive. Phil Goodstein, in South Denver Saga, *writes that Phipps claimed to have undertaken the project in part "to stimulate the local building trades." (Denver Public Library, Western History Department)*

During the Depression, shantytowns became known as Hoovervilles. This "residence" was in Pueblo. (Pueblo Library District)

A Pueblo shanty near Second and Greenwood in April 1938. (Pueblo Library District)

Petertown, in Denver's South Platte River bottomlands about two miles west of Capitol Hill, was featured in The Denver Post, *March 6, 1938, from which this photo was taken. (Colorado Historical Society)*

bank building, once worth nearly $20,000, fetched $540. The *Colorado Springs Gazette* explained, "The price for bankless bank buildings in rural communities has been deflated."[43]

F. D. Moberly, liquidator of the Bank of Del Norte, which closed October 30, 1931, faced a dilemma. If he foreclosed on farmers, he would ruin them and get virtually nothing for their land. If he did not foreclose, depositors risked everything. He gambled and waited. Not until June 1933 did account holders see any of their money, and then only 10 percent. To avoid the liquidators, citizens in Hotchkiss left their savings in their tottering bank. After a six-day business moratorium in January 1932, savers in Monte Vista decided to keep the Wallace State Bank and the Monte Vista State Bank afloat by maintaining their accounts. They understood that "the whole country surrounding [Monte Vista] would be liquidated if the banks were forced to close."[44]

Such restraint was rare. The Reconstruction Finance Corporation rescued Denver's Colorado National Bank, one of the state's major institutions. Usually, however, banks failed, liquidators swept up the crumbs, depositors waited for pennies, embezzlers killed themselves or went to jail. Federal judge J. Foster Symes told crooked Craig bankers they were "cowards, sneakers and did not have one drop of real manhood blood in their veins." Carrie Rollan of Del Norte judged that the "Pen is too good for them." Account holders at Denver's Italian-American Bank wept when it went broke. Businessman Fred A. Rosenstock recalled, "It was really pitiful. Some people lost their life savings, the result of years of hard work and frugality."[45]

Unpaid depositors, especially the unemployed, had reason to weep, because their savings stood between them and destitution. In desperation, Jenette Beresford, a widow, asked Charles Boettcher for a job. "Now we are actually quite hungry.... I beg your consideration for we are just about losing our courage." With tens of thousands of others trapped in "this thing called depression" — their jobs, crops, savings gone, their courage nearly gone — she struggled to survive as Colorado and the rest of the country searched for solutions.[46]

FOUR

Breakdown and the Rise of Roosevelt

Charity is today strained to the breaking point. Soup kitchens and bread lines are conspicuous in every city. Men beg on all street corners.

Edward P. Costigan
September 11, 1930[1]

The National Geographic sang Colorado's praises in its July 1932 issue, celebrating the grandeur of the state's scenery and the glory of its cities. Reporter McFall Kerbey told of Palisade's peaches, of Pueblo's steel works, of Denver's nationally renowned schools, of the miracle highway called Trail Ridge Road being built through Rocky Mountain National Park. Dozens of photographs graced the article: mountains of sugar beets, a few skiers, three roaming buffalo. Here was the blue-skied West of the nation's imagination, a place where seldom was heard a discouraging word.

Kerbey did not chronicle Colorado Fuel and Iron's declining fortunes as orders for steel rails plunged to levels not seen since the 1890s, a blow that would bankrupt the company in 1933. He did not mention the pay cuts forced on Denver's teachers, or the steep decline of tourism in 1932. There was no place in his effervescent essay for statistics from Colorado Springs showing that 10,974 transients sought a "flop" at the municipal shelter during the first half of 1932, triple the number of 1931. Only one disquieting picture crept in, showing dozens of people learning to pan for gold in the South Platte River near Denver. The caption explained, "Men and women who cannot find other work are to-day washing out shiny golden grains.... More than a thousand persons in Colorado are enrolled in such classes." Worth a honeycomb of Kerbey's words, the photo proved that all was not well. With their jobs and savings gone, tens of thousands looked to the state, to cities, to churches, and to charities for help. During 1931 and 1932 they often received only spare dimes and platitudes.

Edward P. Costigan implored the U.S. Senate to recognize that federal relief "involves nothing less than the inalienable right of American citizens to life." Herbert Hoover, fiscally prudent and sensitive to states' rights, ignored Costigan, as did most members of Congress until mid-1932. They believed private charities, churches, and states should provide relief. Governor Billy Adams passed the buck by dumping much of Colorado's responsibility on its cities and counties. They, in turn, asked the Red Cross, the Community Chest, and the Salvation Army to clothe the needy, to give tramps a bowl of soup. With the affluent and the middle class squeezing

Gold panners along Denver's South Platte River hoped old-fashioned placer mining would bring them new riches. Few found the work profitable. (Denver Public Library, Western History Department)

their nickels and saving their pennies, charities received less. Flawed in the best of times, the relief hodgepodge collapsed in the worst of times.[2]

At Denver's Grace Methodist Church the Reverend Edgar M. Wahlberg daily fought the Depression. Once an elite haven, Grace had become by the 1930s a community church known for its activism, criticized for being "red and leftist." On taking charge in 1931, Wahlberg found the church in disrepair, the mortgage in arrears, and the men's toilets "with the

Eleven hundred poor children enjoy a free Thanksgiving dinner at Denver's Tivoli Terrace nightclub, 1900 West Thirty-second Avenue, November 28, 1935. (Colorado Historical Society)

worst kinds of obscenity on the walls." He removed the graffiti, fixed the building, and convinced bankers not to foreclose on God.

When a young boy starved to death "in my own neighborhood over which towered the proud steeple of my church," Wahlberg told the child's parents, "Man did this — not God." To undo what man had done, Wahlberg organized the Grace Self-Help Co-operative, which collected and dispensed food, gave free haircuts, supplied firewood, and did repairs. Overwhelmed with donations of cabbage, Wahlberg made sauerkraut — a smelly endeavor that earned Grace the nickname Sauerkraut Community Church. The banker John Evans, grandson of Colorado's second territorial governor, helped finance the operation; his sister, Katherine, served free meals. Clarence F. Holmes, an African-American dentist, donated his time to fix teeth and served as a greeter at Grace. When occasionally a parishioner would hesitate to shake his hand, Holmes responded, "Ah come on, shake hands, it won't come off."[3]

Few places were blessed with churches as amazing as Grace. Instead, they relied upon makeshift programs and crazy-quilt organization to cope with the breakdown. In Palisade the town and churches set up a breadline to feed indigent peach pickers who had been surviving on suckers pulled

Overwhelmed by the Depression and at times threatened with recall, George Begole (1877–1956), Denver's mayor (1931–1935), did not seek re-election. (Colorado Historical Society)

from the Colorado River. Fort Collins looked to its Social Service Bureau, the county commissioners, the Great Western Sugar Company, the agricultural college, the garden club, and the agricultural extension office to provide garden seed for poor people. Gunnison's sheriff doubled as a welfare worker by distributing jack rabbit carcasses to the needy. Larimer County 4-H officials gave the $1,500 they normally awarded in fair prizes to the poor. Some Las Animas County schoolchildren, their normal lunch consisting of a cold pancake, had the Lions Club to thank for half a pint of milk and a graham cracker twice a day. With demands upon it six times greater in early 1932 than in 1931, the Monte Vista Red Cross begged for shoes for barefoot children. Pueblo opened a soup kitchen and helped the Salvation Army feed schoolchildren.[4]

Jesse F. Welborn, former head of Colorado Fuel and Iron (CF&I), faced similar challenges on a larger scale when he took command of Denver's newly formed Citizens' Relief Committee in September 1931. It tried to find work for the unemployed, giving employers who cooperated a red star. Seeing that there were not enough private jobs, Denver put men to work sprucing up Red Rocks Park west of the city. Governor Adams proposed constructing highways in the winter to make work. He called for federal help and urged communities to rescue the starving. Beyond that he would not go, vowing not to raise taxes for relief.[5]

Local governments demurred on fiscal and on philosophical grounds: some were broke, and those with money did not care to spend it on the poor. Many people believed that helping the unemployed constituted futile tinkering with the economy, which, left alone, would recover. Although they admitted that orphans, old people, and the blind had some right to public aid, they balked when asked to help the able-bodied. If they could not find work for the out-of-work, they tried to make it.

Cañon City axed two problems at one woodpile by having needy men chop logs for needy old people. Denver's planning commission proposed employing the unemployed on Cherry Creek flood control projects; Durango's Lions Club suggested road construction. Grand Junction, late in 1931, appropriated $6,000 for public works to relieve "extensive" unemployment; Greeley decided to add water mains, using "mostly hand labor." Fort Collins employed some of its poor in constructing and staffing a soup kitchen and a divided dining room — part for Spanish-speakers, part for English-speakers. Brighton prodded its Hispanic relief recipients to tend gardens. Gardens were cheap and hence appealed to cash-poor communities. The city and the chamber of commerce planned a plot in Walsenburg; CF&I sponsored them in Pueblo. Agricultural College agents promised high yields from 7,500-square-foot tracts: 250 pounds of cabbage, 250 of carrots, 200 of beets, 120 of squash, 150 of turnips, 175 of onions, 170 of greens, and 275 ears of corn. Joseph Payne of Boulder even managed to farm indoors in the winter by growing "depression flowers," crystalline fantasies made from cinders soaked in salt and bluing.[6]

Fearful that the shrinking economic pie would not feed everyone, desperate people fought for crumbs. Denver's African-Americans found their janitorial and shoe-shining jobs threatened: "We are finding keen competition on all hands, and from the very white man and woman whom a decade or so ago looked with disdain upon some work regarded as menial." Learning that some 400 married women worked for Denver schools, a reader of *The Denver Post* suggested that women who "would look better in their homes living on their husband's salaries" be replaced with jobless men.[7]

Fred Lozuaway of Denver offered a more benign, if no more effective, solution. At Thirty-eighth Street and the South Platte River, he ran Fred's Gold Mine, a placer operation where for $1, greenhorn prospectors could buy a gold pan. Fred said there was plenty of pay dirt in the state's rivers. During the spring and summer of 1932 thousands of people, remembering nineteenth-century bonanzas, deluded themselves into believing they, too, could strike it rich. Several thousand took classes from Agricultural College instructors, only to discover panning was no panacea. From Breckenridge, a faded mountain hamlet, came a warning in May: "If the tenderfoot goes broke we are not in a position to give him unlimited food and shelter." A few days later the town's mayor, Thomas C. Coltman, asked Governor Adams to send a couple of tons of flour to feed neophyte prospectors. "It is quite impossible," he told Adams, "for anyone to pan enough gold to make a living."[8]

Resourceful entrepreneurs devised novel ways to make money. June Rice, wife of the administrator of Denver's new Porter's Hospital, left 25-watt bulbs burning in empty rooms so passersby would think the hospital a prosperous facility worthy of patronage. Margaret Reincke, a CU student, invented an improved soup spoon praised by *Rocky Mountain News* reporter Gene Cervi: "The new spoon may be used in either hand without confusing the wielder." Eager to attract ball fans, Denver promoters sponsored motorcycle baseball. With the exception of the pitcher, batter, and catcher all players were on motorcycles. Successful hitters jumped on their cycles to race to first base.[9]

Shwayder Brothers, Denver manufacturers of Samsonite luggage, lost money for the first time in 1932. They diversified, King D. Shwayder recalled, by making "a dogie dinette, a little stand with two bowls in it, and sandboxes, and stilts, among other things, card tables." The sturdy $1 card tables, popular in a decade hooked on board games, sold so well they saved the firm. Unable to get a fair price for his cattle at home, Farrington R. Carpenter, a Hayden rancher, trucked two "samples" to Los Angeles. When a potential buyer refused to leave his seventeenth-floor office to view the merchandise, Carpenter loaded a bull on the elevator. "He [the bull] kind of stopped there a little when he was going in but I was glad he stopped there instead of waiting until he got into Mr. Vale's office." Despite the animal's indiscretion, Carpenter made the sale. Later he loaded up on oranges, convincing roadside vendors to sell a crate for a silver dollar. "We advised [the proprietors] that real money would soon be scarce because the president had closed the banks." The oranges brought Carpenter $3 a crate in Colorado.[10]

"We don't want to rob, only to live," said Howard Macy, a Monte Vista farmer, defending potato growers' efforts to raise prices by withholding crops. Others concluded that eating depended on stealing. Hungry thieves robbed Brush's City Food Store, taking eight pounds of coffee and several cans of pork and beans. Henry Poltster confessed to Colorado Springs police that he filched flour from the Economy Market to feed his pregnant wife and young daughter. The "rumble is close at hand," warned Denver's Roman Catholic bishop, Urban J. Vehr, predicting revolution unless the country embraced a "new social order based on justice and charity."[11]

Adonias Garcia, a Costilla County farmer, hoped for charity. He wrote to Governor Adams: "I dident work last summer, and I made a little crop but I dident raise nothing we dident have no water. So I am very poor now, and I wish you could help me with $10.00." Adams could not hand out $10 bills, nor did he have a cure for the Depression. Chambers of commerce promoted buy-at-home campaigns; city councils protected local merchants by taxing or prohibiting itinerant peddlers. Grand Junction's Prosperity League encouraged residents to write wealthy people, "urging them to come to Grand Junction and the Grand Valley to invest their money and to make their home." A chain letter received by Charles Boettcher promised that repeal of the Eighteenth [Prohibition] Amendment would employ two million men. George W. Frasier, president of Colorado State Teachers College in Greeley, disagreed. "Dollars that buy beer and whiskey can't buy bread for hungry mouths." Gertrude M. Hollingsworth thought curing goiters would help. She informed Billy Adams that "there would be less crime; less insanity and less mental defectives to care for. Money saved in the long run."[12]

The starving could not patiently wait for the end-of-goiters millennium. Ill-served by local governments and private charities, desperate citizens formed self-help cooperatives. Thirty men banded together in Fort Collins in June 1932 offering farmers labor in return for produce. T. J. Nixon organized a cooperative in the Louisville-Longmont area; L. R. Hill put together an association in Colorado Springs. The UW Self Help Co-Operative of Grand Junction told Governor Adams it was harvesting potatoes, onions, and fruit, building a road to a coal mine, and cutting wood. Could the state spare a few National Guard tents for its use? the co-op asked. William C. Danks, head of the National Guard, allowed the "situation may be termed an emergency" and implied that local commanders could lend tents.[13]

Abandoned elephant barns, zebra stalls, and lion cages, vestiges of the Sells-Floto Circus's winter quarters at Thirty-seventh and Hazel Court, sheltered some of Denver's unemployed and their families in the summer of 1932. Members of the Unemployed Citizens League, which, with 22 district offices in Denver, claimed more than 30,000 adherents, had coalesced under the leadership of architect Charles D. Strong and Nathan L. Beatty. Some members worked for farmers for a share of the harvest. Others razed condemned buildings, using the scrap to repair houses. They fetched timber from Jarre Canyon, southwest of the city, to the circus grounds, where they cut it up and stored it for fuel. The police donated crocks confiscated from bootleggers, which the league used to process cabbage into sauerkraut. Chefs "who in another and more prosperous day catered to the elite of the city" cooked up vegetables for the homeless. Reporter Jack Carberry acknowledged that the league's practice of sharing among its members "may smack of Socialism, or Communism, perhaps," but he assured *Rocky Mountain News* readers that the cooperative was "free from the influence of any political party, race or creed or 'ism.' "[14]

The league, at best, provided stopgap help. With unemployment among household heads soaring above 20 percent, demands for federal help grew. One group, the veterans of World War I, had staked a special claim on the U.S. Treasury in 1924, when they had been promised a bonus, averaging $1,000, to be paid in 1945. Frantic for cash in May 1932, they converged on Washington, D.C., petitioning Congress for immediate payment. More than 1,000 veterans waited in Denver's Civic Center in early June as their commander, Joe Maida, finagled transport in Burlington boxcars. Others improvised. William E. Baker of La Veta hijacked a Mississippi tugboat, only to have his piracy foiled by the crew, who beat him up.[15]

In Washington they joined 15,000 other veterans camped on the Anacostia Flats along the Potomac River. Dubbing their neighborhood Larimer Street, they named their lean-tos and tar-paper shacks after Denver buildings: the Brown Palace, the Windsor. William R. Eaton, Denver's Republican congressman, visited to explain his opposition to the bonus. Perhaps as an apology, he gave the campers his lucky $20 gold piece so they could buy tobacco. That was all they were to get; Congress refused to pay the bonus. In late July, President Hoover dispatched General Douglas MacArthur, assisted by Major Dwight D. Eisenhower with army troops to roust the veterans. It was, fumed John A. Martin, candidate for Congress in southern Colorado, "the most damnable outrage in American history."[16]

Back in Denver in August, Maida and several hundred others bivouacked along the South Platte River near Alameda. To dislodge them city officials demanded that Major Alphonse Pierre Ardourel of the National Guard repossess the tents he had lent them. Investigating "Camp Maida," Lee Taylor Casey of the *Rocky Mountain News* found 303 residents, including 63 women and 74 children, living in 81 tents. A clean place with a volunteer nurse and doctor, the camp, in his opinion, posed no threat. He maintained that the squatters were patriots, seeking only food, shelter, and jobs. Children paraded behind the flag "with all the campers observing the proper formalities when the colors pass." Whether spurred by loyalty or afraid to brave the wrath of a society that feared radicals, most veterans stayed within the nation's traditional political and economic bounds. Democrats or Republicans, they remained capitalists all — or almost all.[17]

A thimbleful of Communists and a pocketful of socialists hoped to convince other Coloradans to take up an "ism." Kept alive in the 1920s by disciples such as Frank L. Palmer, who lectured at Grace Church, Communists capitalized in the 1930s on the breakdown, which they reckoned proof of their philosophy. Operating through groups such as the Trade Union Educational League, the Young Communists League, and the International Labor Defense League, a few devotees, including Dorothy and William Dietrich, John and Dorothy Eil, James Allander, and Haydee U. Zeitlin, rallied Denver's unemployed, damned exploitation of farm workers, and backed Denver's African-Americans in one of their first frontal attacks on segregation.[18]

Fretting over the Communist menace, state officials sent spies such as "Agent 57" to track radicals. In early January 1931 the anonymous agent reported that Denver's Unemployed Council had gathered a force of 1,500 to march on the state Capitol demanding relief and that afterward the group in "mob disorder" poured down Sixteenth Street. "There is a possibility of destruction," he warned, "attacks upon warehouses, plants." In February more than 1,400 crowded Denver's Broadway Theater to hear national Communist leader William Z. Foster. "Don't Starve, Fight," proclaimed local organizers. In May the Unemployed Council mustered 1,000 marchers to parade through downtown. In late June bold peace-mongers Solomon J. Greenberg and Michael Shantzek distributed anti-war literature at Fort Logan. Greenberg was beaten; both were arrested and held

Would-be soldiers trained at Citizens Military Training Camp at Fort Logan south of Denver. (Colorado Historical Society)

incommunicado "while the case [sedition charges] was being thoroughly prepared," the adjutant general's office explained.[19]

At the same time, Communists raised funds to help defend nine black youths, the Scottsboro boys, all under death sentence for rape in Alabama. Colorado's African-Americans, in 1930 a small contingent of 11,828, approximately 60 percent of them in Denver's Five Points neighborhood, applauded demands for racial justice, but some black leaders opposed the Reds. Fritz Cansler, executive secretary of the Glenarm Branch of the YMCA, reported that hundreds of Communists "swarmed around the building" the night of August 8, 1931, in the mistaken belief that they could meet there. "There is no doubt," Cansler warned, "that the [Communist] movement is gaining ground and something should be done to counteract the influence they are exerting."[20]

Racism gave radicals a fertile field. A cross-burning designed to frighten a black family out of west Denver in late 1931 was, reported police agent Samuel E. Carey, "being used by agitators to inflame the negro." Angry over segregated swimming pools, blacks damned the tradition that kept them from swimming at Smith Lake in Washington Park. When a few tried to do so in mid-August 1932, a white mob armed with sticks and stones drove them away. *The Denver Post* blamed Communists for encouraging the black bathers, and among African-Americans the Communists took credit for the dramatic challenge to the city's color code. Conservative blacks shunned the agitators and privately described the fray as a "subversive victory," but they, too, insisted African-Americans had the right to swim at any public facility.[21]

Their fight for civil rights brought the Communists little support; indeed, it probably hurt them among whites. Their 1932 senatorial candidate, Raymond D. Richardson, captured only 858 votes, more than half from Denver and Pueblo. In Gilpin, Grand, and Phillips counties he won no backing at all; in most other places he could count his fans on one hand: one vote in Lincoln County, two in Montrose, three in Morgan, four in Delta, five in Adams.

Socialists did better. Split between members of the Socialist Party of America and the Socialist Labor party, they might have remained as marginal as the Communists had it not been for Carle Whitehead, a Denver attorney. The Socialist Labor party, its anemic Denver chapter claiming only five members in 1934, offered scant competition to the dynamic Whitehead, local head of the Socialist Party of America. In 1932 he won more than 8,000 votes in his bid for the U.S. Senate, about 2 percent of the total. Although nearly a third of his ballots came from Denver, he scavenged more than 200 in 14 counties, including Arapahoe, Delta, Mesa, and Weld.[22]

Norman Thomas, the Socialists' presidential candidate, lectured a Macky Auditorium audience in Boulder: "Our present capitalist system is nothing more or less than racketeering." In Denver 6,500 applauded him at the City Auditorium in mid-October. Yet in November, Thomas and all the other third-party presidential candidates combined garnered less than 4 percent of Coloradans' votes. Shifting from 1920s conservatism typified by Hoover and Adams, voters in the early 1930s inched to the left by embracing Democrats — a few liberal, most moderate to conservative.[23]

Billy Adams saw the tornado coming. At age 71 in his third term as governor, he found himself abandoned by many within his party and by such crucial allies as *The Denver Post*. Two years earlier the *Post* had spread the blame for the country's troubles: "We indulged in an orgy of gambling and extravagance. When the bubble burst, we wanted to blame anybody but ourselves." In 1932 the paper focused its criticism on Adams, if not for making the mess, at least for failing to respond to the state's banking crisis. The beleaguered governor, not wanting to hurt his nephew Alva B. Adams's chances to be elected to the U.S. Senate, decided not to run in 1932.[24]

That left the Democratic gubernatorial nomination open to 38-year-old Edwin C. Johnson, popularly known as "Big Ed." Of commanding presence and with folksy charm, Johnson had collected many of the merit badges handy for winning votes in Colorado — homesteader, football player, telegraph operator, grain elevator manager, Mason, Lion, Elk, and Lutheran. He had also honed his political skills as a legislator, as private secretary to Governor Adams, and as lieutenant governor. Although a Democrat, he was no Costigan. The conservative head of the Colorado

Alva B. Adams (1875–1941) of Pueblo and Edwin C. Johnson (1884–1970) of Craig, both Democrats, emerged as two of Colorado's most powerful politicians during the 1930s. (Colorado Historical Society)

National Bank, Harold Kountze, who had little love for most Democrats, remembered Johnson as "a big, honest Swede," and some Republicans came to regard him as one of them.[25]

Smelling victory in November, Democrats jockeyed for position. The death of Republican Senator Charles W. Waterman allowed Adams to appoint Walter Walker, publisher of the Grand Junction *Daily Sentinel,* to the Senate. In November, Walker ran against Karl C. Schuyler, a Denver attorney, for the brief honor of completing Waterman's term, set to expire in March 1933. In the contest for a six-year senatorial berth (1933–1939), Alva B. Adams opposed Schuyler, who ran for both the long and the short terms. Democrats also eyed congressional seats. Denver's Lawrence Lewis hoped to beat William Eaton. In the northeast Fred Cummings counted on his sugar-beet connections to help him vanquish Republican George Bradfield, who had defeated the incumbent congressman Charles B. Timberlake in the primary. John Martin, a former congressman, judged the time right to unseat Guy U. Hardy in southern Colorado. For Martin the choice was clear: "Vote one ticket and eat, or vote the other and go hungry." In the west, long-time representative Edward T. Taylor easily met a nominal challenge from Richard C. Callen.[26]

Herbert Hoover's November 6, 1932, Denver visit did not seriously hurt Franklin Roosevelt. Hoover is with former U.S. senator Lawrence C. Phipps, Sr. (right). (Denver Public Library, Western History Department)

Franklin Delano Roosevelt, the Democratic presidential nominee, hailed from New York and favored abandoning Prohibition — two strikes against him in the eyes of some Coloradans. But unlike Alfred E. Smith, FDR was a Protestant and a patrician. Miners liked his talk of stabilizing silver prices, and sugar-beet growers appreciated Democratic proposals to make the Philippines independent, a move that would allow tariffs to be imposed on Filipino sugar. Thirty thousand people greeted Roosevelt when he motored through downtown Denver on September 15, 1932.

Ducking most issues, he relied on his charm, his smile, and his handshake to win the hearts and votes of common people. "Splendid sunshine you have here in Colorado," he told Billy Adams. A woman in the crowd shouted, "He's our next president."[27]

In Colorado Springs, Roosevelt spoke from a Broadmoor Hotel balcony; in Pueblo, 10,000 cheered his 10-minute speech. Hoover, the first president to visit Denver since Harding in 1923, attracted a crowd to Union Station on November 6 for a short address in which he urged them to be charitable. By then it was too late. Polly, a Denver parrot, had already learned to squawk "Hooray! for Roosevelt!" And 100-year-old William Lloyd, the city's oldest voter, was awaiting election day so he could cast another ballot for a Democrat named Franklin, having given his first to Franklin Pierce in 1852. Sampling the mood in Holyoke, the *Holyoke Enterprise* reported that a straw vote at the Hotel Burge revealed 176 for Roosevelt and 163 for Hoover. People, the paper said, "wanted a change in everything."[28]

Colorado's politics changed dramatically in 1932 as Democrats trounced Republicans. Ed Johnson beat his Republican opponent, James D. Parriott, by more than 70,000 votes. The state Senate turned Democratic, as had the House in 1930. Adams defeated Schuyler for the six-year U.S. Senate slot, although Schuyler edged Walter Walker for the few months left in Waterman's term. Lawrence Lewis, Fred Cummings, John Martin, and Edward Taylor, all Democrats, went to the U.S. House of Representatives. Roosevelt gathered more than 250,000 votes; Hoover harvested 189,617 in an election that drew 50,000 more voters than in 1928.

Without a clear program and hence without a clear mandate, Roosevelt appeared an enigmatic messenger of hope. Echoing the confusion of most people, the *Weld County News* gave the president-elect a half-hearted send off: "It may be that Mr. Roosevelt will do no better than Mr. Hoover has done, altho [*sic*] we think in all sincerity that he cannot do much worse."[29]

FIVE

Fear, Relief, and Politics: 1933–1936

Mr Roosevelt
Dear President

there are 5 in are Flaimely and all they low us is $3 to live on evry 2 weeks they wont give us now work Iem not the only one there is 6000 in the same way. We have a litle Babay that need milk Bad. th Doctor told us that are Baby must have milk By all means But they will not give nothing I wood like to know what we can do about it are childrens crieds all th time fer somthing to eat all th time.

> Louie Bunelen
> July 12, 1933
> Sterling Colo.[1]

"The only thing we have to fear is fear itself," Franklin Roosevelt told the country in his inaugural address March 4, 1933. Fear bred the panic in late 1932 and early 1933 that led to runs on banks, many without reserves to satisfy their depositors. To forestall total breakdown, some governors, including those in the financially pivotal states of New York and Illinois, closed all banks. In Colorado on March 3, Ed Johnson asserted with more bravado than evidence, "The banks of this state are perfectly sound." The next day, as Federal Reserve banks across the nation closed, he ordered the state's institutions to do likewise.[2]

Roosevelt ratified the governors' actions by declaring a national bank moratorium on March 6. Examiners hastily inspected banks, hoping to speedily reopen the salvageable ones. For a few days Coloradans got along with the cash they had on hand. Bookies and bootleggers who insisted on cash payment suffered. Restaurants, hotels, and theaters accepted IOU's and checks. By May 14 stronger banks in Denver, Pueblo, and Colorado Springs reopened, followed soon after by stable institutions in smaller towns. Others were put on probation in an attempt to avert panic withdrawals. The Farmers State Bank of Cope limited withdrawals to $100; the Durango Trust could pay up to $50. Fort Collins's First National fell under the spell of a conservator who froze its deposits until May 1934.[3]

The Emergency Banking Relief Act of March 9, 1933, confirmed FDR's right to close banks and empowered him to regulate gold and silver. Abetted and sometimes pushed by advocates of inflation and by apostles of silver, the president decoupled the value of the dollar from the price of gold, seized gold coins, and manipulated the price of silver and gold. Ordered to trade their gold in excess of $100 for paper money, some

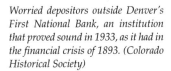

Worried depositors outside Denver's First National Bank, an institution that proved sound in 1933, as it had in the financial crisis of 1893. (Colorado Historical Society)

Coloradans balked. Former U.S. senator Charles S. Thomas informed U.S. Attorney Ralph L. Carr that he had "$120 in gold, which I have acquired in order to qualify myself for the penitentiary pursuant to the recent edict of the President of the United States." The Justice Department declined to prosecute the feeble octogenarian, but Thomas continued to jab at "white livered cowards" in Congress and at Franklin Roosevelt, "as much a dictator as Mussolini or Stalin." Others, unwilling to risk 10 years in Leavenworth, surrendered their treasure. Bankers kissed their gold good-bye in March 1933 as federal agents spirited it away, first to fill Federal Reserve bank vaults, later to entomb much of it at the Denver Mint.[4]

Whatever objections Coloradans had to FDR's gold grab, they thanked him for increasing the price of both gold and silver. By late 1933 gold stood at more than $34 an ounce, 70 percent more than in 1932. Silver also soared, rising overnight by 21¢ to 64¢ an ounce in early 1934, thanks to a presidential decree. To celebrate silver's triumph, *Time* reported, Leadville miners "filled with moonshine" shot off their revolvers in the street. Gold production rose by more than 50 percent between 1933 and 1941, and the value of silver output skyrocketed by 900 percent between 1933 and 1940.

Charles S. Thomas (1849–1934), Colorado's governor (1899–1901) and one of its U.S. senators (1913–1921), refused to part with his gold. The Rocky Mountain News, *June 25, 1934, reported that on his deathbed Thomas joked, "Everybody's told me to go to hell, so I'd like to go down and see what it looks like." (Denver Public Library, Western History Department)*

Mining picked up; mountain towns perked up. So many men were working near Alma in 1935 (600 in lode mines and 150 on placers) that they could not find houses to rent. Day and night shifts toiled at Como, and two dredges scoured for gold near Breckenridge. Leadville's population increased by more than 1,000 people, reaching nearly 5,000 in 1940. Cripple Creek went from 1,427 in 1930 to 2,358 a decade later. Telluride doubled its population, and Aspen, which had 705 residents in 1930, breathed a little easier in 1940 with 777. Although not a boom of nineteenth-century dimensions and not totally dependent on precious metals, the mining revival of the 1930s gave hope to many and jobs to some. Unfortunately, as historian William D. Leuchtenburg has pointed out, FDR's flirtation with silver, an industry nationally "less important than chewing gum, spaghetti or the output of 'Eskimo Pies,' " benefited only a few and cost $1.5 billion.[5]

As silver flowed from Colorado's mines, beer gushed from its breweries. Prohibition, a failed experiment of nearly 18 years' duration in Colorado, died in 1933. At one minute past midnight on April 7, 1933, the state's two major breweries — Denver's Tivoli Union, and Coors in Golden — began shipping beer. Coors, which had 750,000 bottles ready to go, dispatched a fleet of 70 trucks and a 20-car beer train to distribute the brew. Within a day, Coloradans bought 50,000 cases and revenue agents raked in more than $15,000 in license fees. Later in the year, repeal of the Eighteenth Amendment to the U.S. Constitution ended the federal ban on hard liquor.[6]

By supporting repeal of Prohibition, Roosevelt pleased most people. By favoring silver and gold, he made Colorado's hard-rock miners happy. By rescuing the banks, he bought time he needed to rush recovery measures through Congress. In the 100 days between March 9 and June 16,

1933, lawmakers passed reams of legislation embracing the creation of the Civilian Conservation Corps (CCC) to employ young men in the greening of the nation, the Agricultural Adjustment Administration (AAA) to stabilize farm prices, the National Recovery Administration (NRA) to revive business by fixing fair prices and wages, and the Public Works Administration (PWA) to prime the economy by spending billions on public projects.

To provide immediate relief Congress established the Federal Emergency Relief Administration (FERA). Run by Harry Hopkins, one of Roosevelt's closest advisors, FERA initially planned to spend half a billion dollars — half in grants to states, half in matching funds, with state and local governments expected to provide three dollars for each federal dollar. Hoover's Reconstruction Finance Corporation (RFC) had allowed states to borrow for relief: Colorado received its first payment of $250,000 in September 1932, which it used to help 5,000 farm families on the plains. FERA went further. By directly involving the federal government in local relief, Roosevelt and his New Dealers wrote a new chapter in federal-state relations — one destined to shape Colorado's politics and to mold its response to the New Deal.

Reporting that "the relief business constitutes the state's largest industry — if it can be called an industry," Gene Cervi of the *Rocky Mountain News* described FERA in late 1934 as "the life-line of the state," providing help to some 250,000 people, one in every four Coloradans. In some counties 60 percent of all people were on relief; only in Mineral (1930 population 640) were assistance rolls blank. FERA gave small doles to the destitute, made grants to self-help cooperatives, set up camps for transients, and distributed surplus food to the hungry. Supplemented by the short-lived (November 1933–March 1934) Civil Works Administration (CWA), it also made jobs for the jobless.[7]

Denver's relief army, estimated by Cervi at 60,000, ate a big wedge of the federal pie. Riprapping the banks of Cherry Creek and the South Platte promised to prevent floods and to employ more than 1,000 men. Finding that the poor needed mattresses, the Denver Board of Public Welfare hired 119 women and men to make mattresses in a disused automobile plant at Eleventh and Cherokee. At just one meeting in January 1935 the Colorado State Relief Committee approved more than 200 projects: $1,215 to Otero County to conserve and hatch fish, $388 to Kit Carson for a town well, $308 to Logan County for collecting and repairing shoes, a paltry $12 to Douglas County for road repair.[8]

Labor-intensive projects appealed to FERA and CWA administrators, who tried to put large numbers to work quickly. In December 1933, Alice E. van Diest, CWA's director of women's work, reported more than 450 women, most making around 50¢ an hour, working on CWA projects — 215 taking an unemployment census in Denver, 12 helping the State Historical Society interview pioneers, two mending books in Brighton, one doing the same thing in Mesa County. Although willing to buck conventional attitudes that decreed that women would stay at home, FERA still

gave the bulk of its work to men, concentrating on tasks demanding heavy labor. Loveland renovated its library, laid bridges over ditches, and improved its ballpark. Sterling resurfaced streets and modernized its airport. Las Animas put in a storm sewer; Brush landscaped a six-acre addition to its cemetery; Alamosa built a new entrance to its jail. Grand Junction landed an airport project that crashed when CWA funds ran out and the city council balked at spending local money on a field that was only used once a month. In Denver, unemployed architects created a scale-model of Denver in the early 1860s for the State Historical Society.[9]

Between its birth in 1933 and its death in late 1935, FERA spent $4.12 billion nationally, with the states providing approximately 29 percent. Massachusetts, for example, funded nearly 48 percent of the $219 million expended there. In Colorado, as in many southern states and some other western states where officials could not or would not raise taxes to match FERA grants, stinginess paid a dividend. Of the $46,663,546 spent in the state, nearly 85 percent came from the federal government.[10]

Pueblo CWA workers in front of the City Auditorium, February 14, 1934. Created on November 9, 1933, the Civil Works Administration put more than 4.2 million people to work nationally by mid-January 1934. (Pueblo Library District)

Diorama of Denver in the early 1860s created by FERA workers between 1934 and the summer of 1935. In 1993 it still enthralled visitors to the Colorado Historical Society. (Denver Public Library, Western History Department)

Assuming responsibility for destitute vagrants, FERA picked up the tab for transient relief. That pleased Colorado, which attracted large numbers of homeless travelers, especially in the summer months. Its railroad connections, coupled with its reputation as a healthy place — factors once considered assets — proved partial liabilities in the 1930s as tens of thousands flocked to the state. Some were tramps and bums; many others were ordinary poor people, men and women, girls and boys. Uprooted by the Depression, most of them rode the rails into transportation hubs such as Denver, Colorado Springs, La Junta, Pueblo, Trinidad, and Grand Junction.

By October 1934, FERA had established 20 Colorado transient stations, which that month cared for 12,650 people. Finding many TB sufferers among its clients, the division ran a convalescent camp in the Black Forest north of Colorado Springs, housing it in the former sanatorium of Yosemite Nabona, a herbalist healer. In Denver, boys were cared for in two houses. In the mountains near Bailey, transients were put to work building cottages. At Monument Lake near Trinidad they raised the dam so the shallow pond would better harbor fish, a project applauded by the Izaak Walton League and condemned by union leaders who resented hoboes taking jobs from locals. One of Grand Junction's stations, located in the center of town, also drew complaints, for it attracted tramps, "a nuisance and a flagrant lot" according to Congressman Edward Taylor, which presented "an awful spectacle of debauchery adjoining the homes of a great many respectable people and women and children." Taylor asked that the center be moved, and FERA quickly accommodated him.[11]

The Transient Division in August 1934 received only $70,000 from a Colorado FERA budget of nearly $1.9 million. Hence it could not offer much. Earlier that summer Lorena Hickok, an investigator working for Harry Hopkins, found "some decidedly promising camps" in Colorado, but she judged the overburdened Denver center "awful." Writing from La Junta, Charles E. Johnson described his fellow camp residents as "the forgotten men" who were promised "shelter, food, clothes and ninety cents per week in return for six hours work five days a week" and wound up with "a dirty bed and very poor meals." Being on the bum, Johnson mused, might be better than being in the camps: "We wouldn't be wearing out our few clothes as fast. . . . We could have a greater sense of independence. It is a fact that we can't get a job any place, still we could kid ourselves that we are trying."[12]

Despite transient aid, despite the civic improvements to its credit, despite the relief it gave, FERA was not much loved. Private charities, which helped dole out federal relief in 1933, complained in early 1934 when FERA field agent Benjamin Glassberg insisted that only public agencies disburse public money. Speaking for his own Catholic Charities as well as Denver's Red Cross and Central Jewish Aid, the Reverend John R. Mulroy asked Hopkins to countermand Glassberg, "otherwise our agencies practically cease to function and much ill will be created." FERA stuck to its principles. Aubrey Williams, the agency's assistant administrator, wired Mulroy: "Central agencies such as we have practically everywhere is the only fair arrangement to clients and to public expending body."[13]

Frugal Coloradans held their noses when they caught a whiff of scandal from Baca County, where commodity distributors tried to sink their sins by chucking moldy government cheese down a well. FERA squirmed around in that mess for a time. It did better in avoiding blame when a dam it had built on Horse Creek 10 miles north of Holly broke on August 28, 1935, flooding the town. That would not have happened, FERA engineer L. E. Truehart explained, if Holly politicians had not insisted on keeping water in the lake, rather than using it as it was designed, exclusively for flood control.[14]

FERA also came under fire for helping some people and for not helping others. William Dumm of Denver fretted about social workers who give "jobs to Mexicans who blow in here from old Mexico" — a charge denied by the Denver Bureau of Public Welfare. With more sympathy toward Hispanos, Helen Fischer of Boulder faulted the local relief operation: "Beet workers, who are largely Spanish-American and who have been living in this county for several generations, seem to be the least understood and are really discriminated against."[15]

Ed Johnson and many of his constituents disliked FERA because it offended their conservative sensibilities by giving money away, because they resented federal trespassing on Colorado turf, and because they correctly viewed it as friendly to Senator Edward Costigan, who, as time wore on, increasingly feuded with Johnson. Legislators welcomed federal money but resisted raising taxes to provide matching funds, and when they tardily approved an automobile tax, the state Supreme Court voided it. Hopkins kept the federal spigot open through 1933, patiently waiting for Colorado to chip in. To gain leverage with the legislature, unpopularly known as the "Twiddling Twenty-ninth," Johnson privately asked Hopkins in December 1933 to punish the state unless it provided matching dollars. He assured Hopkins, "Firm position at this time will result in adequate prompt legislation."[16]

Hopkins agreed to play the governor's game by stopping relief as of December 31, a draconian measure he rarely used. He wired Johnson, "When legislature acts to cooperate on reasonable basis will be very happy to make further appropriations." The strategy worked. Destitute Denverites marched on the Capitol on January 3, 1934, demanding that the legislature act. Instead, lawmakers fled as the mob briefly took over. "A genuine Communist meeting followed," Frank C. Cross of *The Nation* reported, "the first Communist meeting to be held under the dome of any state Capitol in the United States." The Methodist minister Edgar M. Wahlberg remembered the fracas differently, contending that "there was no revolution in Colorado." Whatever happened, the General Assembly got the message and raised the gasoline tax.[17]

That opened the door for other taxes for relief, roads, pensions, schools, and the burgeoning cost of government. On March 1, 1935, Coloradans began paying a 2-percent sales tax on everything except cigarettes and small purchases of bread and milk, a levy calculated to raise up to $6 million a year. But that did not satisfy the tax monster, which, three years later, started feeding on state income taxes, with top rates of 6 percent on annual net income in excess of $10,000. Local governments also grubbed for money. Denver's zoo started charging admission in 1937, and the city council pondered taxing outdoor clocks.[18]

The question was not only one of financing relief but also of controlling it. Johnson's first appointee to head the Colorado State Relief Committee, Richard M. Broad, Jr., a Republican state senator from Golden, proposed jettisoning professional social workers by assigning aid distribution to the counties. "It would be fatal to turn the relief administration over to the kind of county commissioners they have in Colorado," Pierce Williams, a FERA field representative, wrote Hopkins.[19]

Statistics supported Williams's fear. Perhaps no place gave truly adequate relief, but some counties were far more generous than others.

JONNIE GRIMES AND HIS FAMOUS BRAHMA BULL "NEW DEAL" COLO. STATE FAIR. PUEBLO. (DOUBLEDAY)

Between March 1933 and March 1934, per capita relief costs in Denver were $8.67, with more than 30 percent being paid from local funds. In Sedgwick County, where an October 1933 report revealed "malnutrition exists in larger families, especially among the foreign born," the county expended $1.98 per capita in 1933–1934, less than 5 percent being local funds. Montrose, with 30 percent of its relief children undernourished, scraped by on $1.52 per capita, with only 13¢ coming from local coffers. Even in relatively generous places, relief fell short. Helen Fischer of Boulder told Hopkins of the failure of "reactionary politicians" to help the needy. Grace A. Blair lodged a similar complaint against Denver's program, which she urged be put under federal control. Lorena Hickok, Hopkins's roving investigator, found Pueblo's welfare operation dominated by the Colorado Fuel and Iron Company (CF&I), controlled by multi-millionaire John D. Rockefeller, which funneled CF&I workers' relief money to company stores to pay off old debts. To eat they had to borrow more. "In other words," Hickok wrote Hopkins, "we are right now in the position of subsidizing John D. Rockefeller!"[20]

Broad's antipathy toward social workers extended to the top of the state relief apparatus, where he warred with Jessie I. Lummis, executive director of relief. "I expect her to take care of detail work," Broad complained to Aubrey Williams. "So far my cooperative spirit is not appreciated." Nor did Hopkins — who once received a seven-page letter from

The New Deal came to Pueblo in the form of a Brahma Bull named "New Deal" featured at the Colorado State Fair. (Pueblo Library District)

Broad, which after 2,000 introductory words declared, "and now to the real purpose of this letter" — appreciate the long-winded Republican. When Colorado attorney general Paul P. Prosser questioned the legality of legislators serving on the relief committee, Hopkins forced Broad to resign.[21]

Governor Johnson countered by replacing Broad with Herbert Fairall, a Denver auto insurance agent and a conservative Democrat reputedly hostile to Costigan. Hopkins initially refused to recognize the appointment, and on January 23, 1934, he made Casper D. Shawver, a Fort Collins druggist and a Costigan partisan, relief chief. That angered Johnson, who also resented the limitations imposed on Fairall and his state relief committee, which Hopkins reduced to an advisory group. Travers J. Edmonds, a FERA field agent, explained to Hopkins in January 1934 that the governor had forsaken his 1932 alliance with the Costigan-Adams forces and had "slipped over to the other side." By mid-1934, when Costigan's ally Josephine A. Roche challenged Johnson in the Democratic gubernatorial primary, any semblance of harmony between the liberal senator and the conservative governor had evaporated.[22]

Roche announced her candidacy in Washington, D.C., in late May 1934. An ardent New Dealer, she had gone to school with Frances Perkins, FDR's secretary of labor, and sipped tea with Eleanor Roosevelt shortly before declaring her intention to run. In Colorado she could count on considerable labor support and the backing of liberal Democrats who applauded her "Roche, Roosevelt, and Recovery" rhetoric. Nonetheless, party bigwigs shunned her. John A. Carroll, who became her campaign manager, recalled, "By God, they [the Costigan faction] couldn't get anybody of any stature to nominate her so they asked me to do that." At the state Democratic convention in July she took 32 percent of the votes, trailing Johnson but edging former governor Billy Adams, who was attempting a comeback. Energetically campaigning in August, she called for a progressive state income tax and faulted Johnson for throwing bricks at the New Deal.[23]

Her backers cited her many accomplishments: policewoman, probation officer, relief worker in Belgium, Rocky Mountain Fuel president. "To countless workers," said Edward Costigan, "she is a new Joan of Arc." When her opponents called her radical, Edgar Wahlberg responded, "Luther, Lincoln, Washington, and Jesus . . . were branded as radicals." When some questioned the ability of a woman to be governor, John Carroll retorted, "A wide-awake woman is better than a drowsy man." When *The Denver Post* attacked her, Costigan damned the paper as "Public Enemy Number One."[24]

Billy Adams's withdrawal from the primary helped Johnson because conservative Democrats of Adams's ilk were more likely to vote for Johnson than for Roche. Alamosa and Pueblo counties, Adams bastions, went for Johnson. Roche won decisively in Denver and narrowly beat Johnson in Boulder, Grand, and Gunnison counties. She also took Mesa County, as hot a bed of liberalism as any bed got in western Colorado, but

Josephine A. Roche (1886–1976) resigned her post as assistant secretary of the treasury in October 1937 and returned to Colorado to oversee Rocky Mountain Fuel. In an April 3, 1946, Rocky Mountain News interview, she noted: "I never was in politics. There were certain principles some of us thought were worth fighting for and we used the political mechanism to do it." (Colorado Historical Society)

she trailed Johnson in every other county. *The Denver Post* savored Big Ed's victory, which, it exulted, "halted the Red march."[25]

Roche captured a big consolation prize. In December 1934 Roosevelt named her assistant secretary of the treasury in charge of the Public Health Service, making her, after Frances Perkins, the second-highest-ranking woman in the federal government. She resigned after three years, returning to Denver to again take command at Rocky Mountain Fuel. Slowly she faded from public view, although she remained active as a United Mine Worker pension fund director. Asked in 1975 whether she was thinking of writing a book, she snapped, "Who in hell would want to read it?" In 1976, at age 90, she died in Washington, D.C.[26]

Johnson's primary triumph was tantamount to election. In November he defeated the Republican nominee, Nate C. Warren, a Fort Collins banker, by nearly 65,000 votes. Pierce Williams, FERA field agent, had described Johnson in 1933 as having "no judgment whatever to guide him in handling situations in which political relations are involved." Yet, Big Ed showed in 1936 that he understood Coloradans better than did the Washington bureaucrats. As his victory booty he demanded a trophy — relief administrator Casper Shawver's head.[27]

Getting it was made easier by relief riots in Denver. On October 29, 1934, 500 "relief strikers" assembled at the state Capitol demanding that FERA restore relief budgets, that it pay union wages, and that African-Americans and Hispanos be treated fairly. The next morning 300 picketers marched upon a FERA project at West Jewell Avenue and the South Platte, where they urged 125 men working on the riverbank to strike. When they refused, the marchers threw the workers' tools into the river. After the police arrested several picketers, a mob attacked the officers, who then fired upon the crowd, wounding one man in the hip. Other arrests followed as the police jailed agitators. FERA workers, they promised, would be protected the next day by 300 officers armed with machine guns. That ended the immediate threat but did nothing to enhance Shawver's or FERA's reputation. Embarrassed by the strike, which received national attention, Aubrey Williams demanded that Shawver submit "an immediate report . . . to go to Mr. Hopkins so he can take it to the White House."[28]

Johnson fired Shawver on November 8, 1934. "My action," he told Williams, "is based on [Shawver's] political activity, absolute inefficiency, total lack of ability to do the job, absolute refusal to cooperate with state agencies and with anybody in his department." FERA bowed to Johnson by dispatching a non-political professional, Robert W. Kelso, to manage Colorado relief. It was a capitulation made easier by the agency's own misgivings about Shawver. Benjamin Glassberg wrote Hopkins, "I am convinced that he probably is a splendid small town druggist, but in no sense is an organizer or administrator." Alice E. van Diest shared Glassberg's opinion, calling Shawver "ineffectual and inefficient."[29]

Under Kelso and his successor, Ralph O. Baird, FERA struggled through most of 1935. "Without these government funds the majority of those on relief would be in dire want and riots would be certainties," editorialized Grand Junction's *Daily Sentinel*. The fear was real, as demonstrated by the Capitol takeover of January 1934, the relief melee of October, and mini-revolutions such as Denver's anti-eviction riot of April 14, 1933, in which 21 were jailed. Still, Coloradans longed for something better than the dole and the make-work project. Catching the mood of the country, Roosevelt in January 1935 declared, "The Federal Government must and shall quit this business of relief." In May the president appointed Harry Hopkins to head the Works Progress Administration (WPA), a work program without doles. FERA gradually wilted, making its last Colorado payments in December 1935.[30]

The state, in theory, was to fill the relief vacuum created by FERA's demise. Those unable to work were told to seek help from their counties as they had before FERA was invented. And Herbert Fairall, made largely powerless by Hopkins, again gained considerable sway over relief. To cement his victory Ed Johnson kicked the dying FERA in late 1935 by demanding an audit of its books. FERA officials guessed that the governor's attack was calculated to embarrass Costigan, whose Senate seat, it was rumored, Johnson coveted.[31]

By late 1935 Costigan had good reason to fear Johnson. The senator had won some friends by co-sponsoring the Jones-Costigan Sugar Act, which propped up sugar prices, and by helping secure an army air force flight-training school (later named Lowry Air Force Base) for Denver. His fight to protect African-Americans from lynching, his attacks on Wall

Street, and his support for FDR's recovery programs made him a prince among liberals nationally. But in Colorado, where Roosevelt's coattails were shorter than in many other states and justice for blacks little prized, Costigan's reputation could be turned against him. Wasn't he spending too much time on national matters? Didn't he care about the people back home? The relief muddle hurt him, as did Roche's defeat. Facing an arduous 1936 campaign, he had also to think of his health. Suffering from asthma, victim of a 1934 stroke, and overworked, he suffered a heart attack in late March 1936, followed by a blood clot that forced amputation of one leg. In early April 1936 his wife Mabel and two of his closest allies, Josephine Roche and Oscar Chapman, announced that the senator would not seek re-election.[32]

Ed Johnson said, "I deeply regret to learn of the illness of Senator Costigan. I have nothing further to say." A few days later he declared that he would run for Costigan's Senate seat. Distraught liberals scrambled to find a candidate. Roche had been defeated once; Chapman bowed out; so did Justice Benjamin C. Hilliard of the Colorado Supreme Court. Merle D. Vincent, a long-time Roche ally, fell by the wayside. In the end, liberals backed William E. Sweet, a former governor (1923–1925) whose father, Channing, had been a socialist. Johnson swallowed Sweet in the Democratic primary. In the general election he defeated the Republicans' sacrificial candidate, Raymond L. Sauter, by more than 133,000 votes. Franklin Roosevelt himself did not do that well in Colorado in 1936 — he out-polled Republican Alf Landon by some 114,000.[33]

Shattered Costiganites contented themselves with one major victory: the election of Teller Ammons to succeed Johnson as governor. Costigan protégés Oscar Chapman and Charles F. Brannan wisely stayed in Washington, where they both eventually gained cabinet posts in Truman's administration, Chapman as secretary of the interior and Brannan as secretary of agriculture. John Carroll took a minor prize, becoming Denver district attorney in 1937, but rose from the ashes of the Costigan camp to be elected Denver's congressman (1947–1951) and a U.S. Senator (1957–1963).

"So far as possible without betraying or neglecting the interests of my own state, I expect to follow his [Roosevelt's] wise and courageous leadership," Johnson pledged at the outset of his campaign. Once in the Senate, his fleeting loyalty to Roosevelt turned to Jell-O as both he and Alva Adams often voted with Republicans and conservative Democrats. It was a posture that served Johnson well. He won re-election to the Senate in 1942 and 1948 and, on coming home, he again became governor (1955–1957). Before Big Ed emerged, Billy Adams laid claim to being the most successful politician in twentieth-century Colorado. By the time Johnson retired, the crown belonged to him. He wore it proudly until his death, at age 86, in 1970.[34]

Costigan, self-described as "a lightning-shattered pine," could make no such boast, although his intellectual legacy and civil rights commitment lived in such successors as John Carroll. Back in his Denver home, which he and his wife Mabel shared with Josephine Roche, Costigan went into seclusion from late 1937 until he died, at 64, early in 1939. "So while my trunk shall pass away," he wrote,

> To pitchy black or ashen grey,
> Flame-charioted I, heart of pine,
> Will search the earth for hearts
> like mine.

Of those hearts, few were more touched than Josephine Roche's. Thirty-six years after he died, she reminisced, "After him every man seemed very dull."[35]

Dead before its third birthday, FERA, like Costigan, had suffered much. Plagued by disorganization and sometimes mismanaged by local officials hostile to relief, it was ill served by its friends who politicized it. "I am very sympathetic to Senator Costigan," field agent Glassberg warned Hopkins, "but it seems to me most important to keep CWA and FERA administration completely clear of both wings of the Democratic party." On-again, off-again funding did not help either. "I don't know the straight of this relief muddle at Denver," Congressman John A. Martin of Pueblo wired Hopkins shortly before the November 1934 elections. "I do know the hundred times more serious effect of cutting our work relief. . . . It is just raising billyhell."[36]

Martin was correct, but FERA's problems went even deeper. Its annual expenditures dwarfed the state's pre-Depression budgets; to its administrators all Colorado hearkened, yet the agency could not fully relieve distress. Louie Bunelen of Sterling could not buy milk for his baby on the $3 he got every two weeks, nor could others, particularly in rural areas where doles were often far lower than in Denver, Pueblo, and Colorado Springs. By promising help that it failed to consistently deliver, FERA became the focus of discontent. It also angered many people, for in attempting to save their bacon, it failed to save their pride. Ed Johnson's attacks on the agency would not have helped him reap nearly 300,000 votes in 1936 had his jibes appealed only to the rich and to a few state-rights purists. His barbs drew blood because many Coloradans, as much as they needed federal assistance, nevertheless resented it for endangering their independence and shattering their dreams.

Often they appeared ungrateful for the help they received, unmindful that Colorado had captured more than its share of FERA money. In later years, when they thought back on the New Deal, they tended to forget welfare czars Broad, Fairall, Shawver, Kelso, and Baird; relief riots, transient camps, and mattress factories; and FERA itself, which once helped feed, clothe, and house a fourth of the state's people. Instead they recalled more popular programs, such as the Civilian Conservation Corps, an experiment ennobled in part by its conservation mission, by the great outdoors, and by plenty of fresh air.

SIX

The Civilian Conservation Corps

Dear Ma and Sis:

I received the package Monday. Was I glad when I seen that towel and soap oh! boy, I been drying my face with may handkerchief until now. ... Send me them gloves too. We sure have been cutting down plenty trees.

Vic M.
Lake George, Colo.
C.C.C. 802nd
Camp No. F-13[1]

When Vic M., a Civilian Conservation Corps recruit from Las Animas County, reached Lake George, 19 miles west of Woodland Park, in mid-1933, he was, officials reported, so "thin and emaciated" that "even the ten year olds wouldn't let him play with them on their baseball team." Six months transformed Vic. His weight shot up from 90 to 138, and he was asked to join the baseball team. "From a sick, dull boy, he has become a physically sound and mentally alert young man." More than that, "the twenty-five dollars a month has taken his family from dull penury to comfort. . . . President Roosevelt and his C.C.C. camps are counted very highly among the blessings for which they thank God."[2]

The first enrollees in Denver also thanked FDR for the Civilian Conservation Corps (CCC), naming their temporary quarters at Fort Logan, "Camp Roosevelt." Authorized by Congress on March 31, 1933, the CCC became one of the most popular New Deal programs and still lingers in fond historical memory. William E. Doyle, later a judge of the Tenth U.S. Circuit Court of Appeals in Denver, remembered his days as a CCC foreman: "It had all sorts of intangible values. It helped you grow up." Wayne N. Aspinall, Speaker of the Colorado House of Representatives (1937) and later a durable Democratic congressman (1949–1973), called it "one of the great political institutions of Colorado."[3]

Like the Peace Corps of the 1960s, the CCC appealed to American idealism, albeit an idealism bounded by prejudices. Women could not join, and Colorado's African-Americans were often sent to segregated outfits in New Mexico, Texas, and Arizona. Hispanos, an estimated 40 percent of the state's recruits by 1938, often found themselves concentrated in heavily Hispanic units. Young men, mainly between 18 and 25, were asked to serve their country by conserving its farms, sprucing up its forests and parks, and protecting its grazing lands. In return, Uncle Sam offered soldiers in his "bug army" $30 a month, of which $25 went to dependents back home, or, if the man had none, $22 per month was put in escrow for his use on discharge.

CCC recruits at Denver's City and County Building on their way to Fort Logan, April 1933. (Colorado Historical Society)

Enrollees, who initially joined for six months, could survive on low wages because they received free housing, free meals, free health care, free vocational and high school educations, and free government-issue clothing.[4]

The state's first regular camp at Trout Creek, 14 miles northeast of Buena Vista, opened on May 9, 1933. Its last, a forestry operation at Monument, closed in 1942. In the intervening years, 32,501 Coloradans, including some World War I veterans exempted from normal age restrictions, and a few hundred Native Americans who worked at home on the Southern Ute Reservation, joined the relief army. A state of more than 100,000 square miles, about one-third federally owned, much of it forest, farm, or grazing land, Colorado offered ample opportunity for the agency to live up to its motto: "Save the Soil, Save the Forests, Save the Young Men."[5]

Because enrollments were limited by a population-based quota, many out-of-staters staffed the state's projects. In 1938, of 7,400 CCCers, Colorado claimed less than half as citizens. "Kentucky gentlemen" in Company 2552 enjoyed the scenery at Estes Park, Company 2547 at Elbert brought Ohioans and West Virginians to Colorado, and Texans breathed mountain air at Pagosa Springs. On the other hand, at Red Feather Lakes in north-central Colorado, Fort Collins area recruits found an outdoors near home, as did the cadre at South Fork, many of them Hispanos from the San Luis Valley. In a decade, the CCC established, abolished, sometimes re-established, and eventually disbanded more than 170 Colorado camps, most housing companies of 150 to 200 men.[6]

On arriving at Lake George, Vic M. found no bathing facilities, but he reassured his mother "some of the men are now starting to make a bath house. It will be keen then." Harried army officers, assigned to construct and administer the camps, scrambled during the spring and summer of 1933 to accommodate some 7,000 men. They outfitted them with World War I surplus uniforms and housed them however they could — some in hastily constructed barracks, some in old hospital tents. "We live in tents," wrote Vic M., "seven in one tent me and Joe Menepace and Metro Morgan are in the same tent." At the hastily organized Rocky Mountain National Park camp, recruits, who for a time lacked adequate blankets and sufficient food, braved two blizzards in May 1933. The second one tore some of their tents to shreds. Gradually, but not universally, conditions improved. At Morrison well-made barracks survived into the 1990s.[7]

Inspectors checked on latrines, literacy, lice, and literature. At Buffalo Creek in mid-December 1934 investigator James C. Reddoch found 121 men at work on projects ranging from fence-building to trail maintenance. He uncovered no bedbugs, no communistic propaganda, no illiterate recruits. He did discover that three men had eloped, and he criticized the camps' quarters in a "summer resort hotel . . . wholly unsuited for winter occupancy." He was even less impressed with Company 1842 at Delta, which he inspected August 12, 1937. The camp, mainly tents, offered its denizens a recreation hall "practically bare," made enrollees pay 50¢ a month for laundry, charged its doctor $5 a month for his tent, and gave its men only two suits of summer underwear. He thought more highly of the Idaho Springs camp, which he toured in the summer of 1940. Because the camp was located in town, the CCCers could attend movies three nights a week. He rated morale, shoes, clothes, barracks, kitchen, and the canteen as excellent, and he recommended that the commander, Edward A. Hazlett, be given a raise.[8]

"We don't do much work," Vic M. noted. "We get up at 6:30 breakfast at 7:30 and start to work at 8:00 and work until 11:30 dinner at 12:00 afternoon start work at 1:00, quit at 4:00. supper at 4:45, put out the lights at 9:00 at nite." During the day, and often in the evening or on weekends, corpsmen found time for education and recreation. At Vallecito, north of Bayfield, recruits could take grade school and high school classes, learn auto mechanics and carpentry, and dabble in photography and leather craft. Their 900-volume library also included six daily newspapers and 53 magazines. At Norwood enrollees could take correspondence courses to finish high school and could choose among 14 vocational classes. Many companies boasted newspapers, often mimeographed sheets: the *Ballyhoo* in Boulder, the *Dam-An-Furrow* in Hugo, the *Yawns and Gaps* in Colorado Springs, the *Rocket Echoes* in Castle Rock.[9]

Some enrollees grumbled about the food: "Plentiful and wholesome, it is often unappetizing." A 1934 report from Larimer County told of 24 boys threatening "to walk out and go home unless the food was improved." Despite lapses, the Corps took its culinary responsibilities seri-

CCC Company 801 at Beulah southwest of Pueblo. Pueblo, Denver, Boulder, and Colorado Springs used the CCC to improve mountain parks. (Pueblo Library District)

ously. On Sunday, August 1, 1937, Company 2803 in Grand Junction breakfasted on peaches, cream of wheat, and hotcakes; lunched on cold cuts, cabbage and apple salad, pickles, onions, bread, cheese, Jell-O; and dined on roast pork, mashed potatoes, green beans, lettuce salad, and coconut cream pie. Advising recruiters on employing cooks, CCC officials gave clear directions: "The primary basis for selection of this group is the ability to COOK."[10]

Perhaps a few deserted because of the food; most had more serious reasons. After James W. left the Gunnison camp, the foreman found letters indicating that his "stepfather was beating his mother and taking the allotment money." Edwin G.'s wife's pregnancy seemingly caused him to desert. Alfonso M. "married a widow with four children and apparently sought more remunerative employment outside of the corps." After 1937 increasing numbers of young men found more lucrative work outside of the Corps, which was paying around 10¢ an hour, so the CCC dropped its requirement that its men be on relief and allowed more African-Americans to join.[11]

Headquartered at Fort Logan, the Corps worked with the Forest Service, the National Parks Service, the Bureau of Reclamation, the Soil Conservation Service, the Division of Grazing of the Interior Department, and municipal parks throughout the state. On the plains, CCCers improved ditches, sowed cover crops, demonstrated contour plowing, planted trees as windbreaks, and helped kill grasshoppers. In the mountains they planted trees, built roads and trails, strung telephone lines, and fought fires, including the intractable 1934 burn north of DeBeque, which ignited surface oil shale. Declaring war on pests, they killed Black Hills bark beetles, which proliferated in Colorado in 1933, scattered poisoned oats to eradicate rodents, battled toxic larkspur in the White River National Forest, and murdered porcupines at Mesa Verde. They crusaded against deadly hemlock at the old mining town of Leando in the Holy Cross Forest and eradicated mistletoe in Boulder. Near Palisade they lined irrigation canals with concrete to retard erosion. North of Craig near the Snake River, they dug wells and built water tanks. By 1938, when it reached its halfway mark, the CCC had compiled a remarkable record in Colorado, including the planting of 9,609,400 trees, the construction of 86,887 check dams, and the stocking of 2,676,500 fish.[12]

Among the CCC's beneficiaries, the Interior Department's Division of Grazing owed the Corps special thanks, for without CCC help, the Division would have been hard-pressed to fulfill the conservation mandate it acquired in 1934 when Colorado congressman Edward T. Taylor won congressional approval of the Taylor Grazing Act. For decades rangeland had been abused by cattlemen and sheepmen. To prevent and reverse range destruction, the Taylor Act set up grazing districts managed by local stockmen charged with wisely using the public domain. Prodded by Farrington R. Carpenter, a Republican rancher from Hayden who became the first director of the Grazing Division, sheep and cattle ranchers cooperated. By building fences, trails, and stock watering holes, the CCC helped assure the success of Taylor's law.[13]

Stock tanks and irrigation ditches were not things of obvious beauty, but other CCC projects became long-term joys. The spectacular 25-mile Rimrock Drive auto road penetrating Colorado National Monument west of Grand Junction owed its creation to CCC and Civil Works Administration (CWA) laborers, nine of the CWAers dying in a rock slide on the road December 12, 1933. The Triple C's checked the St. Charles River south of Pueblo with a 104-foot-high, 700-foot-long earthen dam, behind which rose Lake San Isabel. On the lakefront, corpsmen built piers, a boathouse, a community house, and picnic tables. CCCers made Highline Drive in Colorado Springs's Garden of the Gods and constructed the Rampart Range Road north from the Garden to Devil's Head and farther north to connect with State Highway 67. West of Boulder on Flagstaff Mountain, James P. Solan and his masonry crew helped make the Sunrise Circle outdoor theater in 1934. Later Solan worked on a similar, grander project, Denver's Red Rocks Amphitheater, a 10,000-seat masterwork constructed by Morrison's CCC Company 1848 between 1936 and 1941.[14]

George E. Cranmer, after mid-1935, Denver's manager of Parks and Improvements, spearheaded creation of the theater. The city had purchased the magnificent assemblage of sandstone outcroppings at the base of the Front Range in the late 1920s. In 1931 a visitors' center, modeled on New Mexico pueblos, was built near the larger rocks. For a while Denver left the area in its natural state, an arrangement no doubt palatable to frugal Benjamin F. Stapleton, Denver's mayor from 1923 to 1931 and again

CCC Camp F-51-C, Company 831, near Norrie on the Fryingpan River. Camp designation "F" indicated that the facility was associated with the Forest Service. (Denver Public Library, Western History Department)

from 1935 to 1947. As George Cranmer remembered it, Stapleton was something of a Puritan, who found theaters faintly evil. Cranmer, on the other hand, had seen the ancient amphitheater at Taormina in Sicily and envisioned something like it for Denver. Utilizing the architectural talents of Burnham Hoyt and labor from the CCC and the Works Progress Administration, Cranmer got the amphitheater built and roads and parking lots constructed. "The last place I looked for money," Cranmer recalled, "was the Denver city treasury."[15]

The assault on Mother Nature at Red Rocks, where huge boulders were dynamited to create a seating terrace, did not trouble the Corps, which defined its conservation mission broadly. After the Memorial Day flood of 1935, CCCers helped dig the towns of Kiowa and Elbert out of the mud. In Colorado Springs they policed devastated neighborhoods with such zeal that they refused Governor Ed Johnson access without a pass. At Two Buttes, 200 corpsmen searched for Steve Benson, a three-year-old lost in a dust storm; in Fort Collins they saved two-year-old Albert Delehoy from the icy Poudre River. In Gardner, northwest of Walsenburg, they ignored separation of church and state long enough to build pews for Sacred Heart Catholic Church.[16]

Employing young men by the tens of thousands, plus thousands of others including cooks, foremen, doctors, and teachers, the CCC shored up local economies. "My mother was delighted when I joined the CCC, for

the first time she would have a steady income of $25 a month. The money supported my mother and four brothers and sisters," Bernard Valdez, later Denver's housing manager, recalled. Corpsmen's "pocket money" often wound up in cash registers at local drugstores, pool halls, and movie houses. The organization needed lumber for its buildings and food for its workers. "My father, Frank Brady, manager of Boulder Lumber, was happy to get a CCC order," the Reverend John F. Brady, S.J., remembered in 1992, nearly 60 years after the CCC built its Boulder barracks. Some estimates put CCC camps' local expenditures as high as $5,000 a month.[17]

Conservation work pleased Coloradans, who appreciated having their land preserved and made accessible. Who could fault the CCC's efforts to help more people enjoy America's "purple mountains' majesty" and its "amber waves of grain?" Who could question FDR's magnaminity in helping young men assist their families and learn skills? Normally CCC enrollees did not displace other laborers and thereby risk the ire of labor unions. Had the Corps not constructed Red Rocks Amphitheater, Denver

Before the CCC created Red Rocks Amphitheater by making seats for 10,000, the area was a big rock garden. (Denver Public Library, Western History Department)

likely would have left it as a big rock garden. And if one of the "boys," as recruits were often called, leaned on a shovel north of Gunnison or west of Grand Junction, the likelihood that a *Denver Post* reporter would discover the sluggard was remote.

Still, the relief army attracted detractors. Some mothers suspected that the government wanted to train their sons for war. Warwick Downing of Denver worried about the safety of unprotected women living north of Genesee Mountain near the Mount Vernon Country Club, where the CCC proposed to put a camp: "The presence of a large number of young men at our entrance will cause much apprehension."[18]

Others choked on political vapors. Denver officials, Republican-leaning during the mayoralty of George D. Begole (1931–1935), charged in June 1933 that CCC supervisory jobs were going to "broken-down politicians, men entirely too feeble to stand the rigors of forestation work." They had a point: Democrats favored Democrats. James Solan, masonry supervisor on the Flagstaff amphitheater project, was a good Democrat. William E. Doyle, a foreman at Evergreen and later at Boulder, was not only a Democrat, he was also brother-in-law of John A. Carroll, one of Costigan's chief lieutenants. When George A. Carlson, a well-qualified landscape engineer, needed a job in 1933, he went to Carroll. "He [Carroll] said, 'George, you're already branded. But I'll see what I can do. Will you be loyal to us?'" Carlson responded: "You're darned right I'll be loyal to you. I need to eat." Political bickering led to the transfer of CCC camps from Denver's mountain parks in 1933, but in 1934 Begole invited them back.[19]

The town of Hugo's 1938 mini-revolt against the CCC was triggered less by patronage politics than by small-town factionalism. When Buck Owens's Roving Ranger Dog and Pony Show's trucks got mired in a mud hole north of Hugo, CCCers helped pull them out. Owens, reportedly, did not say thanks. That evening, after dinner, corpsmen drifted into Hugo, where they heard that Owens was saying nasty things about them. In retaliation they went to the fairgrounds and collapsed the Roving Ranger tent by slashing its support ropes. Owens later accepted $20 in damages from camp commander Captain Earl J. Yates, who reprimanded his men. The incident also sparked a petition, signed by 62 people, requesting a federal inquiry.

Investigator E. L. Creager talked with some 50 Hugoans late in August 1938. Many petitioners said that they signed simply because they were asked, that they had no bone to pick with the CCC and no firsthand knowledge of the fracas. Mr. Paul Papke, a rancher, did testify that CCC boys cursed in the streets "several years back; that the local authorities did not arrest the boys for such misconduct." He also charged that "the boys are always 'slopped up on booze' which makes the streets of Hugo unfit for girls." Ralph Brockway, another rancher, called the petition "a lot of 'bunk'" and pointed out that the CCC "is a help to the town." Mrs. J. C. Cave, a woman "about ninety years old," said she signed the petition to please a friend, that "she does not know a thing against the CCC; that she could not

even recognize a CCC boy if she saw one and does not remember having ever seen one." Creager concluded that "there appears to be in the town of Hugo two factions: one consisting of substantial citizens of the town, who readily recognize the benefit to the community occasioned by the presence of the Civilian Conservation Corps; and the other consisting of people who are chronically dissatisfied." He recommended that no action be taken.[20]

CCC Company 868 at Palisade. (Denver Public Library, Western History Department)

As Hugo went, so went Colorado. Most people saw more advantages than disadvantages from the Corps, and hence they winked at transgressions. They especially liked the more than $56 million that flowed into the state between 1933 and 1941 to support the "tree monkeys." Many corpsmen also found the experience rewarding. Decades after he helped build the dam at Lake San Isabel, Orlando Romero of Trinidad returned to find his initials still visible on the concrete spillway. "I took my wife and my son and his wife and our grandson to show them where I had been and what I had done. And I felt rather comfortable in showing them that. It's something that people are still using."

Coloradans welcomed the CCC, its projects, and most of all its money. Other poor people, especially if they were Hispanic, were less well received. Aware of Coloradans' hostility toward "Mexicans," Governor Johnson snatched up the state's welcome mats and in 1936 blockaded its southern border to prevent "indigent and alien labor" from entering.[21]

SEVEN

Blockade

This martial law along our border is an infernal nuisance to tourists and business travelers. American citizens simply don't like being stopped on the roadside by armed men. This is not Europe, in spite of all the apeing of European mannerisms that some of our jackass politicians can manage to put across.

Durango Herald-Democrat
April 28, 1936

Late in April 1936 General Neil West Kimball, commander of the Colorado National Guard, took up quarters in the bridal suite of Trinidad's Columbian Hotel. Drawn there neither by honeymoon nor anniversary, Kimball and his staff bravely bore the rigors of army life: wake-up calls from the front desk, refreshments from room service. Acting at Governor Johnson's behest he dispatched his troops to the Colorado–New Mexico line south of Trinidad and to other southern border-crossings. Their mission: to resist invasion.[1]

The enemy, mostly Hispanos, without generals, without arms, without room service, moved north toward Colorado in the spring of 1936 as it had in springs past. Its intent was also manifest, to get work for its troops — men, women, and children. For decades Colorado farmers, railroads, and sheep raisers had welcomed their labor. Others, including Ed Johnson, viewed them with alarm. Why, they asked, should aliens and indigents take local jobs and depress wages? Why, they wondered, should the state welcome more poor people?

The questions frequently sprang from a deep dislike of Hispanos, some of them recent arrivals from Mexico, some long-term residents of Colorado without citizenship papers, some descendants of seventeenth-century Spanish settlers of New Mexico. Lumped together as "Mexicans," they found that their poverty, their culture, their Catholicism, their language, all told against them. Had their numbers remained constant and their communities stayed concentrated in southern Colorado, they might, perhaps, have been spared the full force of bigotry. But the demand for cheap labor, particularly for workers so poor they would toil with the back-breaking short hoe, called the *mata Cristiano*, "Christian killer," attracted large numbers of Hispanos to northern Colorado. In 1930, census takers found that nearly 5 percent (57,676) of the state's population was Mexican-born. More than 10 percent of them (6,837) resided in Denver, and thousands more lived in sugar beet–producing counties such as Weld (8,792) and Larimer (2,054).

Studying South Platte beet districts in the late 1920s, economist Paul S. Taylor found "Mexicans" barred from many small-town barbershops, drugstores, and restaurants and segregated in theaters. Farmers were warned to house them at a distance from the main house: "There are always children, sometimes quite a number, and if the houses are too close there is sure to be trouble." One woman told Taylor, "We had one Mexican who ate with the family, but he was specially clean." A theater owner stated, "We keep the Mexicans separately seated and let them know that they are not wanted. We don't give them service. . . . I doubt if the Mexicans

Hudson, Colorado, September 1938, "Great Western Sugar company's colony for sugar beet workers . . ." Caption from Farm Security Administration (FSA) photo by Allison. (FSA, Library of Congress)

Beet workers' shack in Colorado, 1938. (Photo by Allison, FSA, Library of Congress)

will ever get sufficiently educated and clean." Nor did most city-dwellers appreciate the newcomers. One Denverite complained to Ed Johnson, "West Denver was once the home owners domain but now the copper hides are littering the alleys with broken glass, stones, and Junior Mexico."[2]

Before the 1930s, farmers balanced their antipathy toward Hispanos against their need for labor. The "Mexicans" worked for a pittance, annually earning between $600 and $800 per family, which some supplemented by taking winter jobs in coal mines or by working for railroads. Those were the good times. In 1932 workers estimated their yearly beet pay would

Hudson, Colorado, September 1938, adobe houses of farm workers. (Photo by Allison, FSA, Library of Congress)

amount to only about $100 before expenses. Finding conditions "deplorable beyond belief," J. R. Ruberson, an investigator for Colorado's Industrial Commission, wondered "how any man can live and maintain his family on the price that is offered the beet workers." Seasonal laborers, he said, suffered "a condition of industrial slavery far worse than the chattel slavery of old."[3]

Some "slaves" considered revolting in May 1932 when labor organizers encouraged them to strike. The *Colorado Labor Advocate* reported that "approximately 95 percent of the workers announced that they would refuse to work in the fields." Strike spokesmen demanded reinstatement of the $23-per-acre pay workers had received in the late 1920s. They insisted on being paid in cash, and they wanted their pay guaranteed. Claiming that it usually had "a kindly feeling for those who represent the laboring people," Greeley's *Weld County News* had no mercy for "ill advised, if not malicious agitators." They should, insisted the paper, "be dealt with severely." Weld County's sheriff, W. W. Wyatt, agreed. He quickly jailed union organizers. In late May the *Brighton Blade* reported that the "communistic leaders from Denver have about given up."[4]

Organizers struck at the right moment in the wrong year. Farmers needed lots of workers in May to thin and block the sprouting beets, but in 1932 they faced declining payments from Great Western Sugar, which was itself battling huge losses. Farmers had no reason to raise pay because unemployed laborers were so plentiful that counties were pressuring Mexican nationals to go home.

Thousands left. The *Brighton Blade* reported that "33 automobiles carrying 202 Mexicans went through Adams County early Thursday morning [May 19, 1932] on their way to Juarez." Another 2,000, the paper said, had "shipped by train to Juarez from Denver and Northern Colorado." The *Fort Collins Express-Courier* explained that it was better to export aliens than to give them relief. Bent County dispatched 91 Mexicans, "many in area for a number of years," providing them with 200 loaves of bread and 150 pounds of bologna with which to make sandwiches on their trip south.[5]

Exporting aliens seemed sensible to taxpayers. The Federal Emergency Relief Administration (FERA), on the other hand, helped them. Hispanos with large families allegedly found that relief paid more than field work. "For two summers," the Colorado Bureau of Public Welfare observed in 1935, "there was very little beet work, and the FERA used no pressure upon these families to accept this type of employment with the result that very few left the city [Denver]." O. Edgar Abbott, a disgruntled Denverite, informed Hopkins that "relief recipients are not only foreigners, but are aliens — some alien enemies." Mexicans, he reported, "who formerly bought bulk coffee at 20 cents a pound now insist on Hill Brothers Coffee at 35 cents a pound. 'I am as good as anybody else,' they say; 'why shouldn't I have the best?'"[6]

Aware of the hostility toward Hispanos, Governor Johnson attacked FERA in March 1935 for assisting indigent aliens, more than 2,000 of whom, he claimed, were feeding at the public trough. Such persons, he insisted, should be deported, a process he offered to hasten by rounding up the interlopers, mostly Mexican nationals, and putting them in a concentration camp on South Table Mountain near Golden. There, it was argued, they could be fed cheaply until sent away. The Mexican ambassador to the United States objected when Johnson ejected 32 Hispanos: 20 of them, said the diplomat, were U.S. citizens. The State Department apologized to Mexico, and FERA told Johnson that it would help indigents regardless of citizenship.[7]

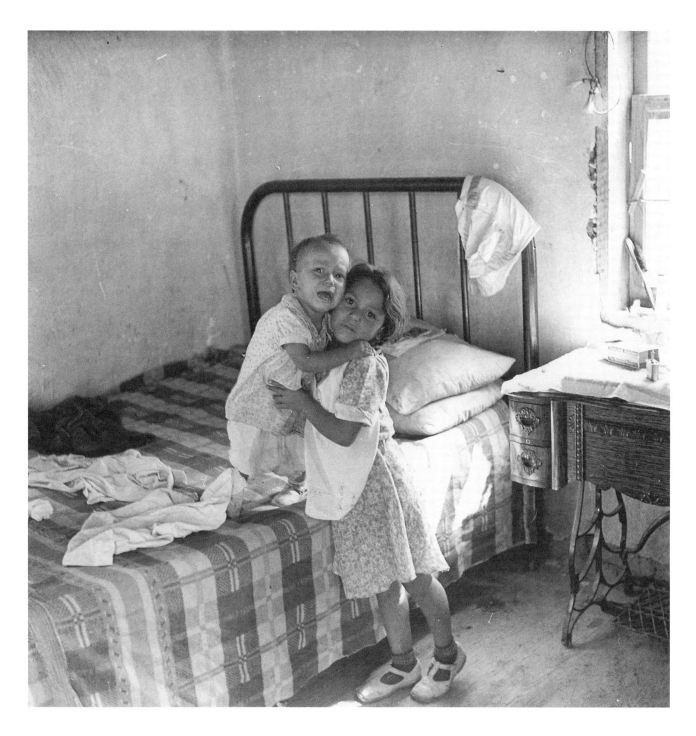

Big Ed counterattacked in 1936. Instead of evicting those he considered undesirable, he decided not to let them in. On Saturday, April 18, 1936, he proclaimed that the state faced an invasion from "aliens and indigent persons" looking for jobs. The onslaught, he warned, could trigger unrest because "it is impossible for large numbers of our own citizens to find employment." To counter the trespassers, he ordered the National Guard to seal Colorado's 365-mile-long southern border, where they were to turn away non-citizens and poor travelers.[8]

Hudson, Colorado, September 1938, farm workers' children. (Photo by Allison, FSA, Library of Congress)

Colorado National Guard officers, some of them summoned from a military ball, plan the blockade. From left to right, sitting: R. C. Royal, J. E. Ryan, E. C. Austin, William O. Perry, Neil Kimball; standing, E. G. Egan, Roy Qualls, Virgil D. Stone. Caption derived from The Denver Post, *April 19, 1936. (Colorado Historical Society)*

"Colorado National Guard companies E and B, 168th Field Artillery, and Forty-fifth tank division lined up at the guard headquarters at East Third avenue and Logan street Sunday before departing for the 'front.' " Caption from The Denver Post, *April 20, 1936. (Colorado Historical Society)*

General Kimball mobilized quickly, summoning some of his tuxedo-clad officers from a military ball to plan strategy. Late on Sunday, April 19, he registered his 16-man contingent at the Columbian, the finest hostelry in Trinidad. The next morning, refreshed after a tavern breakfast, he moved south to Raton Pass, where by 6:00 A.M. he had established Camp Johnson near the Colorado–New Mexico line. In the meantime, local lawmen had been enforcing the governor's edict. On Sunday, Las Animas undersheriff Harry Jones turned back a truck with six poor laborers. When one of them objected and said that he "stood on the constitution," Jones told him "go

Guardsmen posting sign. (Colorado Historical Society)

ahead and stand on it, but that he should do his standing on the New Mexico side of the border."[9]

War correspondents, outnumbering Kimball's force by two, recorded the day's events. Soldiers put up large signs: "Martial Law — Slow — Stop." With military precision, they met and vanquished the first invaders: nine people crammed into a broken-down jalopy, among them "Ramone Ruiz, his wife and five children, the youngest, a babe in arms." At first the travelers tried trickery, denying that they could speak English. Guardsmen were not fooled. Finding that Ruiz and friends had only a total of $3, they sent them back to New Mexico. Victory followed victory. By the end of the day, 75 people, many with less than 30¢, had been turned away. Similar reports came from other fronts: from Durango, where Lieutenant Colonel Edward C. Austin established headquarters in the Strater Hotel, from Conejos in the San Luis Valley, from Campo in the southeast. The next day, guardsmen stopped trains and ordered tramps to walk back to Raton. Employing technology and cunning, Kimball surveyed the border from the air and sent spies to snoop in New Mexico. In other parts of Colorado, highway patrolmen monitored entry spots to determine whether paupers were circumventing the southern checkpoints.

Guardsmen on the Colorado-Oklahoma border south of Campo prepare to stop aliens and indigents. (Photo by Arthur Rothstein, April 1936, FSA, Library of Congress)

Occasionally the operation faltered, as when Kimball snared a suspected indigent only to find that she had $5,000 in cash. Charles E. Lounsbury, editor of the *Rocky Mountain News*, an opponent of the exercise, chuckled, "We cannot resist, knowing the Adjutant General as well as we do, saying that this is the largest amount of money he has ever beheld in one chunk." The misstep, however, was minor, and Kimball recovered. "We have a job to do here," he said, "a mighty serious job." Within 24 hours of the blockade's inception, *The Denver Post* hailed Johnson for saving more than 1,000 jobs for residents. By April 23 more than 400 outsiders had been rebuffed; uncounted others had not even tried to enter. Only a few Coloradans, the governor reported, had complained. Others delighted in his decision, seeing it as sanctioning their prejudices. From southwestern Colorado he heard praise: "Down here in the sunny San Juan Basin we feel we have more than our share of Mexicans."[11]

Poor migrants could not counterattack. Their only choice was to turn around. But they had allies, including New Mexico governor Clyde Tingley. "You would think," he said, "that New Mexico had been cut off from the United States and was a foreign country." New Mexicans, he reminded Johnson, "are not aliens any more than the citizens of Colorado are aliens. . . . They are descendants of people who settled this country when Colorado was still part of New Mexico." Tingley demanded that guardsmen spying in his state get out. He also threatened to ban Colorado products: "We'll stop every truck bringing shipments into New Mexico and force truckers to unload."[12]

Johnson also found enemies at home. Helen Fischer, a Boulder activist, damned the blockade as "Un-American, conducive to race hatred, and unconstitutional." Socialist leader Carle Whitehead and the Methodist minister Edgar M. Wahlberg objected. Johnson explained that he was trying to help workers: "Lincoln didn't free all the slaves in 1863. We have slavery today competing with free labor." The governor had a point — local Hispanos suffered because of the annual influx of out-of-state workers. But because the blockade was seen as anti-Mexican, the governor lost points with Hispanos. David Chavez, Jr., the district attorney of Santa Fe, New Mexico, wrote Johnson that the Spanish-Americans in Colorado think "you are discriminating against them as a class." Beet workers in Greeley certainly thought so; they passed a resolution condemning the blockade.[13]

Others feared economic reprisals. "I will be dead broke on the deal," a woman who had invested in potatoes complained on learning New Mexicans were boycotting Colorado spuds. A distraught citizen asked Johnson to allow an out-of-state sheep shearer in: "If this man can't come in to shear sheep we are just about up aginst it." The *Durango Herald-Democrat* editorialized, "There is no money in this horse play. . . . It drives tourists away. . . . It violates constitutional rights. . . . It is merely a piece of political grandstanding upon the part of the governor and the quicker the governor finds out that the damphool [*sic*] idea isn't even popular, the better off will be our treasury and our people."[14]

On Wednesday, April 30, less than two weeks after declaring martial law, Johnson ended it. "Colorado has always been a good neighbor," he claimed, "and we must not now alienate the friendship of our sister states." *The Denver Post* cast a rosy light on the debacle by praising Johnson's attempt to save jobs for residents. The *Lamar Daily News* suggested that if Big Ed again wanted to get his picture in *The Denver Post*, he "display his manly beauty in bathing trunks. . . . This ought to make a sure hit and it would be cheaper than declaring war on the rest of the United States."

Kimball gave his men medals; Johnson answered letters, such as the following:

> Kind Sir,
>
> I understand you have guards on the border of Colo. stopping all cars. As I am moving to San Luis Valey [*sic*] Colo. with family and a truck load of milk cows (cows are inspected to fill requirement of all laws) I would appreciate a pass of clearance so I will not be held up on the road.
>
> Sincerely yours,
>
> John W. Lowman
> Eagle Point, Oregon

No pass, the governor responded, was needed.[15]

Organized labor, which might have been expected to back Johnson, did not. William E. Sweet, who earned labor's endorsement in the 1936 U.S. Senate Democratic primary contest, castigated the governor for ordering "his brave soldiers [to] stick their bayonets in the empty bellies of the Spanish-Americans who came to Colorado seeking work." Johnson beat Sweet by more than two-to-one. When President Roosevelt stopped at Julesburg in late September 1936 and when he campaigned along the Front Range in mid-October, he had little choice except to embrace Johnson, a maverick who understood his constituents' fears and prejudices. Many Coloradans, although uneasy with the governor's means, approved of his goal in imposing the blockade. Some applauded him out of racism; others out of desperation. In 1936, as in 1933, they still lacked jobs, still looked for answers. Big Ed, they thought, was at least trying to help.[16]

EIGHT

Work Programs and Pump-Priming

I sometimes wonder just what Pueblo would have done if it had not been for the generosity of the federal government. Our parks are rated as some of the finest in the nation. We have miles of paved streets; miles of curbs and gutters and blocks of sidewalks have been constructed. Practically all streets and alleys have been graded and graveled. We have new buildings for civic activities; the Colorado State Fair has been brought from nothing to a million dollar institution.

Ray H. Talbot
Pueblo County Commissioner
April 2, 1942[1]

"Hello Mr. Luker, I'm glad to see you again," said Franklin D. Roosevelt. "I'm glad to see you again, Mr. President. God bless you. You saved us farmers' lives," Luker responded.

Four years earlier, in 1932, C. E. Luker, had broken through police lines in Denver to talk with Roosevelt. "I'm a farmer," Luker said, "just a common dirt farmer. If you don't help us, Mr. Roosevelt, we're sunk." Roosevelt promised, "If I am elected, with God's aid I will help you, and you will be the first people I will help."

Luker, who harvested a $16,000 wheat crop in 1936, returned to thank FDR for keeping his promise. They chatted for a few minutes before the president's motorcade left Denver's Union Station, passing 25,000 people as it moved through downtown en route to the Capitol grounds. There, 75,000 waited to hear him speak on October 12, 1936.[2]

They came to see the president, to say thanks, to ask his help. Mrs. Anna Carlson of Denver recalled that she went "to keep Fitzsimons open." Roosevelt, who included the army hospital in his visit, pledged, "As long as I am President, this hospital will continue in operation." Colorado, he noted, had benefited greatly from New Deal programs: price supports for sugar, help for mining. He promised it would gain even more from federal dams and reservoirs. "Of course we spent money," he admitted. From the crowd someone yelled, "Spend some more."[3]

The Denver Post hated the New Deal, which it accused of harboring Communists; the *Colorado Springs Gazette* called FDR "reckless and wasteful"; the *Pueblo Chieftain* chided him for proposing unconstitutional laws. Among the state's large-circulation dailies, only the *Rocky Mountain News* favored his re-election. But the crowds that flocked to hear him in Greeley, Denver, Colorado Springs, Pueblo, and La Junta signalled that he would defeat his Republican rival, Alf Landon, governor of Kansas. In Colorado

C. E. Luker of Eastlake north of Denver thanks FDR for helping farmers. Denver, October 12, 1936. (Photo by Harry Rhoads, Denver Public Library, Western History Department)

Springs, Roosevelt reckoned that twice as many people gathered as in 1932. "That's twice as many votes," a bystander quipped. "And I hope you are twice as happy," the president replied.[4]

Many were happier. Colorado's farm income was up 56 percent from its 1932 lows, and Denver's bank clearings rose by 70 percent in the same period. In 1932 only one Coloradan in eight made more than $5,000; in 1936 one in seven did. FDR claimed some credit for the upswing, and he could point to clear successes: Federal Deposit Insurance Corporation protection for savers, Federal Housing Administration mortgages for home buyers, Securities and Exchange Commission vigilance for investors. Attacked for his work programs, Roosevelt retorted, "The wheels of your factories and mills began to turn for the first time — only after the government had begun to spend money and had provided employment for millions of people on all kinds of projects."[5]

Roosevelt's great flop, the National Recovery Administration (NRA), an early New Deal attempt to revive industry and spur employment by

FDR, Eleanor Roosevelt, Ed Johnson, and Denver mayor Benjamin Stapleton, Denver, October 12, 1936. (Denver Public Library, Western History Department)

fixing prices, wages, and hours of work, went unmentioned in his Denver address. Companies that adhered to NRA guidelines displayed the Blue Eagle, the symbol of recovery. The bird proved flightless as businesses evaded NRA rules. In 1935 the U.S. Supreme Court declared NRA, with the major exception of its adjunct, the Public Works Administration, unconstitutional. Governor Edwin C. Johnson kept a fledgling version, the Colorado Industrial Recovery Act, alive locally until it also hit legal snags and died.[6]

By 1936, stripped of NRA and having abandoned the Federal Emergency Relief Administration (FERA), Washington relied on two multi-billion-dollar-programs—the Works Progress Administration (WPA) and the Public Works Administration (PWA) — to absorb the unemployed and to prime the nation's economy. WPA, administered by Harry Hopkins, planned to make jobs by backing small and medium-sized ventures. PWA, directed by Interior Secretary Harold Ickes, concentrated on larger undertakings. FERA had created jobs and given relief. WPA and PWA left relief to the states. Their burden, it was assumed, would gradually be lightened by the Social Security Administration's pensions for retired persons, assistance for the blind, unemployment insurance, and payments to dependent children.

Coloradans helped nudge the nation toward Social Security by backing the Townsend Plan, concocted by California physician Francis F Townsend. He proposed granting $200 monthly to retired persons at age 60, requiring them to spend it within the month. That, he prognosticated, would help old people and give the economy a shot of fiscal Geritol. When local pension leaders, including Denver attorney O. Otto Moore, uncovered chicanery in the Townsend organization, they organized the National Annuity League. They triumphed in 1936 by securing an amendment to Colorado's constitution earmarking 85 percent of sales and liquor taxes to fund pensions of $45 a month to residents 60 or over who lacked other income. Besieged by taxpayers, who demanded lower taxes, and state agencies and universities, who wanted more money, the legislature refused to fully pay the pensioners. Not until 1943 did retirees regularly collect $45 per month.[7]

Unemployed persons under 60 had no cushion except general relief, at best a concrete pillow. Mary H. Isham of the State Relief Committee suggested in 1935 that FERA's demise might rekindle "that old neighborly spirit" in Colorado communities, "which have been willing to let Uncle Sam do it all." Denver's "neighborly spirit" during July 1936 brought relief recipients about $12 per family. Sometimes, as in March and early April 1939, they got nothing. "The only thing that kept some of these people going was a small supply of surplus foods in the federal warehouse," reported Gene H. Harris of the Denver Welfare Bureau. That year Colorado's 38,990 pensioners received an average of $29.55 each month; welfare clients, of whom there were 55,874, survived on $6 each. Disgusted with relief in Denver, the Reverend C. P. Sauter wrote Roosevelt, "God Almighty is not pleased with it." Mortals did not like it either, finding that the stigma of relief often outweighed the pittance they received. Half a century after the Depression ended, Denver journalist Gene Amole still recalled "universal themes with which any kid who grew up in the Depression could identify. Moving in with relatives and sleeping in shifts to avoid going on 'relief' was one of them."[8]

Paltry relief and a sputtering economy left tens of thousands dependent on federal work programs. WPA and PWA tried to sidestep the state-federal quagmires that had sucked FERA into bottomless controversies. Washington ran both agencies, appointing administrators and reviewing proposals. If local officials failed to submit worthy projects or did not put up sufficient matching money, they could twiddle their thumbs and face the political consequences as neighboring towns built schools and other states constructed dams. No one had to play ball with the federal government, but those who did were rewarded with ballfields, bridges, golf courses, schools, paved streets, community centers, sewers, and swimming pools.[9]

That was theory. In fact, Congress expected WPA to quickly reduce unemployment, so sometimes it allowed its workers to plod away on hastily and ill-conceived tasks. In Colorado the agency suffered from an additional handicap. By appointing Paul D. Shriver, a Costigan partisan, to head the state's WPA, Hopkins angered Ed Johnson, who accused the agency of foot-dragging in providing jobs, of employing aliens, of trying to buy people "like so many cattle," of "piddling around with leaf-raking projects."[10]

Shriver, one-time secretary of the Colorado Democratic party's central committee, left his post as a FERA lawyer in Washington, D.C., to return to Colorado in June 1935. He quickly met Johnson's anti-alien salvos. "They must," he said, "be taken care of." He scolded Johnson: "Hunger, unfortunately, is no respecter of persons or of citizenship. I cannot believe that your solution to the alien problem, even if it were possible to determine who were aliens, and who were not, is that such unfortunate people are to be allowed to starve within the boundaries of a state which justly boasts of its friendliness and hospitality." Privately Shriver told Hopkins that Johnson "is merely attempting to use this alien question for publicity purposes." In time the governor's view prevailed: Congress in 1937 ordered WPA to give citizens employment priority — a rule that led to the dismissal of more than 1,000 aliens in Colorado.[11]

To the foot-dragging charge, Shriver had a practical defense: it took time to organize the gigantic program, which Congress authorized on April 8, 1935. "How will office space, furniture and supplies be obtained?" Shriver asked Hopkins in mid-June. Who, Shriver wondered, would appoint subordinate administrators? Answering questions and setting up state headquarters at 810 Fourteenth Street in Denver occupied the agency for several months. By September 7 only 17 persons had gotten WPA jobs. To speed things up, Clinton P. Anderson, a WPA field representative who later became a U.S. senator from New Mexico, registered workers en masse at the Denver City Auditorium, a procedure geared to employ up to 1,500 each day. "They can straighten out the records while the men work," Anderson told WPA officials in Washington. By early November nearly 9,000 were busy; by late December, more than 40,000. The numbers rose to some 43,200 by March 1936 and then, in fits and starts, declined until, renamed the Works Projects Administration, WPA ceased operating in Colorado in March 1943. By then 150,000 Coloradans had been on its rolls.[12]

PWA employed fewer people than WPA, often only a couple of thousand a month. Because they were usually skilled persons hired by private contractors, PWA avoided much of the criticism that dogged WPA. It suffered a tortoise-like start, but Harold Ickes's cautious approach paid dividends, because carefully planned projects backed by local financing, ranging from 55 to 70 percent, insured public support. Paul Shriver at WPA proved a durable, if battle-scarred, administrator. PWA's head, George M. Bull, a respected engineer, was even more fortunate, winning praise at times from the anti–New Deal *Denver Post*.

Johnson's indictment of the WPA's "piddling around with leaf-raking projects" stuck in people's minds because there was some truth in it. The

WPA never confessed to "piddling," but it did admit "project congestion," the problem of having too many workers on a job. Historian Donald D. Wall recalled that it took a small army of WPAers to build an outhouse on his family's farm near Brighton, a waste of labor offensive to his German-Russian father, who, nonetheless, conceded the utility of Uncle Sam's john.[13]

Many disliked WPA for the same reasons that they had resented the Federal Emergency Relief Administration. Both of the federal leviathans threatened to crush the dream of American self-reliance. Both were accused of playing politics. Neither could totally relieve distress. Both suffered from being so large, diverse, and ubiquitous that few could comprehend them. In May 1941, WPA reported having undertaken more than 5,000 Colorado projects since 1935 at a federal cost of some $100 million. Some 400 structures had been built, among them 63 schools, 124 recreation buildings, 22 offices, 26 sewage disposal plants, and 28 dams. Reviewing its road record in 1942, it reported more than 9,000 miles constructed or improved. It had built more than 30,000 outhouses, improved or installed 21 airports, put in 21,241 culverts, served more than 21 million school lunches, produced more than 7 million articles in its sewing rooms, and canned more than 5 million quarts of produce.[14]

Margaret S. Reef, head of WPA's Women's and Professional Division, recalled interviewing men who had lost $10,000-a-year jobs: "That man would sit and talk with me and he would weep because he didn't know how he was going to get along — he was going to lose his home, his children were hungry." To help women and men who could not dig, the WPA supported canning, clerical, sewing, recreational, research, and other professional activities. At Denver General Hospital, WPAers filed birth and death records; at the Denver Public Library they indexed several decades of the *Rocky Mountain News*, mended books, and helped establish a vast bibliographical center. At Grant School in southeast Denver, WPA recreation directors coached football, basketball, and volleyball teams and taught square dancing, cooking, speech, and singing. In Park Hill, club women studied opera with a WPA teacher; in Weld County, foreign-born miners took WPA citizenship classes. Residents of Colorado Springs, unversed in soap carving, learned how from WPA teachers, who also taught swimming at the Broadmoor Pool. In Colorado Springs, as in Denver, the WPA ran nursery schools.[15]

Special projects, often fully federally funded, gave jobs to artists, actors, musicians, and writers. Small compared to the totality of the work programs, the cultural endeavors provided a molehill of employment, sparked a mountain of controversy, and left a legacy of murals, plays, books, and federal involvement with the arts.

The Public Works of Art Project (1933–1934) hired Colorado artists, including Gladys Caldwell, who did friezes for Denver's City and County Building, and Frank E. Mechau, whose "Horses at Night," a mural for the Denver Public Library, helped him secure a national reputation. Later the WPA's Federal Art Project employed a few dozen artists under the direction of Donald Bear, head of the city's art museum. Some fashioned museum displays, built models of Indian habitations, and made woodblock prints illustrating life in Colorado. Red Robin, a young Zuni, created sand paintings that caught the fancy of eastern collectors. Marvin B. Martin sculpted a fountain originally intended for Denver's Morey Junior High School. Pascal F. Quackenbush did murals for Denver schools, and in Grand Junction Alfred Lee Howell recounted western Colorado's past in his large paintings.[16]

The work put food on the table. Charles Tribble, an artist, recalled, "I remember one kid at Chapell House [a Denver Art Museum gallery] in one of these classes who hadn't eaten a solid meal in a week. . . . He was actually getting so thin and so weak that the guy had trouble moving." Although successful at feeding people, the WPA arts project could not guarantee

A WPA canning project in Pueblo.
(Pueblo Library District)

quality output because it was required to employ artists on relief, genius and hack alike. The Treasury Department's Section of Painting and Sculpture avoided the relief trap by sponsoring competitions, open to all, to select artists to embellish public buildings, mainly post offices. Top talents, including Coloradans Frank Mechau and Boardman Robinson, along with out-of-staters such as the Taos painter Ernest L. Blumenschein, vied for the commissions, which usually brought them less than $1,000.[17]

Robinson chaired a committee, which selected Ethel Magafan's "The Horse Corral" for the South Denver Branch Post Office. For the Englewood Post Office, Robinson offered a work of his own. Despite his fame as a muralist, his preliminary sketch of cowboys and their women friends struck Treasury Department critics as frivolous. Asked to base his painting on local history, he responded, "There's no history of this Denver suburb of Englewood, but the thrilling saga of real estate exploitation." For such a place, Robinson made "Colorado Stock Sale," a scene in which nondescript horses look better than the people — flinty farmers and overstuffed women whose stilted children appear doomed to ride in their parents' saddles.[18]

Robinson's satire was not contagious. Other muralists invented scenes dear to the public: an idealized, strife-free, largely agricultural West full of mountains, farmers, cows, and horses. For $600 Blumenschein gave Walsenburg a sensitive rendition of the nearby Spanish Peaks, only to see his canvas overwhelmed when the postmaster painted the surrounding wall light yellow. "Am not ambitious to undertake any more murals except they would be placed in good architectural settings," Blumenschein told Edward B. Rowan, superintendent of the Treasury Department's Section of Painting and Sculpture. For Glenwood Springs, Mechau painted horses; for Colorado Springs he painted horses, cowboys, and Indians. Louise E. Ronnebeck put sturdy peach pickers in her Grand Junction mural. John H. Fraser's "North Platte Country Against the Mountains," a misnamed mural in Littleton, on the South Platte, featured cows, farmers, a couple of silos, and a grain elevator. Bovines ruminated in James Russell Sherman's "Industries Around Loveland" in Loveland, and a cattle herd thundered through Ila McAfee Turner's "The Wealth of the West" in Gunnison. William Victor Higgins of Taos incorporated three horses and a dog in his "The First Crossing at Rocky Ford," which took him more than six years to complete.[19]

Sick of horses, Edward Rowan applauded Colorado Springs artist George Vander Sluis's plan to put sheep in the Rifle Post Office. Before the sheep could safely graze, cattlemen raised such hell that the postmaster swore that he preferred undesecrated walls. Rowan retreated, as did Vander Sluis, who blessed Rifle with a big mountain, a dog, and a few little horses. Denver's main post office, under the aegis of the Treasury Relief Art Program, did get sheep — Gladys Caldwell's monumental sculptures of mountain sheep.[20]

Painting politically acceptable animals did not always shield artists from criticism. Archie Musick of Colorado Springs dabbed all the correct icons — horses, deer, Indians, and Zebulon Pike — on the wall of the Manitou Springs Post Office. Postmaster Gus C. Flake judged it "an attractive addition" but admitted that others "consider it simply a waste of the tax payers money." To such penny-pinching Philistines, Musick responded, "The taxpayers who feel this mural an unjust robbery can compute their losses by figuring just how much of their tax money went into the building, and then figuring what one percent of that would be, and that's what they paid personally. . . . That isn't going to send anyone to the poorhouse and it gives the artist a more solid footing in the social scheme, converting him from a precious parlor monkey to a useful tradesman, so that he may walk on the sidewalk with respectable people."[21]

The Federal Theater Project (FTP) did for a few actors and actresses what the art programs did for artists. Boardman Robinson asked that Colorado Springs be awarded a WPA children's theater, and J. Howard Miller, an FTP administrator, proposed giving Grand Junction a shot of drama. But only Denver got a federal theater, because it alone could muster the threadbare thespians to staff one. Even there, pickings were slim. "We are extremely limited with capable women," Karon Tillman, the state director, told his bosses in Washington. By embracing vaudeville and

Frank E. Mechau's (1904–1946) "Horses at Night," painted in 1934, won praise from Edward Bruce, head of the Public Works of Art program. Restored in the mid-1980s, the painting currently (1993) belongs to the Denver Public Library. Mechau also won federal commissions for post office paintings in Colorado Springs and Glenwood Springs in Colorado, Ogallala in Nebraska, Clifton and Fort Worth in Texas, and the Post Office Department Building in Washington, D.C. (Denver Public Library, Western History Department)

children's productions, FTP employed approximately 50 people, among them sword-swallower George Berton and W. J. Nixon, known as Chandu the Magician.[22]

The Federal Theater acquired a tolerable home in September 1936 at the Baker Theater, 1447 Lawrence Street. It could seat 500 on chairs, which, thanks to a WPA sewing project, were cushioned. *It Can't Happen Here*, Sinclair Lewis's anti-Fascist drama, opened the 1936 season with a thud: critics panned it and audiences shunned it. Far more successful was the second offering, *Me Third* by Mary Coyle Chase, formerly a *Rocky Mountain News* reporter. Her comedy portrayed the trials of Harlan Hazlett, whose mother hired a maid, Grace Dosher, formerly a cashier in a bordello frequented by Hazlett. All ended happily when Hazlett's wife dumped him, thereby freeing him to marry Grace, whose blackmail file promised him political success. For Chase, too, *Me Third* ended well. FTP offered it in San Bernardino, California, and producer Brock Pemberton staged it in New York under the title *Now You've Done It*. Although its run was short, it afforded Chase a stepping-stone on her way to writing *Harvey*, which won the Pulitzer Prize in 1945.[23]

The Baker aimed to uplift local taste by presenting Eugene O'Neill's *Ah! Wilderness* and *Days Without End*. Usually, however, to fill its 25¢ and 40¢ seats, it catered to a public that liked light fare such as Laurie Johnson's *Mary's Other Husband* and Joan and Michael Slane's *The Dragon's Wishbone*, a children's play featuring Chandu the Magician as a rabbit. Sensitive to local attitudes, the Baker gave tickets to orphans and rejected the Communist-oriented John Reed Club's offer to buy every seat for a performance of Conrad Seiler's *Censored*.[24]

Even so, FTP suffered attacks from upset actors and cantankerous reviewers. W. J. Nixon, unpaid for his Chandu outfit, pestered Washington to investigate: "No doubt you know Tillman's theatrical experience is

A scene from Me Third, *Mary Coyle Chase's first play. (National Archives, Photo Section, Washington, D.C.)*

confined to shoe-salesmanship." More damaging were broadsides from Albert DeBernardi, Jr., drama critic for *The Denver Post,* who blasted the Baker for encouraging "stage struck people already employed in other lines of private industry, to throw up those jobs and take a course in acting at the expense of the taxpayer." Reviewing FTP selections in 1939, DeBernardi charged that they were "radical dramas with social implications" and that some "aimed to inflame theater patrons into action against the American system." Heeding the catcalls, Congress rang down the curtain on the Federal Theater in mid-1939. By then the Baker had presented some 500 performances of more than three dozen plays.[25]

Pueblo musicians played for the WPA.
(Pueblo Library District)

The Federal Music Project (FMP) drummed up an even more impressive record. It began making music in Denver on December 2, 1935, and by early June had done 330 public presentations statewide. In Denver it employed 101 out-of-work musicians; in Colorado Springs, 20; in Pueblo, 19. Pueblo's conductor, Robert Gross, entertained more than 33,000 people at 67 concerts in a 14-week period late in 1936. In Colorado Springs, Edwin A. Dietrich presented 14 concerts in December 1936, including one at the Chief Theater, where Santa Claus put in an appearance. In Denver, FMP ran three orchestras, a male vocal unit, a ladies' string ensemble, a string quartet, a symphonietta, a symphonic band, and a concert orchestra, which, taken together, had by late 1937 entertained some 200,000 persons. The project hit a sour note in mid-1936 when many of its players got private jobs. In 1937 Horace E. Tureman, the state's FMP director, reported that defections had forced the band to disband. Yet, despite sour notes, FMP continued giving concerts into 1940.[26]

Unlike the art, theater, and music projects, the Writer's Project maintained a low profile that might have allowed it to slip into safe oblivion had it not published *Colorado: A Guide to the Highest State* in 1941. It gave readers fact-crammed tours, letting them know, among thousands of other tidbits, that legend whispered that Idaho Springs was named for a maiden named Ida who dug gold there with a hoe. Morris M. Cleavenger, a newspaperman from Wray, supervised much of the work on the *Guide*. Anthony Venneri, one of the sub-editors, reported that the book was the "work of more than 100 men and women during the years from October 1935 to January 1940." Venneri resented editors in Washington, D.C., "whose slashing of much historical and valuable written material was owing to their instructions to confine the whole into a limited and specified number of pages." Washington ordered local writers to forswear trite words such as "scenic" and insisted that sections on the Indians be fair to Native Americans. Much of the final rewrite was done by George F. Willison, whose 1931 story of Colorado's mining frontier *Here They Dug the Gold* had won praise for its prose.[27]

Subsequently hailed by the journalist John Gunther as "one of the two or three best of all the volumes in the American Guide Series" and by historian Thomas J. Noel as "the finest guidebook ever done for Colorado," the book initially suffered a scathing review by Denver poet Thomas Hornsby Ferril, who found it "riddled with error, clumsily organized, badly indexed and the maps are downright wretched." The guide does have faults: Mechau's "Horses at Night" is called "Horses at Morning," and, as Noel points out, *tumbleweeds* is misspelled *tumblewoods*. Those peccadilloes and others, in Noel's opinion, hardly merited Ferril's fury. When in 1947 Hastings House published *Ghost Towns of Colorado*, the last gasp of the Writer's Project, Ferril damned it as "interesting in a slip shod way."[28]

Among the supervisors of the Federal Writer's Project was Mary F. Adams, who helped complete the guide. Margaret Reef explained that it made sense to put women in charge of non-construction jobs "because so many women were involved." WPA rejected married women, on the theory that their husbands should provide for them, but it employed single women and those who provided the sole support for their families. In 1936 women constituted 20 percent of its work force, 5,000 of them making shirts, trousers, leather coats, and other clothes for relief recipients. Boasting of its weaving program, WPA claimed that "the Spanish-American people . . . display a natural aptitude for the work." In Alamosa, Denver, Durango, Greeley, Pueblo, and Walsenburg, women canned food for welfare clients. They also prepared school lunches and served as housekeeping aids in motherless homes. "The day is not far distant," commented Frances B. Wayne of *The Denver Post*, "when little Orphan Annie whose family is on relief can flip her skirts, tilt her nose and say to the little girl from the big house next door, 'Huh! We've got two maids. That's more'n you've got.' "[29]

Young people, male and female, found part-time employment through the National Youth Administration (NYA), which was technically part of the WPA until mid-1939. Some were out-of-school youths given federally subsidized jobs. Others were students employed part-time. In December 1938 more than 2,500 high school students and nearly 1,300 collegians, one in ten of the state's undergraduates, were getting NYA pay, on average $6 a month for high schoolers and approximately $5 more for collegians, who worked as teacher's helpers and library and laboratory

A San Luis Valley WPA project. (Denver Public Library, Western History Department)

assistants. Often those small stipends allowed students to remain in school. Nelson E. Cantril, head of the Hayden High School, asked NYA administrators to help Edith S.: "She walks eleven miles to school daily and her parents are barely able to keep her in school." L. S. Leeper, superintendent in dust-choked Springfield, wrote, " I have so many students that are in absolute need . . . that I hardly know who to select and who to leave out."[30]

WPA faced the same dilemma. It could not make work for every needy applicant, even at its 1937 pay rate of $45 a month for unskilled persons in rural areas. To stretch its budget it limited hours and hired on an intermittent basis, often forcing people to go on relief or to accept private jobs, no matter how low the pay. In early 1936 it dropped more than 10,000

— married women and Hispanic farmworkers being among the first axed. "There will no doubt be considerable suffering," a WPA official reported, "as the counties are not in a position to give adequate compensation and relief." Removed from WPA rolls, Estanislado Valverde asked for reinstatement: "I got a wife and six children. I was unable to send them to school because none of them has any shoes."[31]

Workers bombarded the WPA with complaints. Eunice H. Raymond of Denver wrote Harry Hopkins of her supervisor's "unfair and personal advances," a charge echoed by seven other "girls." The manager resigned, but Paul Shriver also removed whistle-blower Raymond because "it has been our policy in Colorado not to employ married women when their husbands were capable of supporting them." Women in Springfield fumed about supervisors who, allegedly, did not allow employees to talk or whisper and who forbade them to report conditions to county authorities.[32]

LeJean Clark, secretary of Denver's Young Negroes Progressive League, charged that African-American sewing women were segregated by being assigned to Whittier School. Mary F. Adams admitted that "many colored workers are assigned to Whittier," which, she said, "indicates merely an attempt at making convenient transportation arrangements for the colored people who live in the near vicinity of the school." Shriver explained to his bosses in Washington that at one time "colored women were segregated as a result of their own desire." But he insisted that Colorado's WPA had made "a particular effort . . . to avoid any possibility of racial discrimination." Such statements may have rung hollow with African-American NYA youths who found themselves shunted into a city program to teach auto-repair, an "occupational field" that the NYA judged "open to this minority group" and to those who made up the NYA African-American choir. "Our negro jitterbug dancers and our Spanish songsters are favorites in the community," Mary Coyle Chase, then a NYA publicist, boasted.[33]

Those without work complained because they did not have it; those with work wanted better pay. In Carbondale proud men who stayed off relief found themselves ineligible for jobs building the local school. Leadville workers humbly petitioned Hopkins to rethink WPA's practice of paying laborers in large cities more than those in small: "Now, please to your honor . . . we do not want to misinform you about any thing, nor to couse [sic] Harm to no body, but we are informed that out side this County the wages on Wpa, is all ways from $45.00 up to $55.00 a month."[34]

Others lacked civility. Walsenburg's jobless, 250 strong, seized the Huerfano County courthouse in July 1938 demanding work. At the same time more than 1,000 Denver laborers, angry over pay delays, walked off WPA jobs. George F. Cleaver explained his desperate need for money: "We've got one onion, one potato, a tablespoon of rice and a little of the coffee left. My wife's not very well. She's weak from lack of food." Bill Gillespie told a reporter of his mother's suicide, "just because we never

Blacks pointed out that African-Americans were segregated on a sewing project at Whittier School in northeast Denver. (Denver Public Library, Western History Department)

had enough to eat." Another complained, "I have seven children. We haven't had any food in the house for four days."[35]

July 1938 was not one of Shriver's better months. President Roosevelt visited Pueblo on July 13, after which WPA clerks sent notes on Democratic party letterhead thanking organizations for making the event a success. Upset that federal employees were doing partisan chores, Shriver fired the supervisor. That angered Pueblo's Democratic bosses, who saw nothing wrong in a little politicking. Shriver, said Pueblo commissioner John E. Hill in a letter to FDR, made "Hitler and Mussolini look like pansies."[36]

The Pueblo flap was unusual. Normally city officials appreciated the WPA because it allowed them to make improvements without asking the taxpayers to pay the full cost. Benjamin F. Stapleton, mayor of Denver, estimated the "present and potential value" of WPA works in his city at some $50 million. New parks — Bonnie Brae at Bonnie Brae Boulevard and East Kentucky Avenue, and Garden Center at Alameda and South Kalamath

Beneficiary of more than $400,000 in expenditures during the 1930s, the state fair in Pueblo boasted a new administration building in April 1938, thanks to the WPA. (Pueblo Library District)

Street — blossomed because of WPA. So did an additional nine holes at the Berkeley Park golf course and Monkey Island at the City Park's zoo. Without WPA, Hale Parkway between Colorado Boulevard and Grape Street might not have existed. In 1938 more than 600 men looked forward to building a large athletic field south of South High School, a scheme that was stymied, says historian Phil Goodstein, by the University of Denver, which feared competition with its Hilltop Stadium. Thousands drudged on South Platte and Cherry Creek flood control, bringing riprap stone from South Table Mountain. Others labored on a $104,260 project to extend runways at the municipal airport. City funds amounting to $37,314 went into the first stages of making Red Rocks Amphitheater; WPA in mid-1938 contributed more than $200,000.[37]

Pueblo, heavily dependent on Colorado Fuel and Iron employment and hence hard hit by the soft market for steel, received some $10 million from WPA between July 1, 1935, and September 30, 1939. Its junior college obtained its first permanent home, a $50,000 Spanish-style building on West Orman Avenue, thanks to WPA. Its children frolicked in WPA wading pools at Mineral Palace Park; its stray dogs found sanctuary at the WPA pond; its golfers putted on WPA golf greens, the first eighteen-hole course in southern Colorado. By putting up $747, the city grabbed $4,428 in federal funds to repair shoes for the needy, and nearly $100,000 went to a rug-weaving project. The WPA even built a railroad in Pueblo — a short line to haul excavation dirt at the State Hospital for the Insane.[38]

Denver, Pueblo, and Colorado Springs won substantial projects. They had brigades of unemployed, and they were often home to state and federal institutions, such as the insane asylum in Pueblo, a huge facility housing some 4,000 patients in 1940, with a claim on government money. Sometimes, because of their large populations, they could mount special appeals for federal help. Colorado Springs, ravished by flood in 1935, spent more than $650,000 in local and federal funds to improve the channel of Monument Creek in 1937. By the late 1930s Denver had devoted more than $3 million to Cherry Creek and South Platte River improvement projects, more than 90 percent of it federal money. Medium-sized and small places also did well. Trinidad, its coal miners suffering from high unemployment, had 1,253 men and 155 women on WPA jobs in late 1937 — one of the highest allocations in the state. Grand Junction in 1939 put up $38,000 to get $56,000 from WPA for a paving project. For improvements at Lincoln Park it contributed even less — securing $33,508 with a match of only $3,900.[39]

Because often 80 to 90 percent of a proposal's cost was borne by WPA, it made sense for communities to sponsor projects. Denver inadvertently completed its new City and County Building before WPA help was available. Boulder put finishing touches on its courthouse with WPA money. Julesburg issued $50,000 in bonds for waterworks in 1935, missing an opportunity to pick Uncle Sam's pockets. Other places were luckier, or smarter. George E. Hine of La Junta credited federal programs with pushing the town "ahead between 35 and 40 years in constructive work." The storm sewer system had been doubled; street paving increased by some twenty-fold. H. C. McClintock, Boulder's city manager, judged that without WPA the city's golf course would have been "ten years in the future." O. K. Nabors, mayor of Durango, tallied numerous improvements: drainage ditches, street surfacing, flood control on the Florida River. Arthur Wold, a Grand County commissioner, appreciated WPA food and clothing aid for the indigent because it allowed Grand to shave its per-family relief payments to as low as $10 a month.[40]

Some WPA tasks, including many to landscape parks and cemeteries, smacked of the "leaf-raking" despised by Ed Johnson. Other projects were more substantial, if sometimes less than crucial. Ault got tennis courts; Center a community center; Monte Vista a hospital; Holly an administration building featuring offices, a library, two jail cells and a fire truck garage; Del Norte a courthouse; Lamar a 280-acre park and a home for Southeastern Colorado Junior College. Cheyenne Wells, Clifton, Granada, Hartman, Hugo, La Salle, Meeker, Nederland, Salida, Stratton, Two Buttes, Wiley, and Wiggins, among others, built new schools or refurbished old ones. Olathe had planned a new school in 1921; WPA made it possible in the late 1930s. The Eads school burned, so WPA built a new one in 1939 using locally quarried limestone.[41]

By using local materials, WPA cut costs and increased local employment. Alamosa's WPAers made 750,000 bricks, with which they constructed Lincoln School and a county administration building. At Fruitvale near Grand Junction the WPA manufactured adobe brick for a school. Holly used area limestone, hewn by hand, to make a gymnasium

and community building; the same rock went into a school addition at Granada. Lamar put up a 40-foot observation tower in its city park, building it from native sandstone. Prowers County sandstone went into a city administration building at Eads. Northeast of Walsh in Baca County, WPAers quarried sandstone to build a 140-foot bridge across Bear Creek on State Highway 51.[42]

The Public Works Administration also spent generously on buildings, sometimes financing construction for other federal agencies, sometimes backing state and local proposals. Walsenburg constructed a combined grade and junior high school; Boulder built a half-million-dollar school. Denver captured nearly $200,000 from PWA in 1940 to move its police department from the decrepit old City Hall to a new headquarters at 1245 Champa. The state fashioned a marble-clad tomb at Fourteenth Avenue and Sherman Street to house its bureaucrats; the U.S. Treasury enlarged the New Customs House. When Denverites refused to finance 24 school projects, Claude Boettcher rescued one proposal by donating $192,500 to

WPA built a mountain lodge at Monument Lake west of Trinidad. (Denver Public Library, Western History Department)

For the Alamosa County Building, WPA workers made bricks. (Denver Public Library, Western History Department)

secure a PWA grant of $157,500 for a school for disabled children. In an eleemosynary mood, Lawrence C. Phipps parted with $137,500 to land a PWA grant of $112,500 for construction of Phipps Auditorium at the Colorado Museum of Natural History.[43]

Colleges and universities found a friend in PWA, one they badly needed, as legislators put higher education low on the list for state funds. President George Norlin of the University of Colorado finagled PWA money to build or enlarge 15 university buildings, including a library, a field house, a natural history museum, and a faculty club. Colorado State College of Agriculture in Fort Collins and Western State in Gunnison built dormitories. Adams State in Alamosa constructed Casa Bonita and Kit Carson Hall. When these buildings did not fill with students, the college rented rooms to the public, to the dismay of local landlords. The Colorado School of Mines in Golden constructed a house for its president; Colorado State College of Education in Greeley put up faculty apartments.[44]

Water, far more than college buildings, preoccupied Coloradans during the drought-ridden 1930s. Often they asked Uncle Sam's help and often they received it from PWA, from WPA, from the Bureau of Reclamation, and from the Army Corps of Engineers. Denver's first PWA request was for water — Western Slope water from the Fraser River, which the city proposed to bring through the unused 6.4-mile Pioneer Bore, which paralleled the Moffat railroad tunnel. Poor precipitation in the fall and early winter of 1932–1933 panicked officials into starting construction, an expensive task that they abandoned when March and April snows blanketed the Front Range, assuring water for the summer. Fearing that the reprieve was temporary, the city in July 1933 asked PWA to back completion of the Moffat diversion. Federal approval took two years, construction nearly three. Water first flowed through the tunnel in 1936, but not until 1938 was the $9.5-million venture finished. Two years later Denver expanded its

By using federal funds, George Norlin (1871–1942) constructed many of the buildings necessary to accommodate the University of Colorado's student body, which tripled in size during his long presidency (1917–1939). (Colorado Historical Society)

supply with the completion of the $1.1-million Jones Pass Tunnel, another PWA effort, which tapped the Williams Fork of the Colorado River.[45]

Colorado Springs also watched its water. As early as 1908 it had envisioned reservoirs on the North Slope of Pikes Peak, a dream the PWA made real with a 1933 grant. Four years later, on September 12, 1937, officials dedicated North Slope reservoirs, which impounded nearly two billion gallons of Crystal and South Catamount creeks' water, boosting the city's reserves by 90 percent. To the south, farmers in Crowley County on the Arkansas River thirsted for Western Slope water more than 200 miles away. Using a Reconstruction Finance Corporation loan, they diverted water in 1935 from east of Aspen through a four-mile tunnel under Independence Pass to Twin Lakes south of Leadville and thence through the Arkansas River to the parched plains.[46]

Eastern Coloradans claimed a right to unused Western Slope water that was escaping to California. Outnumbered and beleaguered Western Slope residents argued that without water their development would one day be checked, a sentiment effectively echoed by their powerful congressman, Edward T. Taylor. When South Platte River valley farmers asked Congress in 1936 to authorize loans to finance the Colorado–Big Thompson project to pump Colorado River water from the west to the east, Taylor killed the idea. That pleased both the Western Slope and National Parks officials fearful that the diversion might damage Rocky Mountain National Park.

To resurrect Colorado–Big Thompson, easterners in 1937 agreed to pay for the Green Mountain Reservoir, designed in part for compensatory Western Slope storage. That persuaded westerners to support the creation of Shadow Mountain, Willow Creek, and Lake Granby reservoirs, which sent Colorado River water through Grand Lake into the 13.1-mile Alva B. Adams Tunnel under Rocky Mountain National Park into Mary's Lake, Lake Estes, and the Big Thompson River, from whence it ran through streams, lakes, canals, and power plants, generating electricity and eventually filling Eastern Slope reservoirs, including Carter Lake, southwest of Loveland, and Horsetooth, west of Fort Collins.[47]

Colorado–Big Thompson, at its inception the largest project ever undertaken by the Bureau of Reclamation, took some 20 years to complete at a cost of more than $160 million. It promised to benefit northeastern Colorado well into the twenty-first century, fulfilling the hopes of one of its major boosters, Charles Hansen, editor of the *Greeley Daily Tribune,* who was mildly immortalized by two canals named for him. Construction did not begin until the late 1930s — and water did not flow through the Adams Tunnel until 1947 — so its Depression-era impact was limited, although after the 1938 Green Mountain Dam ground-breaking, Kremmling's population perked up, its 1940 count of 567 being more than twice its 1930 tally. The letting of contracts to build the Caddoa Dam (renamed John Martin Dam in 1940 to honor Congressman John A. Martin, who died in office in 1939) on the Arkansas River, an Army Corps of Engineers undertaking, gave hope late in 1939 to Las Animas and Lamar, while little Caddoa enjoyed glory days until rising water flooded it.[48]

Congressman Taylor, chairman of the House Appropriations Committee after February 1937, saw to it that the Western Slope shared in water projects. The collapse of the Fruit Growers' Reservoir near Delta on June 13, 1937, commanded presidential attention as Interior Secretary Harold Ickes wrote Roosevelt: "The pressure for immediate construction is very heavy. . . . Congressman Edward T. Taylor will communicate with you concerning this allocation." FDR quickly shifted $200,000 in WPA funds to the Bureau of Reclamation, which replaced the dam. That job was small compared to other multi-million-dollar reclamation ventures in Western Colorado, including the Pine River project with the Vallecito Dam north of Bayfield, additions to the Grand Valley project west of Grand Junction, and the Taylor Park reservoir northeast of Gunnison.[49]

Getting and storing water was only half the battle. Many places found their supplies unsafe. "One of the marks of civilization," Edward N. Chapman, M.D., of Colorado Springs said in 1933, "is the proper disposal of human excreta." By that standard Colorado had advanced little beyond the Middle Ages. In 1930 most of its towns and cities simply flushed untreated waste into rivers, polluting every major waterway. Cities and towns coped by filtering water and lacing it with chlorine, lime, and alum. "If this treatment of our water kills the bugs and sometimes the gold fish, what does it do to us?" wondered the *Pueblo Chieftain.* In rural areas, sewage filled farm ditches from which people drank. If, somehow, they managed to get pure water, they, and their city cousins, still risked disease from eating unwashed produce contaminated by sewage. California, which insisted on high-quality irrigation water, posted a 1931 typhoid death rate one-third of Colorado's. There infants faced half the risk of dying from diarrhea and enteritis as those in Colorado.[50]

The *Pueblo Chieftain* revealed in January 1934 that Pueblo's 12 sewers so badly fouled the Arkansas River that between La Junta and the Kansas line it was 90 percent sewage at best, 100 percent when the water was low. Colorado Springs dispatched its sewage southward toward Pueblo via the Fountain River and subterranean gravel beds, which enriched the Steel City's already rich air. Denver did no better. According to Dr. Chapman, the South Platte entered the city relatively clean. The untreated waste from more than a quarter-million people, combined with industrial effluent, made the river into a putrid ribbon "grossly contaminated by sewage." As a result, Chapman argued, Weld County's young children suffered a death rate from from diarrhea and enteritis well above the state's average, seven times higher than California's.[51]

Both WPA and PWA cleaned up rivers. By October 1938, WPA had spent more than $200,000 for disposal plants in Berthoud, Brush, Eaton, Hayden, Sterling, Sugar City, and Windsor and at Camp George West near Golden. At Brighton, PWA cooperated with WPA, the former helping finance the disposal system, the latter providing laborers to construct gravel filter beds. An uncommonly small PWA grant of $2,500 helped Steamboat Springs construct a disposal plant, $20,489 went to Boulder, $42,075 to Greeley, and $1,602,900 to Denver. Because PWA required matching funds of from 30 to 45 percent, additional local millions went into sewage treatment. Denver spent more than the federal government to complete its $3.4-million disposal facility in 1939. In addition to building treatment plants, WPA brought city neighborhoods into the twentieth century by giving them sewers: Denver got more than 12 miles, Pueblo nearly 5 miles. Results were impressive. Even before Denver completed its plant, typhoid, diarrhea, and enteritis death rates started falling. By 1940 nearly 75 percent of Coloradans who used sewers treated their waste completely, while another 10 percent partially did so.[52]

WPA and PWA also backed water purification and distribution systems. "We are getting pure water, something we have never enjoyed before," reported Louie Eickenrodt, mayor of Del Norte. The PWA water list reads like a Colorado gazetteer: waterworks for Cheyenne Wells ($2,618), Colorado Springs ($412,000 — total cost $1,700,939), Denver ($2,556,225 — total cost $5,868,347), Fort Collins ($33,000), Frederick ($4,500), Loveland ($26,767), Morrison ($6,302), Olathe ($6,415), Ordway ($25,336), Silverton ($2,663), and Wellington ($1,454). Help in laying water mains went to Boulder ($16,449), Carbondale ($10,292), Fruita ($12,807), Monte Vista ($300,000 loan), and Yuma ($2,887). Cities and towns also took advantage of WPA's willingness to finance swimming pools: Aguilar,

Earl L. Mosley (1883–1966), Colorado Springs's city manager (1930–1947), used federal money for civic improvements, including flood control. Later he worked for the Denver Water Board (1950–1966). (Local History Collection, Pikes Peak Library District)

Akron, Burlington, Cheyenne Wells, Cripple Creek, Deer Trail, Haxtun, Holyoke, and Hugo all procured pools. Capitalizing on its hot springs, Salida splashed in style, thanks to $169,000 in WPA aid.[53]

Coloradans often had to be shamed into cleaning up their water. They thought more highly of highways. WPA paved streets, built and patched up bridges (1,800 of them by early 1939), and constructed roads. By extending Denver's Alameda Avenue 12 miles west from Knox Court, the WPA assured easy access to Red Rocks Amphitheater. It rebuilt part of State Highway 115 between Colorado Springs and Cañon City and made State Highway 10 an all-weather route between Walsenburg and La Junta. Utilizing a disused rail grade, WPAers made the scenic Phantom Canyon route between Victor and U.S. Highway 50, which opened on July 4, 1938.[54]

Short of money and often unable to provide skilled workers, WPA left major road jobs to the state, to PWA, and to the Bureau of Public Roads. Prodded by Governor Johnson, the legislature in 1935 agreed to finance highways by borrowing against anticipated gasoline tax revenues. That gave highway-makers $25 million to add to sizeable grants from PWA and the Bureau of Public Roads — the latter agency alone spent more than $28 million in Colorado between 1933 and 1939. Despite feuding between Johnson and chief highway engineer Charles D. Vail, the state got good mileage from its money.

In 1930, Colorado motorists braved a crazy array of roads, many unimproved, some graded and graveled. Of more than 8,000 miles of

roads, fewer than 500 were paved. Drivers could travel on the narrow, hard-surfaced U.S. Highway 85 from the Wyoming border through Denver and Colorado Springs to Pueblo. The road then turned to gravel until paving resumed at Aguilar, running from there to Trinidad, where it again stopped. From Fort Collins, Boulder, Golden, and Evergreen, pavement led to Denver. Motorists on U.S. Highway 40 drove on a hard surface from near Evergreen to Denver; east of Denver the road was gravel. From Colorado Springs, pavement extended west for only a few miles to Manitou Springs; no hard-surfaced road ran east from the city. Scattered paved stretches of U.S. Highway 50 east of Pueblo allowed motorists a smooth ride, as did a few miles of the same road near Cañon City. The rest of Colorado, with the exception of a few miles of asphalted road near Alamosa and Grand Junction, relied on rutted and pocked, gravel-surfaced washboards, which sometimes made the highway speed limit of 35 m.p.h. seem unsafe. Asked to attend an April 1934 water meeting in Grand Junction, Charles Hansen

George E. Cranmer (1884–1975), Denver's manager of Parks and Improvements (1935–1947), found federal money crucial in creating Winter Park ski area and Red Rocks Amphitheater. (Denver Public Library, Western History Department)

of Greeley complained of the day-and-a-half journey: "So much of it is mountain roads."[55]

At least in late April, Hansen could hope to negotiate Berthoud Pass, which was often blocked by snow in the winter. Loveland Pass, crossed by an unimproved road in 1930, made marginal motoring sense in the summer, none in the winter. Hoosier Pass, south of Breckenridge, was unusable in the winter; so were Monarch east of Gunnison, Rabbit Ears east of Steamboat Springs, Independence east of Aspen, and Wolf Creek north of Pagosa Springs. The Carlton Tunnel, an old rail bore nearly two miles long, gave motorists a convenient summer route from Leadville to Basalt, but it was useless in winter.

The abandonment of rail lines made highways even more vital. A Reconstruction Finance Corporation loan allowed the Denver and Rio Grande Railroad (D&RG) to complete the Dotsero cutoff in 1934. That gave the D&RG a fairly direct route west from Denver to Ogden, Utah, with its connections to the West Coast, thereby forging a new link in the transcontinental rail system. The accomplishment was offset by the abandonment of some 600 miles of track within the state in the 1930s, including the Colorado and Southern Railroad's jettisoning of almost all of the old Denver South Park and Pacific line, which linked Denver with Leadville.[56]

Money remade the highway map. By 1940 Colorado boasted more than 4,000 miles of paved and 4,200 miles of graveled road. Almost continuous hard-surfaced arteries linked most important towns, although Loveland, Monarch, and Wolf Creek passes still awaited paving. Sometimes Loveland and Red Mountain passes were closed in winter, but Berthoud, Rabbit Ears, Hoosier, and Monarch were normally kept open. The Denver–Colorado Springs highway, the oldest paved highway in the state, had been widened in places, and it was possible in summer to drive to the summit of Mount Evans. Tourists appreciated that high-altitude adventure, as they did trips to Rocky Mountain National Park, which counted 183,658 automobiles in 1940, an increase of more than 100,000 since 1929. At Mesa Verde only 4,224 autos visited in 1929; more than 10,000 came in 1940.[57]

As early as 1937 large amounts of WPA money went into defense projects. By late that year more WPAers were working on converting the Agnes [Phipps] Memorial Sanatorium into Lowry Field, a technical school for the Army Air Corps, than on any other single job in the state. In mid-1938 Lowry drank up more than $1 million in WPA funds, a similar amount from PWA, and $1.5 million from the army. By 1939 WPA had spent $3.6 million on the installation. Improvements in civilian airports from Denver to Grand Junction costing nearly $2 million also beefed up the nation's defenses, as did the more than $2 million WPA had expended by 1939 on Fort Logan, Fitzsimons General Hospital, and the National Guard's Camp George West near Golden.[58]

Defense spending and the boost it gave the economy increased employment and decreased the need for work programs, which were,

The number of horses and colts on Colorado farms peaked at 440,000 in 1919 and then declined to 222,000 by 1939. (Undated FSA photo with no photographer identified on caption, Library of Congress)

consequently, phased out by Congress. After 1939 PWA focused largely on defense. Congress shut down the Federal Theater in 1939 and consigned other federally funded enterprises such as the writers' program to state sponsorship. That year average monthly employment on Colorado WPA jobs dropped to 22,000. The entry of the United States into World War II in December 1941 turned the vanishing labor surplus into a labor shortage. Between January 1941 and January 1942 WPA cut its rolls by nearly half, from 22,236 to 11,857. At the end of 1942 only 60 laborers still worked for WPA. On March 31, 1943, WPA, for nearly half a decade the state's largest single employer, closed its doors. Paul Shriver, like many of the people who had worked for him, went off to war.[59]

Historians and economists still hotly debate the merits of the New Deal, with much of the heat being generated by discussions of its work programs. Would the country have recovered faster had the federal government not employed the starving? Might taxpayer dollars used to fund make-work jobs have done more good in the hands of the taxpayers? Did federal theaters, orchestras, and art projects make economic sense? Did "piddling around with leaf-raking projects" make any sense?

On the national level the half-century-old discussion will likely continue for another half century. Certainly there is much to be said for the position advanced by historian James E. Sherow and others that massive federal water projects such as the John Martin Dam were, in the long run, misguided. Mother Nature, Sherow insightfully argues in *Watering the Valley: Development Along the High Plains Arkansas River, 1870–1950*, cannot be fooled forever. Farmers profited for a time, but by the 1980s many of their high hopes had been dashed, despite the big dams.[60]

Nevertheless, from a parochial standpoint, the humanitarian and the economic case for the New Deal in Colorado appears strong. Uncle Sam in six years (1933–1939) allocated the state $362.06 per resident. Only Washington, among states with more people than Colorado, received more non-repayable federal dollars on a per capita basis; overall, Colorado ranked tenth among the 48 states. New York, for example, took in $205.06, California $266.28, and Kentucky, typical of the South, got less than half as much as Colorado.

From the Bureau of Reclamation it received $5.29 per capita, giving it a national rank of eleventh; from the Forest Service $3.04, with a rank of eighth; from the Bureau of Public Roads $27.78, with a rank of tenth; from Social Security $18.96, with a rank of first. Larger programs were also kind. FERA's $38.94 gave the state ninth rank; Civilian Conservation Corps expenditures of $41.27 put Colorado tenth nationally; the Veterans Administration's $58.96 made the state fourth; WPA spent $72.60, giving Colorado sixth place.[61]

Its reputation as a healthy place, its geography, its diversity, its politics, all helped fuel Colorado's New Deal cornucopia. Long regarded as a haven for TB sufferers, the state attracted military veterans to hospitals such as Fort Lyon and Fitzsimons. Many recovered and remained, their

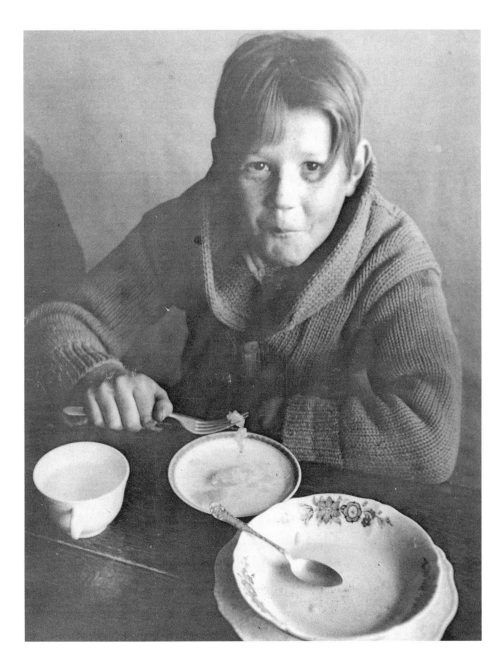

WPA provided hot lunches for school-children as part of Project 853 in Denver. (Denver Public Library, Western History Department)

benefits sustaining them and propping up the economy. Nearly one in every six federal dollars spent in the state flowed from the Veterans Administration.

Colorado, with slightly more than 104,000 square miles, ranked seventh nationally in size among the states. More than 32,000 square miles were federally owned, some as national parks and monuments, much more as forest and grazing land. It was a natural place to put CCC camps and to spend Forest Service money. Its size and rugged terrain gave it an almost unquenchable appetite for roads, for which even its tightwad taxpayers were willing to partially pay. Its under-utilized water resources, maldistributed, according to drought-plagued residents of the Eastern

With backing from organized labor, Ray H. Talbot (1896–1955) won many offices, including Pueblo County commissioner (1933–1946) and later Pueblo postmaster. (Colorado Historical Society)

Slope, made it thirsty for reclamation projects. With its farms, ranches, mines, and cities, the state was positioned to take advantage of New Deal programs crafted for different sectors of the economy. Denver, the twenty-ninth largest city in the country and the metropolis of the Mountain West, was large enough to sustain professional projects and was an attractive and sensible place to headquarter regional offices of federal agencies.

Colorado's liberal senator Edward Costigan fought for federal pork such as the Air Corps Technical School at Denver's Lowry Field; its conservative governor Ed Johnson complained about FERA and WPA, but he willingly fed at the federal trough. His successor as governor, Teller Ammons, a Democrat more in tune with the New Deal, gladly accepted federal money. Ammons's successor, the Republican Ralph L. Carr, did not let politics prevent him from taking federal aid. Early in the New Deal, Colorado got more than its share of FERA money by refusing to properly match federal appropriations. Unwilling to let people starve, Washington sent money. Had the state spent $10 or $20 million more on relief in 1932–1935, it would have relieved suffering, but it might then have lacked money for PWA and WPA matches. Coloradans squeezed WPA, as they had FERA. Harry Hopkins spoke with Paul Shriver by phone on January 27, 1936:

Hopkins: On the merits of the case, where is the trouble? Is it central or all over the state?

Shriver: The trouble is the biggest problem in Colorado. The trouble arises because Colorado instead of assuming part of the obligation depends almost entirely on the Federal government. It is just the attitude of the people, not a political matter. They tend to yell for the Federal government whenever they want anything done.

Yelling paid dividends. Between 1932 and 1939 Coloradans got back $2.78 for each tax dollar they sent to Washington. Don Reading, an economist, found that states such as Colorado that suffered the greatest decline in per capita income between 1929 and 1933 did the best in capturing federal money between 1933 and 1939. Rather than a leftist realignment of U.S. society, Reading suggests that the New Deal was an attempt to return to a pre-1929 economic status quo.[62]

It also may be that the New Deal was animated less by philosophy than by politics and bureaucratic pragmatism. Recognizing that squeaky wheels get oil, Coloradans squeaked loudly after 1929. They also temporarily abandoned their traditional Republicanism, an apostasy that served their interests in Washington after 1932. Washington, on its part, gave generously not simply to mollify powerful Democrats such as Costigan, Taylor, Johnson, and Adams, but also because the West's needs conformed with national and bureaucratic aspirations. Harry Hopkins ordered his WPA administrators to go after the money: "The Western states are going to get government money for conservation purposes. I want our office and our program identified with that. . . . I don't want to miss any bets."[63]

Coloradans did not want to miss any bets either. Setting aside philosophical objections to the New Deal, the state clamored for roads, reservoirs, and work programs. Well positioned to rake in federal dollars, it unabashedly did. It knew that its city dwellers, its miners, and its farmers needed help. If Washington were willing to foot the bill for that help, Coloradans certainly did not mind.

NINE

Down on the Farm

No cracked earth, no blistering sun, no burning wind, no grasshoppers are a permanent match for the indomitable spirit of America's farmers and stockmen and their wives and children who have carried on through desperate days, and inspire us with their self-reliance, their tenacity, and their courage. It was their fathers' task to make homes: it is their task to keep those homes, It is our task to help them with their fight.

Franklin D. Roosevelt
Fireside Chat
September 6, 1936[1]

Towner, a hamlet north of Holly and east of Eads, would rank scarcely a line in the annals of Colorado were it not for a tragedy and a hero.

Driven by 76-mile-per-hour winds, a blizzard swept the plains on March 26, 1931, prompting the principal of the Pleasant Hill School 10 miles south of Towner to order bus driver Carl Miller to take 20 children home early. Unable to see in the blinding snow, he drove into a ditch, where his bus stalled. For 21 hours he stayed with the children, keeping them moving so they would not freeze. Then with some, including his daughter Mary, near death he went for help, a mistake that cost him his life. For the next 10 hours, 13-year-old Bryan Untiedt kept the other youngsters active. By the time rescuers arrived on March 27 three children had perished; two others died soon after. Without young Untiedt all might have frozen. Lionized by the press, Bryan was invited to the White House.[2]

Hobnobbing with Herbert Hoover did little more for Bryan than it did for Colorado's farmers. A reporter interviewing Untiedt in 1935 found that lack of money had forced him to drop out of high school to work on the family farm, "and the prospect is slim that the isolated dairy farm over which dust storms have whirled steadily for weeks will yield enough funds to send him back to his studies." His situation was typical as drought, grasshoppers, dust, and low prices crushed many farmers.[3]

Hot, dry, and unpredictable weather cursed Colorado for most of the 1930s: 1934 was so dry that nearly half the state's agricultural acres produced no crops. Robert B. Rogerson, a North Park rancher, remembered:

I would take a good spy glass and from the top of the mountains where I ran the sheep in summer I could look from any peak and see all over the park, 75 to 125 miles in all directions. I could see only a few green spots where there were irrigated meadows, springs, or soaky land. The rest of the country was all brown as there had been no rain all summer and very little snow all the winter before. The ground was so dry that

the grass did not even start in the spring. It was like a great parched desert.

In 1935 the rain god showered more than the usual amount of moisture on Colorado's northwest, a blessing the fickle deity bestowed on the southeast in 1938, but not in 1939. The southeast, the center of Colorado's dust bowl, got 126 inches of moisture between 1930 and 1939: 20 percent less than in the 1920s and well below the 18 inches annually needed to grow wheat.[4]

Irrigation complicated the picture, allowing one farmer to survive while, nearby, another did not. Only 8.87 inches of precipitation fell in Fort Collins in 1933, but the *Fort Collins Express-Courier* wrung good news from the bad: The "brighter side is that even in such a year irrigation held up remarkably well." From Durango came a tale of feast and famine in 1936. Officials reported that a tract 15 miles wide running the length of Archuleta and La Plata counties was "in sore distress from drought" but that irrigated

Survivors of the Towner bus tragedy were brought to Denver by The Denver Post, *two weeks after five of their classmates froze to death. "If Colonel Lindbergh, Robin Hood and Little Orphan Annie had come to town all at the same time their reception would not have been more enthusiastic than that given the fifteen little heroes and heroines," said the* Post, *as it kicked off a week of festivities for the still-recovering children. Pictured standing, left to right, Ome Untiedt, Max Huffaker, Bryan Untiedt, Rosemary Brown. (Colorado Historical Society)*

lands to the north "have abundant crops." Hatfield Chilson, a water attorney, contrasted the fate of dry-land farmers near Loveland, whom he doubted made enough money in the mid-1930s to buy seed, with those owning senior water rights: "Under that ditch company there was only one farm that was lost during the depression. That farm was lost because the farmer got mad at his wife, went to bed, stayed there for three years, and refused to farm." Nevertheless, irrigation was not always protection against drought. In late March 1935 the Arkansas River went dry in Pueblo, threatening to leave irrigators as bereft as those without ditches.[5]

Dry-land farmers predominated in much of eastern Colorado, particularly in areas not touched by the South Platte and the Arkansas rivers. When sod busters grabbed homesteads in desolate reaches of northeastern Weld County in the late 1880s, the *Colorado Farmer* warned, "Theory says that this country is a desert and that it is not possible to raise crops successfully or sufficient to sustain a farming population; that this country is only fit for grazing." Unconvinced by theories and undaunted by the drought of the 1890s, optimists in overalls prayed for rain as they denuded the land of native grasses that anchored the soil. Between 1900 and 1930 the number of farm owners in the state rose by 110 percent, farm tenants by 270 percent. In those boom years, which fed on the demand for U.S. food sparked by World War I, Baca County in the state's southeast corner grew in population from 759 to 10,570, Logan County in the northeast quintupled its population, and east-central Kit Carson County mushroomed by 600 percent.

The U.S. Weather Bureau's monthly reports gauged the deflation of eastern Colorado during the 1930s. "Remarkably warm and dry," the May 1932 report noted. August registered among the warmest on record. The year 1933 followed suit, with June the warmest known and the 111 degrees at Las Animas the highest June temperature measured since 1889. July saw evenly distributed rain, so "crops made good progress." August rains burst the Castlewood Dam southeast of Denver, unloosing a wall of water that killed two and did $1 million in damage. October, herald of the year to come, proved exceedingly hot and dry.[7]

The "hot and dry" litany droned through 1934, "the warmest and driest in the 47 years of climatic history," reported the Weather Bureau. In July, as the drought dragged into its fourteenth month, farmers in the southeast sank wells to get drinking water, an exercise that revealed subsoil moisture depleted to a great depth. A hot August seared crops in the east; on the Western Slope better conditions promised a bountiful Elberta peach harvest. Rain west of Denver brought floods along Bear Creek, killing six. A cooler than normal September was followed by the warmest and driest October on record, its 0.10 inch of moisture only 8 percent of normal.[8]

As weather-watchers looked back in February 1935, they found that in only one month since June 1933 had temperatures dipped below normal. The *Lamar Daily News* joked that two inches of rain had fallen in Las Animas, explaining that the drops were two inches apart. Making a contest

of calamity, Glenn V. Culp of Lamar offered $5 to the first child who collected a gallon of rainwater. Governor Ed Johnson proclaimed May 22 a day of prayer, "that the earth may again bring forth its increase and that sickness and suffering may be relieved."[9]

Rain came before Johnson prayed. April 18 saw 1.16 inches in Alamosa, 1.95 in Boulder, 1.65 in Haxtun. Confronted with an order for an umbrella, the first in three years, clerks at the Springfield Department Store searched for the one they recalled having in stock. Children doffed dust masks and donned galoshes; farmers bought second-hand tractors. "Baca County," the Springfield *Democrat-Herald* gushed, "can come back quicker than any other county in the United States."[10]

By late May it appeared Johnson had overly rattled heaven's gates. Cloudbursts in the northeast and east-central plains — nine inches at Seibert in two hours, nearly three inches in Colorado Springs on Memorial Day, May 30 — overburdened rivers, most of them ordinarily mere trickles. South of Wray the Arickaree washed away Beecher Island, burying the

Morrison suffered several Bear Creek floods in the 1930s, one of them in early September 1938. (Denver Public Library, Western History Department)

marker memorializing the 1868 battle there between the Cheyenne and U.S. troops. People in Brush expected the Burlington railroad embankment to shield them. Instead it backed up water and then broke, inundating the town. At Fort Morgan high water disabled the municipal power plant. South of Denver the flood ripped out the Amarillo-Denver natural gas pipeline. A 20-foot wall of water hit Elbert; Kiowa, too, was smashed.[11]

With bridges, highways, railroads, and telephone and telegraph lines washed out, many plains towns found themselves isolated. The *Wray Rattler* reported the tortured travels of Tom Grant, who left Wray for Burlington, 55 miles distant, on Thursday, May 30, before the storm broke. He intended to return no later than Friday morning, but the flood trapped him in Burlington until Monday, June 3, when he

> drove his truck 18 miles north to the Launchman where he left the truck and started out on foot. He waded the Launchman and then walked almost to Idalia when he caught a ride. He waded through the flood waters of the South Fork, and continued on his way. Finally he hired a man with a car to take him to Beecher Island where he was able to cross the Arickaree in a wagon. Then he came into town in a car with a friend.[12]

Earl L. Mosley, Colorado Springs's city manager, faced a monumental task as he tried to undo in June what Monument and Fountain creeks had done in May. Water stood 12 feet deep in the municipal power plant; all bridges between east and west Colorado Springs were washed out. In Denver, Cherry Creek spilled over its downtown banks, but both Denver and Pueblo suffered less than Colorado Springs. In July, Ralph Baird of the Federal Emergency Relief Administration told Harry Hopkins that repairing and replacing 452 highway bridges on secondary roads would cost more than $1.5 million and that fixing bridges on major roads would drink up another $1 million. Reviewing the flood, the Weather Bureau reported 19 dead and estimated property damage at up to $10 million.[13]

The downpours of April and May 1935 skewed the precipitation totals for the year, which on balance was hot and dry in the east. So was 1936. More than three inches of moisture fell in parts of the southeast in May 1937, but the year's total of 9.07 inches in that region made it among the driest ever. To add to farmers' distress, grasshoppers by the billions marched on their fields.

The hoppers, a recurring plague, had proven troublesome in 1934. In 1936 they feasted on Denver's lawns and stripped the Livermore Valley northwest of Fort Collins, forcing cattlemen to move their herds. That was prelude to a grim 1937, during which hopper armies munched their way through eastern Colorado, advancing up to a mile and a half a day. John C. Polly, a *Rocky Mountain News* reporter, visited the farm of Max Hutchins, 16 miles southeast of Hugo, in late June. There he saw ground "moving, alive, crawling." There he viewed what had been 50 acres of beans reduced

to a barren patch, even the subsurface stems eaten. "We saw grazing land bare of growth as the kitchen floor in your home. . . . We saw main streets of little towns stained with the marching insect troops." Charles Roughton, a Civilian Conservation Corps recruit at Hugo, recalled, "You wouldn't believe how bad they were. I mean if you were walking on the ground it would be just solid and you could stand still and just feel like the ground was moving underneath you. Then when they took to the sky, it would almost black the sun out, they were that bad."[14]

National Guardsmen trucked sawdust from mountain sawmills to the plains, where farmers mixed 200 pounds of it with 50 pounds of bran, 25 gallons of water, 15 gallons of molasses, 10 gallons of sodium arsenite, and a pint of banana oil — grasshoppers supposedly fancied bananas — to make a lethal meal, which Polly likened to "the bran cereal you feed your children for breakfast." Scattered by spreaders trailed behind old cars, the mix dealt, as Polly put it, "sudden and horrible death to as many grasshoppers as possible." Entomologists painted some of them to trace their

Using a barrel filled with grasshopper poison mounted over a fan, farmers broadcast a lethal mixture. (Denver Public Library, Western History Department)

migration and made post-poison body counts — one square foot in Lincoln County yielded 250 little corpses. Railroads lent boxcars to transport sawdust; Colorado borrowed money; Congress appropriated funds; the Civilian Conservation Corps, the Works Progress Administration, and the Soil Conservation Service all cooperated to partially check what C. G. Zimmerman, an old-timer in Lincoln County, called "the durndest critters I ever saw."[15]

The hoppers returned in 1938; otherwise it was a good, wet year. A dry 1939, drier even than 1934 and 1937 — 1.39 inches of moisture in Buena Vista; 5.15 in Fort Morgan — sparked fears of renewed drought, but plenty of rain in the early 1940s, coupled with World War II demand, triggered a farm boom unmatched since World War I. By restoring ground cover, the sweet rains also brought an end to the Dust Bowl.[16]

Dust followed drought. For Colorado that was nothing new: dust storms in the dry mid-1890s halted rail traffic, killed cattle, and made the snow turn pink. The black blizzards of the 1930s, however, lasted for days, returned annually, ravaged millions of acres, and sandblasted themselves into the national psyche. "Not in the memory of the oldest inhabitant of this community," the Trinidad *Chronicle-News* noted in April 1935, "have there been dust disturbances like these of the past few weeks . . . nothing like the continuous desolating sweep of these dust storms."[17]

Amarillo, Texas, tasted the first serious storm of the 1930s in January 1932. Dusters by the dozen, usually of limited scope, marred 1932; in November 1933 a massive storm swept the Midwest. In Colorado sand blew around in the Gunnison River valley in May 1933, but not until early 1934 did the dirt blizzards grow commonplace, and not until 1935 were they fully recognized as disasters. Soil on the eastern plains, too hard and dry to plow in January 1935, fell prey to the winds. In February dust-laden skies caused towns to switch on their street lights at midday. Unable to see through the soupy haze, railroad crews on handcars collided near Arriba, killing one person. Winds of 77 miles per hour raked Denver in mid-March, subjecting the city to its up-to-then worst dust storm. In Fort Collins and Loveland freshly plowed soil blew away, endangering cherry trees by exposing their roots. Poor visibility kept airplanes from landing in Denver on April 9, and hospital operating rooms shut down because patients could not breathe. Around noon it started to rain "dirty brown beads of thin mud." On April 12, *The Denver Post* reported that a storm in southeastern Colorado had lifted, giving Springfield its first dust-free day in a month.[18]

The respite was brief. "The dust was so terrible you could not see across the street," Charles Boettcher, writing from Denver, noted in mid-April. In Edler, southwest of Springfield, a dense dust cloud on April 14 made it impossible for Mrs. Elmer Collins to see her five-year-old son after he let go of her hand. Five hours later he was found, lying in a field, clutching a handkerchief over his mouth, missing one shoe, his cap, and coat, but alive. Poor visibility also vexed pilot Laura Ingalls. Speeding eastward on April 16 in her sleek Vendetta monoplane, she hoped to beat

Dust dimmed day on Denver's Sixteenth Street in late May 1935. (Colorado Historical Society)

Amelia Earhart's 17-hour-7-minute Los Angeles to New York flight record. A sea of dust boiling above New Mexico and Kansas wrecked her plan. Flying blind nearly as far as Wichita, she turned back when her motors flagged. Unable to land in Albuquerque, she sighted mountains in Colorado and put down in Alamosa.[19]

The dust that grounded Ingalls billowed so high that at 22,000 feet she was unable to evade it. Wafted aloft by the winds, the dust went where the winds went — ships in the Atlantic reported light sprinklings. But mostly it drifted in southeastern Colorado, western Kansas, eastern New Mexico, and in the panhandles of Texas and Oklahoma, a vast region of some 50 million acres that came to be called the Dust Bowl. Colorado's topsoil sifted down on Kansas; New Mexico's sand fell on Colorado. Discovering a speck of humor in the migrating dirt, Will Rogers joked about the lawsuits states could bring against each other to recover their errant land.[20]

The grit got into almost everything. John F. Brady, a student at Regis College in the mid-1930s, recalled that the dust wrecked his watch. Fred M. Betz, Sr., editor of the *Lamar Daily News*, remembered forty years later,

A Prowers County duster, April 14, 1935. (FSA, Library of Congress, no photographer identified)

"I've had one or two cars completely ruined by it." Wind-driven dust in Pueblo stripped paint from cars. Motorists blamed static electricity generated by wind and dust for disabling their ignition systems. To prevent shocks they grounded their cars by trailing chains. To keep dust out of their eyes, they wore goggles; to keep it out of their lungs, they fashioned masks of wet towels secured with rubber bands and paper clips. By the late spring of 1935 dozens of cases of dust pneumonia had been diagnosed in Baca and Prowers counties, prompting the Red Cross to send masks, goggles, and nurses to Springfield and Walsh. The April deaths of five-year-old James Walt and seven-year-old William Drake in Springfield as well as that of an infant, William Owenby, at Campo, south of Springfield, were all blamed on dust. Workers tightly sealed the Walsh High School gymnasium so coughing children hospitalized there could get relief. Rabbits perished by the thousands; birds sought protection in the shadows of telephone poles. Wondering why his cows died, rancher Edmund Sipes of Branson in Las Animas County cut several open and found their stomachs filled with mud balls.[21]

In 1981, Mayme Stagner recalled a storm that smothered the Stagner farm near Campo:

> It was one of the most horrifying things I have ever seen in my life. Like a great big black wall coming in. There were brown spots in it and sort of greenish-looking spots, and it looked like a million whirlwinds all right in each other, and just in one big whirl. . . . And rabbits were

running in front of it and birds were flying and even a coyote went across our place. Everything was horrified.

A wall of dust approaches Burlington in eastern Colorado. (Colorado Historical Society)

 The Stagners fled into their house:

We shut the door and bolted it just as the thing hit the front part of it. There was no wind with it, just a crawling thing that went over the top of us and we kept waiting for the wind for we just knew there had to be some wind somewhere. It didn't start blowing until it was dark in the house. Our little coal lamp was just a little blaze in the room. It threw no light out.[22]

The dust drifted 14 to 20 feet deep against houses, and it covered trees in Baca County. In the midst of the desolation, Mayme, then dreading the birth of her fourth child, had a vision:

I saw a big white barn and a chicken house, then later some long sheds out east of the barn. Then I saw a garden out south of the house, tall corn and I saw a lady standing in the west end of the garden, who seemed to be in a strawberry patch picking strawberries. . . . I saw chickens and turkeys and such playing in the yard. Out east of the yard I saw lambs jumping around. There were pretty trees and a stream of water. I saw all this as plain as day — just like it was being painted before my eyes I saw this lady stand up and put a strawberry into her mouth. Then I looked and it was me standing in that garden![23]

A late May 1937 storm on Highway 59 south of Lamar. (Colorado Historical Society)

Others coped by stuffing rags under doors, sealing windows with tape, canceling school, honking their horns as they inched along highways. Sometimes they stopped to ponder the oddities of the storms. Normally wind brought dust, but sometimes dirt slithered along in a quiet cloud such as the one that enveloped Trinidad on April 14, 1935. Normally the storms were black or brown, but the duster that hit Pueblo on February 23, 1936, shifted from russet to blue to orange and then to black. Red snow, dyed by New Mexico dust, fell at Mesa Verde in April 1936.[24]

People joked about the prairie dog that dug a hole six feet in the air. They managed to smile at the story of a man who sandblasted his dishes clean by holding them near his front door keyhole. From Great Bend, Kansas, came news of a storm so thick that had Lady Godiva chosen to ride through town, even her horse could not have seen her. A switchman on the Colorado and Southern Railroad in Trinidad groused, "Even the d — weather is going democratic."[25]

Denizens of southeastern Colorado debated whether it was wiser to quietly bear the weather or to broadcast their woes. The truth would scare away investors and newcomers; stoicism could lead to reduced federal aid. "We cannot agree," said the *Lamar Daily News*, with the "wisdom of 'kidding yourself.' . . . Chamber of Commerce resolutions will not make the grass grow." The debate became academic in March 1935 as reporters, along with Pathe and Paramount newsreel crews, rained on southeastern Colorado. Their reports convinced the nation of the severity of the Colorado storms.[26]

Rexford G. Tugwell, one of the New Deal's chief medicine men, visited Springfield in mid-August 1936. He could not drum up what farmers wanted most — sustained rain. Instead, FDR's advisors proposed to modify the economic climate by doing a fancy dance, which they titled "relief, recovery, and reform."

The Agricultural Adjustment Administration (AAA), the keystone of the New Deal farm recovery program, hatched in May 1933. It focused on raising prices by paying farmers to cut production. To speedily reduce livestock oversupply, it bought animals and killed them, distributing usable meat to relief recipients. Sugar-beet growers, initially left out of AAA, got a slice of the pie in 1934, thanks to the Jones-Costigan Sugar Act, co-sponsored by Senator Edward P. Costigan, which paid beet growers to trim production. The public did not like AAA's practice of murdering piglets and shooting cows, nor did it always see logic in limiting production while people starved. There was no national mourning when the U.S. Supreme Court declared some of AAA's operations unconstitutional in early 1936. To salvage palatable parts of the program, the Department of Agriculture used the Soil Conservation Act (1935), which paid farmers to idle land for conservation purposes, a procedure that cut production as AAA had. In 1938 Congress passed a second Agricultural Adjustment Act, crafted to pass constitutional muster. Reworking of the Jones-Costigan Sugar Act in 1937 aimed to control beet output, raise workers' wages, and prevent child labor.[27]

Colorado's farmers and ranchers, many of whom were not raising much anyway between 1933 and 1935, found salvation through AAA. Lorena Hickok, Harry Hopkins's roving investigator, wrote him in 1934 that AAA's "wheat allotment checks represented the only income many of these farmers got last year." Rancher Robert Rogerson complained, "The government took six hundred of them [ewes] and paid $2.00 each for them. We had to kill and skin the other six hundred and turn their pelts in. In my opinion, that was the craziest, dirtest [*sic*] deal ever pulled by those in charge of dictating to the general American public." But Rogerson, like others, accepted the money: "That $2,400 went farther and done more good than any other I ever got a hold of."[28]

Spending less than $3 million in Colorado during the 1930s, the Soil Conservation Service (SCS) seemed a David in comparison to the Goliath-sized problems it tackled. Unlike David it only stunned its enemy, and, according to historian Paul Bonnifield, its aim was sometimes faulty. The SCS promoted contour plowing, a procedure that captured precious rainwater. It introduced drought-resistant crops, pushed agricultural diversification, and restored barren land. But Bonnifield argues that the agency occasionally thwarted sensible conservation and that it was lax in developing technology. Where SCS failed, individuals succeeded. Charles T. Peacock, a Colorado farmer, invented a device to make small check dams as a farmer plowed and A. E. McClymonds of Springfield devised a better plow.[29]

Parts of southeastern Colorado turned to desert in the wake of drought and dust. (Colorado Historical Society)

If SCS were the New Deal's David, then the Rural Electrification Administration (REA) was its Tom Thumb. A popular little agency, REA lent $1.2 million between 1935 and 1939 to Colorado cooperatives organized to bring electricity to rural areas. The Grand Valley Project, incorporated in August 1936, the first REA endeavor west of the Mississippi, had extended its lines more than 215 miles by late 1939 to serve 706 families outside Grand Junction. By then REA had electrified more than 4,000 other farm homes in Colorado, bringing them a world of radios, electric irons, refrigerators, washing machines, and electric pumps.[30]

REA made loans, a time-honored governmental way of helping farmers. In June 1933 the little-heralded Farm Credit Administration (FCA) consolidated many federal farm-loan programs. In the following six years, FCA lent Coloradans nearly $67 million, making it one of the largest, albeit among the quietest, of the federal programs. For Fred Betz, Sr., of Lamar, government lending meant a job, as he became chairman of the board of the Federal Land Bank's Wichita district in early 1935.[31]

AAA, SCS, and FCA promoted recovery. Relief for farm as well as city folk came through the Federal Emergency Relief Administration, through state relief, through Works Progress Administration jobs, through the Civilian Conservation Corps, and from the National Youth Administration. Symptomatic of the extent of farm distress, 1934 figures showed 49.7 percent of all residents in Baca County on relief, compared to less than 20 percent in Denver.[32]

More than many New Deal initiatives, the Resettlement Administration (1935), headed until early 1937 by Rexford Tugwell, aimed at reform. Like the FCA, it made loans, but it was willing to back basket cases, farmers without other sources of credit. Borrowers paid dearly for the help. Not only did they have to repay the low-interest loans, they also had to follow federal strictures designed to make them good farmers. For his loan, Onofie Quintana, of Sanford in the San Luis Valley, promised to cultivate a garden, can vegetables, clean his corrals, and clear brushland for farming. Thousands of others faced visits from U.S. Department of Agriculture agents who checked cellars and peered into larders as they compiled large reports on small borrowers.[33]

The Resettlement Administration placed much of the blame for the Dust Bowl on farmers' misuse of land, a point it made in the film *The Plow That Broke the Plains,* in which the plow played the villain. To undo the plow's doing, Uncle Sam bought marginal farmland and put it to grass, laying the groundwork for the Comanche National Grassland, more than 600 square miles in Baca, Las Animas, and Otero counties, and the Pawnee National Grassland, more than 300 square miles in Weld County. Farmers, many broken by drought and dust, were encouraged to move, some to tracts near Grand Junction, which, like similar experiments in Delta, Montrose, and Alamosa counties, rerooted a few of the uprooted.[34]

By early 1938 the federal government had purchased 85,000 acres near Briggsdale in Weld County. Once home to 800 families, only 84 farmsteads remained. Milt Warner of Carr worried that the program would destroy the area's schools, but H. L. Likes argued that "the purchase plan is the only thing to keep the foolhardy from farming where only grazing should be done." Connie Will of Cornish agreed. In mid-1939 he visited Hank Speaker, resettled on the President Roosevelt Project near Grand Junction. Will found the Speaker family living in "a six-room house, all modern. Electric ice box, lights, pressure system, house nicely plastered. . . . They don't care if it rains or not as they have plenty of water at all times." Will concluded, "What a paradise it must have been for Mr. and Mrs. Speaker to have moved to this 80-acre farm; to leave the sand hills behind and live surrounded by mountains!"[35]

Shaken by the dust storms in Baca County, one of which shattered a window pane above her children's bed, Mayme Stagner wrote President Roosevelt: "I told him that we were wanting to get out of there and wanted a place of our own and we were not asking for anything to be given to us. We were willing to pay, but we were wanting a chance, being able to have a home and a decent life." Her husband Bert told her that FDR was a busy man, but she mailed the letter anyway. Within a week she received a reply from the president suggesting that the Stagners apply for resettlement. Accepted as part of the Waverly-Bowen Project, a scattering of farms southwest of Alamosa, they received federal loans to reclaim the land and to build a farmstead. Some years after getting established, Mayme was working in her garden:

> I was picking strawberries in a bowl. I was taking one of the biggest ones and going to eat it, and I saw the lambkins jumping out in the pasture and then a turkey or two going across the yard. I saw the flowers around the house and I thought, 'I've been here before.' That was the scene I had seen standing in our doorway many years before [in Baca County]. . . . I stood there, even in a pink dress and a straw hat, it was quite an experience![36]

Mayme Stagner's happy-ending story was not everyone's. Neither the Resettlement Administration nor its 1937 successor, the Farm Security Administration, had sufficient money to promote extensive relocation. In 1940 the Grand Junction *Daily Sentinel* reported only 88 resettlement families in Mesa, Delta, and Montrose counties. Farmers on the Waverly-Bowen Project — in 1938 there were 76 — faced unprofitable years as the government cleared titles to land that also needed to be drained and restored. Dust still blew in the late 1930s, but the Soil Conservation Service could take credit for stabilizing some land. Despite AAA, most farm prices were low in 1939, compared to the early 1920s, but they were better than in 1933. Wheat, which sank to 31¢ a bushel shortly before Roosevelt took office in 1932, hit $1.04 when he was re-elected in 1936. In August of 1939 it was 45¢, at best a feeble endorsement for his farm policies.[37]

All the New Deal's programs and all of its money could not put Colorado's agricultural economy together again. Farmers' cash income in 1939 stood slightly below $143 million, well shy of the nearly $213 million registered in 1929. During the 1930s, thousands fled the eastern plains, defeated by drought, dust, and depression. The state's population grew 8 percent in the decade, better than the 7 percent national average. But in plains farm counties, distress took its toll: Baca lost 4,363 people, 41 percent of its 1930 population; Kit Carson, 2,213; and Logan, 1,576. Some drifted to Denver, which grew by 12 percent in the decade; others went to the Western Slope — Mesa County added 7,883, a growth of 30 percent. Some left the state. California in 1940 reported that 107,000 of its white citizens were Colorado-born, up 27,000 from the 1930 tabulation. "Just what has become of the people is not known," the *Holyoke Enterprise* observed, "but the number of empty houses and business buildings is evidence that the people are not here."[38]

Despite the exodus, thousands stayed on their farms. Some added acres as land prices fell. In Baca County the average farm grew from 644

acres in 1930 to 1,180 in 1940. For their good fortune, the survivors thanked their God, their luck, their intelligence, their hard work, their perseverance, and, if they were honest, they nodded in the direction of Washington, D.C., from where they had gotten more than $125 million in grants and loans between 1933 and 1939. Mayme Stagner, for one, was grateful: "To me, it was the best thing that ever happened to us."[39]

A farmhouse such as this one on the San Luis Valley Farms, a Farm Security Administration project, delighted Mayme Stagner. (Photo by Arthur Rothstein, October 1939, FSA, Library of Congress.)

Good times in the 1940s dimmed recollections of bad times in the 1930s, and the mythology of western self-reliance blurred remembrance of New Deal aid. Lusting after $2-a-bushel wheat, farmers forgot the lessons of drought and dust. Accepting conservation when it paid, they exploited the land when that approach favored their bank accounts. Historian Donald Worster concludes, "Conservation as a cultural reform had come to be accepted only where and insofar as it helped the plains culture reach its traditional expansionary aims. If that was not failure, then success had a strangely dusty smell about it."[40]

However mixed the merits of New Deal agricultural programs, one endeavor, no larger than a mustard seed, staked a long-term claim on the public's memory. Beginning in the mid-1930s, the Resettlement Administration's Historical Section, headed by Roy Emerson Stryker, dispatched photographers to record rural life. Among the tens of thousands of pictures they took are hundreds of Colorado, a few of which have been widely reproduced, many more of which deserve to be.

TEN

An Album of FSA Photographs

Remember Steinbeck's famous lines — "We ain't gonna die out. People is goin' on."? That's the feeling which comes through in those pictures. Every single one.

Roy Emerson Stryker
ca. 1962[1]

Roy Emerson Stryker, born November 5, 1893, in Great Bend, Kansas, bred in Montrose, Colorado — a rancher, Colorado School of Mines student, World War I veteran — left his adopted state in 1921 for New York City. With his wife, Alice, he cared for slum kids at the Union Settlement House while he studied at Columbia, receiving a B.A. in 1924 and an M.A. in 1926. Advancing from an assistantship to an instructorship, he taught economics at Columbia, enlivening classes by taking students on field trips and by illustrating lectures with photographs. When Rexford G. Tugwell, one of his former professors, planned publication of a textbook, he asked Stryker to gather pictures for it. The collaboration yielded *American Economic Life* (Harcourt, Brace, 1925). It also helped cement Stryker's relationship with Tugwell, a connection destined to shape Stryker's life. "Roy," Tugwell told Stryker, "you'll never make an economist. But you can teach in a better way you know, with pictures."[2]

During the 1932 presidential campaign Tugwell advised Roosevelt on economics, becoming part of an informal advisory group tagged the "brains trust" by the press. FDR took Tugwell to Washington, D.C., where he took command of the Resettlement Administration (RA), an agency designed to help tenant and small farmers, as well as migrant workers. Anxious to document RA's work, Tugwell in mid-1935 asked Stryker to head the agency's Historical Section. For the next eight years Stryker did what he did best: gathered pictures and taught with them.[3]

Stryker was no photographer. "My aunt and I once shot a family reunion. Her ten-dollar Brownie got everything while I drew blanks. I never snapped a shutter after that." What Stryker did well was organize, cut red tape, and recognize talent. With infectious enthusiasm he dispatched a small cadre of photographers whose ostensible mission was to document RA's activities. In fact, they took the pictures they and he wanted, going far beyond narrow public relations work. "We succeeded," wrote Stryker, "in doing exactly what Rex Tugwell said we should do: We introduced America to Americans."[4]

That introduction was long and detailed. Stryker's crew took more than 100,000 photographs, of which more than 75,000 prints survive in the Prints and Photographs Division of the Library of Congress as the Farm

Security Administration–Office of War Information (FSA-OWI) Collection, the name reflective of administrative reshuffles that brought RA's Historical Section into the Farm Security Administration (FSA) in 1937 and put it under the umbrella of the Office of War Information (OWI) in 1942. Some photographs show city life; most depict the rural United States: county fairs, farmers feeding pigs, housewives holding pickle jars as if they were royal crowns, small-town main streets, kids at Labor Day parades, billboards, graveyards, cows, horses, tractors, combines, peanuts, sugar beets, corn, and cotton. Absent are the rich and famous; present are the people.[5]

Stryker hired outstanding photographers, or at least those with great potential. Ben Shahn's reputation now rests on his painting rather than on his photography, and Marion Post traded her camera for domestic duties after her marriage in 1941. Many of the other principal Historical Section photographers — Walker Evans, Dorothea Lange, Russell Lee, Carl Mydans, Arthur Rothstein, and John Vachon — continued as photographers after they left the government. Still, much of their fame rests on their Depression-era images, such as Lange's *Migrant Mother* and Rothstein's *Dust Storm, Cimarron County, Oklahoma.* Those pictures and dozens of others have become enduring icons of the decade.

Photographs of sweating sharecroppers, bleached bones on cracked earth, gaunt mountain-folk, and sad-faced children, however, constitute only part of the FSA collection, which, on the whole, presents a moderately rosy view of small-town and rural America. Depicting the ill-clad, the ill-housed, and the ill-fed no doubt well served the New Deal's political purposes for a time. When he sent Arthur Rothstein into the Dust Bowl in the summer of 1936, Stryker relished the possibilities of getting heart-wrenching pictures: "I do hope you have the good luck to be on hand when some family is packing up, ready to leave for parts more moist." But by the late 1930s and early 1940s, the period of most FSA shutter-clicking in Colorado, the Historical Section was focusing more on the country's promise than on its problems.[6]

Arthur Rothstein (1915–1985), one of Stryker's former students at Columbia, became his first employee at the Resettlement Administration in mid-1935. Initially in charge of the photo lab, he soon escaped into the sunlight to take pictures. "Roy made everyone who worked with him, including me, read a great deal. . . . He was a great catalyst and a great stimulator, and he made people think about their work." When Rothstein photographed National Guardsmen blockading Colorado's border in April 1936, Stryker facetiously offered him a civics lesson: "I am sorry that they did not arrest you at the Colorado State line. It would have been a good liberal education on your rights as a citizen."[7]

On revisiting Colorado in the autumn of 1939, Rothstein found a more hospitable atmosphere. In mid-September, Stryker contacted him at the Hotel Tallcorn in Marshalltown, Iowa, where Rothstein was waiting for the corn to ripen, telling him to go to Colorado, where the potato and sugar-beet harvests promised good pictures. He reached Denver in late September and checked into the Hotel Auditorium at Fourteenth and Stout, "The Newest and Most Complete Moderate Priced Hotel in Denver." He wrote Stryker that Duane B. Wilson of the local FSA office was "sitting on the edge of his chair ready to take off. We expect to cover the state thoroughly and have already left a trail of flash bulbs in Weld County." Rothstein traveled in Wilson's car because a large vehicle was needed for "my cameras, his cameras, our luggage, and the various county supervisors that we haul around to point out the successful rehabilitation clients. . . . It looks like I'm going to be in a frenzy of shutter clicking until the middle of October."[8]

An exceedingly dry 1939 hurt many Colorado farmers, but Rothstein's pictures revealed little of their distress. A few shots of Keota, the bones of a town in Weld County, bespoke the farm bust, and a stark image of a lonely cow suggested desolation on the plains. For the most part Rothstein's view was positive. The migrant laborers he photographed with the cooperation of the Great Western Sugar Company looked healthy, even sometimes happy. Near Kersey, FSA clients Mr. and Mrs. Andy Bihain carefully positioned themselves in front of a cottonwood tree as Rothstein made a half-second exposure at f/16, using slow film to capture in detail their proud contentment as they held melons, tomatoes, and corn. Of all the products of his frenzy of shutter-clicking, it turned out among his best and most often reproduced.[9]

Stryker wanted photos of small towns. Rothstein provided a few: Jaroso, San Pablo, and Monte Vista in the San Luis Valley; Akron on the plains; Georgetown in the mountains. From Montrose, where he stayed at The Belvedere, "One of Colorado's Good Hotels — Modern in Every Respect," he apologetically wrote Stryker, "The hurried nature of this trip means that I'm getting only a few superficial things in an area that is full of interesting material." Despite his complaints, he had much to show for a few weeks' work. In addition to taking hundreds of photos, he had the honor of meeting a memorable madam in Salida: "Laura Evans who runs the 'line,' which, by the way is on the same block as the FSA office. . . . The stories she tells about some of Colorado's oldest families are priceless." He had hoped to go to Durango, but warnings of a polio epidemic dissuaded him. In mid-October he returned to Iowa.[10]

Russell Lee (1903–1986) also visited Colorado in 1939. Trained as a chemical engineer, he decided in 1929 to become an artist. In 1935 he took up photography and in 1936 went to work for the Resettlement Administration. In August 1939, he and Stryker, who were good friends, traveled together through parts of Oklahoma, Texas, New Mexico, Arizona, and then into Colorado, where Stryker vacationed and Lee took pictures. "Didn't realize how much of a Westerner I am until I got out on this particular trip," Stryker wrote Dorothea Lange. "I almost wish I had money enough to buy a cattle ranch and give up photography."[11]

Lee's 1939 photographs, mainly taken on the plains in September and October, were prelude to his more productive visit in the autumn of 1940,

"Left to right: John Vachon, Arthur Rothstein, Russell Lee, and Roy Stryker reviewing photographs in the FSA-OWI collection at the FSA Historical Section." Caption from Library of Congress copy of the photo. (Photo by Beaumont Newhall, ca. 1938, Library of Congress)

when, concentrating on southwestern Colorado, he filled gaps left by Rothstein. Lee wrote Stryker from Ouray in early September: "Have been busy all week what with getting the shots of labor day at Silverton; a grand barbecue at Ridgway (which was almost spoiled because of rain), trips to Telluride and Ophir and Camp Bird mine. That is certainly wonderful country around Telluride and Ophir." Unfettered by any compulsion to stick to agricultural subjects, he photographed mines and miners, movie houses and mountains. At both Ridgway and Silverton he captured Labor Day festivities, creating a photo story more limited in scope but similar to what he had done in Pietown, New Mexico, in April 1940 and the July 4 pictures he would take in Vale, Oregon, in 1941. "Boy, how I wish I were with you these days!" Stryker wrote, "especially when you were over at Telluride."[12]

Rothstein and Lee took the majority of FSA photos of Colorado, but Marion Post (1910–1990) also contributed substantially to the collection. Previously a photographer for Philadelphia's *The Evening Bulletin*, she joined the Historical Section in 1938. In offering her the job, Stryker stated the pay, $2,300 a year, and promised her $5 a day for expenses. "I know that you have a great deal of experience in the field, and that you are quite competent to take care of yourself, but I do have grave doubts about sending you, for instance, into certain sections of the South. . . . Negro people are put in a very difficult spot when white women attempt to interview or photograph them."[13]

As able as she was, Post nevertheless found her September 1941 Rockies expedition taxing. Combining the trip with a short honeymoon, she and her husband, Leon Wolcott, traveled into Colorado from Cheyenne, Wyoming. She wired Stryker from Craig on September 4: "First good weather in a week." Tolerable weather allowed her some good shots in Montezuma and Leadville. In Aspen she and Leon stayed at the Hotel Jerome. Snow made photography difficult. "At least," she mused, "it made a couple of the ghost towns look ghostlier." It also made travel hazardous. Crossing Independence Pass in her new Buick, without tire chains and without a heater, she got stuck and had to be rescued by a snow plow. "I couldn't see the road at all," she wrote Stryker. "I only knew it was narrow and that on the right was a sheer drop God knows how far."[14]

Post told Stryker "that some ghost towns, particularly those near lead and zinc, are coming to life in 1941 — defense needs I suppose. Montezuma and Leadville are two such places." When John Vachon (1914–1975) snapped a few pictures in Colorado in 1942, war was evident. One of his shots shows two soldiers, another a Washington County billboard proclaiming: "America Needs Sugar: Grow More Beets." By 1942 defense needs had also reshaped the federal government. The FSA had long rankled conservative legislators, who criticized it for "promoting socialized medicine, excessive spending on travel and publicity, and wasting funds on no-account people." To protect his little empire, Stryker lent his photographers to other agencies, such as the Office of War Information, which, in September 1942, took over the Historical Section. Historian F. Jack Hurley reports that Stryker "by the spring of 1943 . . . found himself in a custodial position. He was expected to provide propaganda pictures from those already in the file, but little else." He held on to his job long enough to assure that the FSA-OWI Collection, which some wanted to jettison, would be transferred intact to the Library of Congress.[15]

Stryker left Washington in 1943, exchanging his battered New Deal hat for a corporate tie with Standard Oil of New Jersey, where he documented the company's worldwide activities, building in the process another huge photo file. Then he directed a project that amassed photographs of Pittsburgh, and later he worked for the steel-maker Jones and Laughlin. In 1962 he retired to Montrose, his boyhood home, and in 1968 moved to Grand Junction, where he died in 1975. Lee followed Stryker to Standard Oil, subsequently doing free-lance photography and late in life becoming a University of Texas faculty member. Rothstein worked for *Look* until it folded in 1971. Marion Post Wolcott, on the other hand, abandoned professional photography to please her husband and to raise her family. Asked whether he had any idea when he was growing up that his mother was "an important American photographer," her youngest son, Michael, replied, "Nothing. Absolutely nothing of that."[16]

Her FSA work, like that of the other photographers, insures that she will be remembered, just as it guarantees that rural and small-town America of the late 1930s and early 1940s will not be forgotten.

The photographs that follow retain the captioning, including possible spelling and other errors, found on the original photographs in the Library of Congress's FSA-OWI collection. Periods have been added to month abbreviations, and the designation "Colo.," although usually present in the original caption, has not been included after the town or county name. The album is arranged according to photographer with Rothstein first, Lee second, Post Wolcott third, and Vachon, fourth. Within each grouping photographs are arranged alphabetically by place.

Adams County, Oct. 1939. Sugar beet worker drinking water. (Arthur Rothstein, FSA, Library of Congress)

Adams County, Oct. 1939. Field worker with knife used in topping sugar beets. (Arthur Rothstein, FSA, Library of Congress)

Chaffee County, Oct. 1939. Son of an FSA rehabilitation borrower.
(Arthur Rothstein, FSA, Library of Congress)

*Chaffee County, Oct. 1939. The farm
of Ellsworth Painter, an FSA rehabilitation client. (Arthur Rothstein, FSA,
Library of Congress)*

Chaffee County, Oct. 1939. Elmo Temple, rehabilitation client, with part of his flock of sheep. (Arthur Rothstein, FSA, Library of Congress)

Chaffee County, Oct. 1939. Paul Arnold, son of an FSA rehabilitation client, with a turkey. (Arthur Rothstein, FSA, Library of Congress)

Costilla County, Oct. 1939. Spanish-American farm laborer. (Arthur Rothstein, FSA, Library of Congress)

Delta (vicinity), Oct. 1939. Western slope farms. Mrs. Thomas Beede with a prizewinning rooster. (Arthur Rothstein, FSA, Library of Congress)

Delta (vicinity), Oct. 1939. Western slope farms. Thomas W. Beede, a resettlement client with his youngest daughter. (Arthur Rothstein, FSA, Library of Congress)

Denver, Oct. 1939. Driving sheep into pens in stockyards before shipping to packing plants. (Arthur Rothstein, FSA, Library of Congress)

Denver, Oct. 1939. Ranchers at the stockyards. (Arthur Rothstein, FSA, Library of Congress)

*Georgetown, Oct. 1939. A ghost min-
ing town. Hotel De Paris. (Arthur
Rothstein, FSA, Library of Congress)*

Greeley (vicinity), Oct. 1939. Milton Robinson, an FSA borrower, holding sugar beet, on his farm. (Arthur Rothstein, FSA, Library of Congress)

*Hotchkiss (vicinity), Oct. 1939. Mrs. Tom Reilly, wife of FSA reha-
bilitation borrower, with her daughter and guinea pigs. (Arthur
Rothstein, FSA, Library of Congress)*

Hotchkiss (vicinity), Oct. 1939. Farmstead of Tom Reilly, an FSA borrower. (Arthur Rothstein, FSA, Library of Congress)

Keota, Oct. 1939. (Arthur Rothstein,
FSA, Library of Congress)

Keota, Oct. 1939. Town abandoned because of continuous crop failures. (Arthur Rothstein, FSA, Library of Congress)

Kersey (vicinity), Oct. 1939. Mr. and Mrs. Andy Bahain [sic],
FSA borrowers, on their farm. [Often reproduced, this is probably
the best known of the FSA photos taken in Colorado. Bill Ganzel
in Dust Bowl Descent, *p. 50, gives the spelling as Bihain.]*
(Arthur Rothstein, FSA, Library of Congress)

*Kersey (vicinity), Oct. 1939. Andy Bahain [sic], an FSA borrower
with seed corn. (Arthur Rothstein, FSA, Library of Congress)*

Kersey (vicinity), Oct. 1939. Andy Bahain [sic], an FSA client, on a hay rake on his farm. (Arthur Rothstein, FSA, Library of Congress)

Mesa County, Oct. 1939. Mrs. Alfred Peterson, wife of a tenant purchase borrower with preserved food. (Arthur Rothstein, FSA, Library of Congress)

Rio Grande County, Oct. 1939. Potato picker. (Arthur Rothstein, FSA, Library of Congress)

San Luis (vicinity), Oct. 1939. Spanish-American rehabilitation clients working their farm. (Arthur Rothstein, FSA, Library of Congress) [Rothstein did not name the clients.]

Weld County, Oct. 1939. Arid land.
(Arthur Rothstein, FSA, Library of
Congress)

Weld County, Oct. 1939. Mr. and Mrs. Milton Robinson, with the FSA supervisor. (Arthur Rothstein, FSA, Library of Congress)

Weld County, Oct. 1939. Fred Schmeekle, FSA borrower, drilling wheat on his dry land farm. (Arthur Rothstein, FSA, Library of Congress)

Baca County, Oct. 1939. Mr. Bosley, of the Bosley reorganization unit, feeding a sow. (Russell Lee, FSA, Library of Congress)

Cimarron, Sept. 1940. Sheepherder rolling a cigarette. (Russell Lee, FSA, Library of Congress)

Durango, Sept. 1940. Residential district. Durango is the trading, shipping, and distribution center of southwestern Colorado. (Russell Lee, FSA, Library of Congress)

Garcia, July 1940. School House.
(Russell Lee, FSA, Library of Con-
gress)

La Junta, Jan. 1941. Chain stores on main street. (Russell Lee, FSA, Library of Congress)

*Montrose, Sept. 1940. Main street.
(Russell Lee, FSA, Library of Congress)*

Montrose, Sept. 1940. Theater. (Russell Lee, FSA, Library of Congress)

*Montrose, Sept. 1940. Sign. (Russell
Lee, FSA, Library of Congress)*

Ophir, Sept. 1940. General store. (Russell Lee, FSA, Library of Congress)

Ordway (vicinity), Sept. 1939. Mrs. Ernest W. Kirk, Jr., wife of an FSA client, feeding her chickens on a farm. (Russell Lee, FSA, Library of Congress)

Ordway (vicinity), Sept. 1939. Ernest W. Kirk, Jr., with a team of horses bought with an FSA loan. (Russell Lee, FSA, Library of Congress)

Ouray, Sept. 1940. Railroad station of the Denver and Rio Grande Western railroad. This narrow gauge line formerly had passenger service but is now confined to freight service. (Russell Lee, FSA, Library of Congress)

Ouray, Sept. 1940. Theater. (Russell Lee, FSA, Library of Congress)

*Ouray, Sept. 1940. Store building.
Ouray is the center of a gold mining
region developing as a tourist center.
(Russell Lee, FSA, Library of Congress)*

Ouray County, Sept. 1940. Sheep-herder with his horse and camp outfit. (Russell Lee, FSA, Library of Congress)

Ouray County, Sept. 1940. Sheepherder. (Russell Lee, FSA, Library of Congress)

Ouray County, Sept. 1940. Mountain Valley with Mt. Sneffles [sic] in the background. (Russell Lee, FSA, Library of Congress)

Ridgeway [sic], Sept. 1940. Labor day celebration. Boys' sack race. (Russell Lee, FSA, Library of Congress)

Ridgeway [sic], *Sept. 1940. Labor day celebration. Getting barbecue and coffee. (Russell Lee, FSA, Library of Congress)*

Ridgeway [sic], *Sept. 1940. Labor day celebration.*
Woman and her baby waiting in line for barbecue.
(Russell Lee, FSA, Library of Congress)

San Juan County, Sept. 1940. Railroad leading to abandoned mine.
(Russell Lee, FSA, Library of Congress)

Saw Pit, [no month given on caption; likely Sept.] 1940. The store. (Russell Lee, FSA, Library of Congress)

Saw Pit, Sept. 1940. Sign. (Russell Lee, FSA, Library of Congress)

*Silverton, Sept. 1940. Labor day cele-
brations . . . (Russell Lee, FSA, Library
of Congress)*

*Silverton, Sept. 1940. Labor day cele-
bration. High school band. (Russell
Lee, FSA, Library of Congress)*

Silverton, Sept. 1940. Labor day celebration. Miners with their children. (Russell Lee, FSA, Library of Congress)

Silverton, Sept. 1940. Labor day celebration. Young miner taking a picture. (Russell Lee, FSA, Library of Congress)

Silverton, Sept. 1940. Labor day celebration. Boy watching the miners' contest. (Russell Lee, FSA, Library of Congress)

Silverton, Sept. 1940. Labor day celebration. Spectators at the contests for miners. (Russell Lee, FSA, Library of Congress)

Silverton, Sept. 1940. Labor day cele-
bration. Children watching the pa-
rade. (Russell Lee, FSA, Library of
Congress)

Silverton, Sept. 1940. Labor day celebrations. Gold miner operating a drill in the drilling contest. (Russell Lee, FSA, Library of Congress)

Silverton, Sept. 1940. Old house. This was the type of house built by mine and mill operators in the early days and indicates that the owners thought that the operations would be permanent. (Russell Lee, FSA, Library of Congress)

Silverton, Sept. 1940. Detail of the front of a building. (Russell Lee, FSA, Library of Congress)

*Silverton (vicinity), San Juan County,
Sept. 1940. Abandoned gold mill.
These old mills were always built on
the side of a mountain to take advantage of the law of gravity in processing
the ore. The processing took much
water. (Russell Lee, FSA, Library of
Congress)*

Telluride, Sept. 1940. Post Office. (Russell Lee, FSA, Library of Congress)

Ashcroft, Sept. 1941. Ghost mining town. (Marion Post Wolcott, FSA, Library of Congress)

Aspen, Sept. 1941. Main street during a blizzard. (Marion Post Wolcott, FSA, Library of Congress)

Aspen (vicinity), Sept. 1941. Cow hands' cabin on a ranch after an early fall blizzard in the mountains. (Marion Post Wolcott, FSA, Library of Congress)

Craig, Sept. 1941. Main street of a new and thriving boom town. (Marion Post Wolcott, FSA, Library of Congress)

[Denver vicinity], Sept. 1941. Highway from Denver to Idaho Springs. (Marion Post Wolcott, FSA, Library of Congress)

Leadville, Sept. 1941. Main street in an old mining town. (Marion Post Wolcott, FSA, Library of Congress)

Leadville, Sept. 1941. County judge in front of the mortuary on the main street. (Marion Post Wolcott, FSA, Library of Congress)

Leadville, Sept. 1941. Houses in old mining town. (Marion Post Wolcott, FSA, Library of Congress)

Montezuma, Sept. 1941. Ghost min-
ing town coming to life because of the
defense mining boom. (Marion Post
Wolcott, FSA, Library of Congress)

Central City, May 1942. (John Vachon, FSA, Library of Congress)

Central City, May 1942. (John Vachon, FSA, Library of Congress)

[Denver vicinity], May 1942. Soldiers from Fort Logan, Colorado hitchhiking along U.S. highway #40. (John Vachon, FSA, Library of Congress)

Hayden, May 1942. (John Vachon,
FSA, Library of Congress)

Washington County, May 1942. Sign on U.S. Highway #6. (John Vachon, FSA, Library of Congress)

ELEVEN

Life Goes On

A queer looking creature, said to have been a urodela, excited a lot of
curiosity while it was on display at the N. Dean Henry Rexall drug store
Monday afternoon. . . . This specimen was about eight inches long, had
a large fish-like head, short legs, long fins, and a back suggestive of a
lizard.

Wray Rattler,
March 28, 1935[1]

Dust, grasshoppers, riots, relief: the foreground of the past over-
whelms the background. Melon Day at Rocky Ford, Lettuce Day at Buena
Vista, Chautauqua lectures at Boulder, thousands of other unremarkable
events gave the 1930s substance and flavor. People noticed the lark bunting
more often after it became Colorado's state bird in 1931. Caroline Jones, an
African-American reputed to be 114 years old, perished in a Denver fire in
1935. Civil War veteran Frank H. Benham, Pueblo's last surviving member
of the Grand Army of the Republic, died in 1938.[2]

Happy, sad, and strange occurrences provided grist for the newspapers and topics for conversation. Buffalo Bill Cody's old horse, retired to a
farm southeast of Denver, was shot in the neck in 1932. Colorado celebrated
Thanksgiving twice in 1939: once because of President Roosevelt's procla-
mation setting it on November 23, again on November 30 following state
tradition. Elwood Sherman of Estes Park died in 1936 when the house he
built with his veteran's bonus fell on him. In 1932, Carbon Mountain south
of Durango got the hiccups — belching, roaring, "hurling down debris and
rocks and opening chasms." In 1938 an 18-car runaway Rock Island freight
train reached a speed of 180 miles per hour before being derailed moments
before it reached Colorado Springs's central depot. A urodela showed up
in Wray.[3]

Women made news during the decade. In 1935 Elisa A. Palladino
became the first woman to serve on Denver's city council. In 1938 Irena S.
Ingham of Cripple Creek was appointed a district judge, the first woman
in Colorado to hold such a post. Mrs. Pete Ecker of Walsenburg claimed an
even more unusual honor in 1939 when, having killed 300 rattlesnakes, she
declared herself the state's champion woman rattlesnake hunter.[4]

State governors and federal administrators insured that they would
be remembered by leaving behind mountains of papers. Denver restaurant
owner Albert A. McVittie faced mountains of dirty dishes after staging his
annual Thanksgiving feasts for the poor. He, too, says Denver journalist
Gene Amole, deserves a place in history. So does Frank H. Rice, a Denver
preacher who made himself a bishop in his own Liberal Church. Minister

extraordinaire to the poor, Rice "shared in full the poverty of his parishioners, . . . ate the same food he served to them, and when there was nothing on hand to boil into soup he, too, went hungry." If Edwin C. Johnson merits remembering, does not George C. Cox? He gave Fort Morgan 36 years of service as city superintendent until a 1940 row with the city council led to his being fired. The politicians thanked him, paid him $350 in severance pay, but provided no pension.[5]

Whites strutted through the pages of 1930s newspapers. Blacks got far less coverage. Many Coloradans recognized the state's two most famous white musicians: Glenn Miller, who went to high school in Fort Morgan, and Paul Whiteman, who was born in Denver. Fewer knew of the African-American pianist Eugene Gash, or bandleader George Morrison, famed in the 1920s, working as a messenger in the governor's office in the 1930s. Louise Hill, the matriarch of Denver society, hired African-American musicians to entertain her luncheon guests in September 1939. For her, as for many of her caste and race, the group's name was unimportant. She wrote her daughter-in-law: "Also I had [an African-American] band, which I consider very satisfactory for jazz music."[6]

Minimizing blacks was so common that most whites did not give it any thought. Alberta Pike featured Denver's Five Points black neighborhood in the *Rocky Mountain News* in August 1932. She wrote of Benny Hooper's De Luxe Recreation Parlor and Ex-Service Men's Club, where "the noisy black-and-tan crowd is the sporting, fun-loving, easy-going element that plays so important a role in the life of the colored settlement." Pike did note the neighborhood's cultural life: the book review clubs, the churches, the community's commitment to education. But, in tune with the times, she was unable to forgo stereotypes: "Down the street half-naked [children] play. It's hot today. They like it. The sun makes their dark little bodies gleam as if they were oiled."[7]

Bigotry sometimes bubbled violently. The August 17, 1932, Washington Park race riot in south Denver saw whites attack African-Americans who wanted to use the Smith Lake beach. In 1935 in Colorado Springs, 250 whites surrounded a church where blacks and whites, followers of Harlem's Father Divine, dared to worship together. The *Colorado Springs Gazette* reported, "Cries of 'Let's go in and get 'em' echoed thru the crowd." Police kept some order, although "someone poured gasoline into the street and set fire to it." Two years later Colorado Springs's African-Americans were again put down when whites forbade the use of the Lincoln School grounds building for a "colored" recreation center. Still, despite the friction, African-Americans in Colorado were better off than those in the South. On being asked in 1932 to provide money so Denver's branch of the National Association for the Advancement of Colored People could pay legal fees in a swimming pool desegregation case, the central office in New York replied that it could not help: "We are active in a number of life and death cases in the far South. . . . We are forced, especially during this

"Old Man Depression" hangs in front of Denver's Orpheum Theater at 1537–1543 Welton Street. Opened February 11, 1932, the luxurious 2,563-seat theater, razed in 1967, replaced an earlier Orpheum on the same site. (Denver Public Library, Western History Department)

depression, to lean heavily upon our large, active branches in the 'free sections' so that the work may be carried on."[8]

The Depression dominated the decade, but despite the economic collapse, life went on. Crime and punishment, newspapers and books, movies and soap operas, fads and football, summer tourists and winter skiers, high culture and low, gave Coloradans more to ponder than the rate of employment and the price of potatoes. The *New York Times* on March 2, 1933, reported Hitler's consolidation of his power in Germany and Roosevelt's preparations to take power in the United States. Bracketed between those stories — front page center — was a flash from Denver: "Boettcher Freed by Kidnapers; Payment of Ransom Indicated."

Charles Boettcher II, heir to the family's millions, was snatched by two armed men shortly before midnight, Sunday, February 12, 1933, as he and his wife, Anna Lou, returned to their Denver home at 777 Washington Street. Within days his abductors demanded $60,000 in ransom from his father, Claude. Although ordered to shun the police, Claude sought help from Denver detectives, federal agents, and Irving (Dad) Bruce of Colorado Springs, one of the state's foremost investigators. Assisted by as many as 4,000 volunteers, lawmen searched the city. When gangster Joe Roma was murdered in north Denver — riddled with bullets as he played his mandolin — the police speculated that he was connected to Charles's disappearance, an idea they later abandoned.[9]

From time to time the kidnapers dropped Claude a line telling him Charles was fine, but might not remain so. On March 1, Claude sent his chauffeur and another employee to an isolated bridge between Denver and Brighton, where at 8:30 P.M. they tossed a $60,000 bundle of cash into a dry creek bed. An hour earlier Charles, still blindfolded, had been freed at Thirty-fifth Avenue and Gaylord Street in northeast Denver. Learning of the release, reporters besieged the Boettcher mansion until Claude appeared at the door brandishing a pistol. "Stand back," he warned. "I'm sick and tired of being pestered."[10]

Even angrier at the kidnapers, Claude vowed to pursue them "as long as I live." Informants helped crack the case, as did Charles. His captors had blindfolded him, driven for many hours, and then imprisoned him in a cellar, where they fed him soup and sandwiches for 17 days. Noticing that a plane passed over regularly, he determined the time. Because scheduled flights were rare, the information helped investigators locate the hideaway — a farmhouse in south-central South Dakota near Chamberlain. On January 31, 1934, police captured the leader of the gang, Verne Sankey, as he waited for a haircut in a Chicago barbershop. Taken to Sioux Falls, South Dakota, Sankey avoided trial by knotting together two neckties and hanging himself.[11]

In the wake of the kidnaping, some rich Denverites took to packing guns and looked for chauffeurs who could double as bodyguards. The city reckoned that it spent more than $9,000 to find Charles, but most people probably thought it worth the cost, if only because the excitement helped them take their minds off collapsing banks and hungry children. Throughout the 1930s, Coloradans enjoyed plenty of crime, some of it especially juicy because it reached into high places.[12]

Isaac H. Merritt, secretary to Denver's mayor Benjamin F. Stapleton, launched the decade on a felonious path by embezzling more than $26,000 in city funds. In November 1935, James H. Carr, Colorado's secretary of state, implicated in taking payoffs from liquor distributors, was impeached by the state House of Representatives. He resigned before the state Senate could try him. As Carr relinquished the headlines, Denver's district attorney, Earl Wettengel, took them. Although disbarred by the Colorado Supreme Court in April 1936 for forging a document in order to cover up his connection with gamblers, Wettengel remained on the job. Removing him would have required action by a special session of the legislature at a cost few cared to incur. Until Wettengel's term expired on January 12, 1937, Denver's judicial district was left with a man representing it who could not practice law as a private attorney. Denver's embarrassment, however,

Gambling flourished in the 1930s despite occasional efforts to crack down by cracking up slot machines. (Colorado Historical Society)

paled compared to Trinidad's when in the summer of 1938 a grand jury indicted 18 persons, many of them Las Animas County officials, for illicitly feeding at the public trough.[13]

In an era that hatched *Dick Tracy* comics (1931) and made best-sellers of Erle Stanley Gardner's Perry Mason mysteries, crime, especially murders, sold newspapers. First came stories of bloody events, then tales of brilliant detectives, then trial accounts, and finally, in many cases, front-page, minute-by-minute coverage of executions, of which there were 24 in Colorado during the decade. In July 1886 a visitor to Denver had marveled at the city's carnival atmosphere as thousands of people, served by pop-corn vendors and souvenir hawkers, gathered to watch a hanging. Such barbarous spectacles were not permitted in the more civilized 1930s. Still firmly wedded to the principle of an eye for an eye, or, at least, an eye for an eye unless the accused could afford a skilled attorney, Colorado conducted executions at the Cañon City penitentiary, far from the clamoring crowd. Most people, if they wanted to enjoy a hanging or a gassing, had to buy a newspaper.[14]

Seven hangings in 1930 and the prospect of three more in early 1931 prompted formation of the Colorado League to Abolish Capital Punishment in early 1931. The league hoped to get the state to stop executions before three condemned men, Claude Ray, John Walker, and Andrew

Halliday, were hanged. Known as the Manter bandits because they had robbed a bank in that Kansas town before murdering Kiowa County under-sheriff C. A. Hickman near Eads, Colorado, the trio elicited little sympathy. Lawmakers left the death penalty intact. Late in January, Ray, Walker, and Halliday were hanged, giving Colorado its first triple execution.[15]

Witnesses reported that instead of dying from broken necks, the men strangled to death — often a slow process. A similar fate had befallen Eddie Ives in 1930. Convicted of killing Denver policeman Harry R. Ohle in late 1928, Ives, a habitual criminal, was sentenced to die in 1929. By aiding guards during the 1929 penitentiary riot, he won a brief respite. On January 11, 1930, he was hanged — twice. A small, skinny man weighing only 80 pounds, he could not put enough weight on the rope to make the hanging machine work properly. Instead the rope slipped off a pulley, and Ives, semi-conscious, fell to the floor. He managed to tell his tormentors that they could not legally hang him again, but they strung him up a second time to slowly strangle.[16]

Aghast at the ghastly gallows, state senator Teller Ammons proposed that the doomed be compelled to inhale cyanide gas, a means of killing felons that had proven effective and cheap in Nevada. On April Fool's Day 1933, Governor Johnson signed the gas bill. Because the new law was not retroactive, hangings continued, Walter Jones's late in 1933 being the last.[17]

Warden Roy P. Best tested the three-chair gas chamber in late 1933 to get it shipshape for the asphyxiating of Walter Reppin, an 18-year-old who confessed to slaying a Colorado Springs taxi driver. A 30-pound pig stopped struggling after 47 seconds; an old dog expired after only 10 seconds. Reppin, however, objected to being used for an experiment and, with the help of Denver attorneys Philip Hornbein and David Rosner, won commutation of his sentence to life in prison.[18]

That gave William Kelley the distinction of being the first to use the airtight chamber. Condemned with his partner, Lloyd Frady, for killing rancher Russell Browning, Kelley received more than the usual newspaper attention. Lorena Hickok, an investigator for the Federal Emergency Relief Administration, happened to be in Cañon City in late June 1934 as officials prepared to gas Kelley. Hickok, a close friend of Eleanor Roosevelt, told the first lady that Frady had raised the $200 needed to take his case to the Colorado Supreme Court, where he hoped to get a new trial. Kelley was poor, so he was going to die. "The thing has nearly driven me crazy. How can you have any faith and hope in us if we do things like that in this supposedly enlightened age?" Hickok considered paying the appeal costs, but a relief worker warned that her involvement might be reported and embarrass the Roosevelts. Kelley died on schedule after 12 minutes strapped in the execution chair. Eleanor wrote Hickok, "You mustn't agonize so over things. . . . Your giving the $200 would have been useless."[19]

She misjudged Colorado's quirky justice — normally draconian, but sometimes tempered by mercy or indecision. Perhaps an appeal would have saved Kelley, who maintained his innocence. Frady's appeal succeeded. A

Ralph Carr (left), Arthur Morrison, and in the cowboy hat, Warden Roy Best in June 1939. Best, once Governor Billy Adams's driver, took charge of the Cañon City penitentiary in 1932, ruling it, The Denver Post, later said, "with cowboy justice and the lash." In hot water after 1950 for flogging prisoners and for alleged mismanagement, he fought to hold his job until he died in May 1954. (Colorado Historical Society)

model and enterprising prisoner, he supported his mother and bought property with profits he made by marketing souvenirs made by other convicts. On his release, at age 38, in 1949, he drove away in a new Cadillac. "I learned and earned a lot in prison," he told a reporter.[20]

Few were as fortunate as Frady. Numerous appeals only delayed the execution of Joe Arridy, a mentally retarded man convicted of participating in the raping and slaying of 15-year-old Dorothy Drain of Pueblo. Arridy, an escapee from the State Home for Mental Defectives at the time of his crime, did not seem to understand that he had done something wrong. On the day of his execution, June 6, 1939, he was given ice cream, which he shared with the other prisoners. He told Warden Best that he wanted "to raise chickens in heaven." He was, Best recalled, "the happiest man ever to live in the Death Row." It took him six-and-a-half-minutes to die. "A child rather than a man was executed," said his lawyer, Gail Ireland.[21]

Executions, like murders, sold newspapers. Many of the state's smaller papers needed all the help they could get. Outside of Denver, only four dailies reckoned circulations of more than 7,000 in 1939. The *Pueblo Star-Journal* (12,456), an evening paper, and the *Pueblo Chieftain* (9,097), a

morning sheet, were both published by Frank S. Hoag, Sr., a staunch anti-Roosevelt Republican. In Colorado Springs, Clarence C. Hamlin, twice a delegate to the Republican National Convention, published the *Colorado Springs Gazette* (4,729) in the morning and the *Telegraph* (12,391) in the evening. Grand Junction's *Daily Sentinel* (8,212), edited by Walter Walker, was one of the strongest Democratic voices in the state. Boulder also harbored Democrats: Lucius Carver Paddock and his son, Alva Adams Paddock, who owned and operated the *Boulder Daily Camera,* an influential paper of nearly 4,000 daily circulation.[22]

With a daily circulation of 154,959 and 266,731 on Sunday, *The Denver Post* outsold all the other newspapers in the state combined. The *Rocky Mountain News,* a Scripps-Howard publication, struggled through the decade with less than a third of the *Post*'s daily circulation, and not even a sixth of its Sunday figure. As impressive as the *Post*'s 1939 numbers were, they were not as high as in 1930, when Sunday circulation reached nearly 300,000. The decline reflected the Depression and competition from movies and radio, but at least a little of the slippage may be attributed to the death of *Post* publisher Frederick G. Bonfils early in 1933.

Bonfils and his partner, Henry H. Tammen, who died in 1924, gave the public the circus-journalism they seemed to want: sensational stories, lots of pictures, scandal, big headlines, and ballyhoo. Critics charged Bonfils with skullduggery, poked fun at his vanity, and called him names: cuttlefish, crook, and cootie-covered rat. Occasionally Bonfils struck back; once he beat up the editor of the *Rocky Mountain News.* But usually he did

not waste much time swatting mosquitoes: he needed his spare moments
to count his money.

The *Rocky Mountain News,* however, infuriated Bonfils in August 1932
by reporting remarks Walter Walker made to a group of Democrats in
Denver. Angry at the *Post* for its attacks on retiring governor Billy Adams,
Walker predicted, "F. G. Bonfils will be remembered as the vilest man who
ever dealt in the newspaper business. . . . Bonfils is a public enemy and has
left the trail of a slimy serpent across Colorado for 30 years." Likening F. G.
to a vulture, a dog, and a rattlesnake, Walker declared, "Frederick G.
Bonfils is the only one of his kind in the world and the mould was broken
after him." The *News* published Walker's diatribe. Bonfils sued for libel.[23]

Denver attorney Philip S. Van Cise, famed for his 1920s fight against
the Ku Klux Klan, represented the *News.* He hired investigators including
the husband-and-wife team, Wallis M. and Margaret S. Reef, to dig up dirt
on Bonfils, which he hoped would demonstrate that Walker's remarks
were true. As his past was probed, Bonfils squirmed. Contracting an ear
infection in late January 1933, he died, at age 72, on February 2.

The *Post* claimed, "Colorado Has Lost Its Greatest Citizen," and it
reported that President Hoover was "deeply grieved." Others remembered
"many came to his [Bonfils's] funeral to see for themselves if he were really
dead — and hoping that he was buried deep." His death ended an era of
swashbuckling journalism, although *Post* editor William C. Shepherd,
assisted by a galaxy of writers such as Jack Carberry, Bruce A. Gustin, Ralph
Radetsky, Walden E. Sweet, and Frances B. Wayne, continued many of the
paper's traditions. Shepherd also kept the *Post* profitable, making millions
for Bonfils's daughters, Helen and May. Helen, who controlled the paper,
spent much of the Bonfils Foundation's money promoting culture. Beginning in 1934 she sponsored summer musicals, billed as operas although
they were usually lighter fare, in Cheesman Park.[24]

The decade was less kind to many other newspapers. The 1931 Ayer's
Directory of Newspapers and Periodicals listed papers in Kersey, Kim,
Manassa, New Raymer, Norwood, Two Buttes, Walsh, Weldona, and Wiley.
None of those places rated an entry in the 1940 Ayer's, although some
editors may have failed to make reports. Many other papers barely stayed
afloat. Between 1930 and 1939 the Arvada *Enterprise* lost 11 percent of its
circulation, the Niwot *Tribune* more than 20; the Montrose *Enterprise* more
than 50. By early 1933 the *Pueblo Chieftain* had been forced to reduce its size,
and in February it was purchased by the Star-Journal Publishing Company,
which also published the *Pueblo Star-Journal.*[25]

Advertisers in Denver, not wanting the *Post* to have a monopoly, fed
the *News* enough revenue to keep it alive, but not enough to make it fat.
Some of its wounds were self-inflicted. Roy Howard, head of Scripps-
Howard, castigated editor Charles E. Lounsbury in January 1934, telling
him that the paper was "lazily and slovenly edited," that "your art work is
lousy," and that the "paper indicates to me a slovenly state of mind on the
part of the editor." Between Lounsbury's exit in 1935 and Jack C. Foster's

entrance in 1940, the *News* swallowed five editors. Fortunately, it boasted able journalists, including Lee Taylor Casey, Robert L. Chase, and Gene Cervi.[26]

Competition from radio and movies also cut into newspaper profits. The "well-equipped modern home," said the *Rocky Mountain News*, "needs at least three sets . . . a midget set for the upstairs rooms as well as a handsome and decorative console model for the living room, in addition to the one for the motor car." At the beginning of the decade, nearly 40 percent of Colorado's families owned radios, upon which they could pick up programs from more than a dozen local stations. At night, AM broadcasts came from faraway places including Chicago and Los Angeles. By the end of the decade, statisticians guessed that more than 80 percent of the state's families had radios.[27]

As a bearer of quick news the radio surpassed the newspapers; as an entertainment medium it threatened them. People who once lingered over their evening paper found other end-of-day delights in the 1930s: comedies such as *Amos and Andy* (1928), *George Burns and Gracie Allen* (1932), *Fibber McGee and Molly* (1935), dramas, mysteries, westerns. For Colorado chauvinists, there were news broadcasts by Lowell Thomas, one of the state's best-known former residents. During the day, radio fans could immerse themselves in slow-moving episodes of *The Romance of Helen Trent* (1933), *Ma Perkins* (1933), and *Our Gal Sunday* (1937), all part of a bathetic kingdom dominated by detergent manufacturers, which writer James Thurber dubbed "soapland."[28]

Movies offered Coloradans much the same escape that radio did. Going to a movie also gave people a chance to enjoy a stately pleasure dome of a theater for 25¢ or less. In 1940 Denver's 40 theaters could seat 36,279, clearly outdistancing Colorado Springs, where 12 theaters sat 6,345, and Pueblo, where 9 theaters could accommodate 6,802. Most towns of any respectable size boasted a theater. Indeed, a theater was a badge of respectability; there were 253 in the state in 1940. Often they were the brightest buildings in town; sometimes they were the newest. Grand Junction's Mesa Theater redecorated in 1930 by brilliantly lighting the foyer and marquee. Sterling's new Fox Theater merited front-page attention from the *Sterling Farm Journal* in 1938. It was, said the paper, "designed in a thousand-and-one minute details to give Sterling and all of Northeastern Colorado a show house attuned to the modern ideas of the amusement world." Among those attunements were a separate smoking section and soft seats covered with imitation leather.[29]

Theaters offered more than just movies. At Denver's Orpheum, an art-deco building opened on the site of the old Orpheum in 1932, comedy and vaudeville acts rotated with motion pictures. To draw crowds, managers ran all sorts of promotions. Ralph J. Batschelet, manager of Denver's Bluebird Theater, recalled bringing in a butcher to carve up a side of beef, the parts becoming prizes. Once he gave away a live pig; weekly he offered

A Pueblo itinerant probably made a few dollars for advertising Girl of the Golden West. *(Pueblo Library District)*

"Bluebird Deluxe Country Store Nights," dispensing, in 600 weeks, 32,200 Hostess Cupcakes.[30]

Most people, although happy with cupcakes, went to the movies to see the movies: grand spectacles such as *King Kong* (1932–1933) and *San Francisco* (1936), timeless comedies from the Marx Brothers and W. C. Fields, enduring works such as *Snow White and the Seven Dwarfs* (1937) and *The Wizard of Oz* (1939), and plenty of forgettable fluff. Perhaps a few attended to cheer stars with Colorado connections: Spring Byington of Colorado Springs and Denver; Ward Bond, who parlayed small parts in the 1930s into later TV stardom; the fading Douglas Fairbanks, Sr. At the end of the decade, Hattie McDaniel, an African-American actress who spent some of her early years in Denver, gained an Oscar for her role in *Gone With the Wind* (1939). Glenn Morris, a Coloradan from Simla, won a 1936 Olympic gold medal in the decathlon, which got him brief film glory as Tarzan, co-starring with Eleanor Holm. The *Fort Collins Express-Courier* told fans what to expect in *Tarzan's Revenge* (1938): "Among other scenes, she swims to safety in a pool full of crocodiles, and he swings from tree to tree with Eleanor under his arm." Outranked in the Hollywood jungle by Johnny Weismuller, Morris did not swing long as Tarzan.[31]

Movies made money. Harry E. Huffman who operated the Bluebird and nine other Denver theaters, including the Aladdin, Rialto, Broadway, and the Tabor, flaunted his wealth in 1937 by building Shangri-La. Modeled on a Tibetan monastery in the film *Lost Horizon* (1937), the modernistic mansion, set on a hill at 150 South Bellaire Street, dominated the area and became a Denver landmark until subsequent construction blocked it from view. Frank H. Ricketson, Jr., another movie mogul, built his first theater in Montrose in 1925. Along with Charles Yeager, Ricketson created Bank Night, a promotion that lured audiences with promises of cash drawings. Catching on nationwide, the idea helped the movies fend off the Depression.[32]

Theaters, like newspapers, worried about competition. Not only could people listen to the radio, play Monopoly or bridge, or put together a jigsaw puzzle, they could also, if they had the stamina, participate in a walkathon or a dancethon. Such endurance contests, promising big rewards to the last person moving, offended Pueblo's theater owners so much that they pressured the city council to ban the events. The *Pueblo Star-Journal* supported the prohibition and suggested that it be extended to carnivals, "one of the worst forms of amusement with which the public is afflicted."[33]

The Post Office was also afflicted with a fad — chain letters. Such pyramid schemes predated the 1930s. In April of 1935, however, the normally innocuous vagary mushroomed into a postman's nightmare. For weeks a "send-a-dime" chain letter, which appeared to have originated in Denver, clogged the nation's mails. Starting in April, Denverites began receiving letters asking them to send a dime to the top person on a list of six, to then remove that person's name, and to enter their own name at the end of the list. The letter promised that those who reached the top would reap 15,620 dimes — a respectable sum in 1935 when a dime could buy a movie ticket.

The Post Office groaned. In the first 15 days of the chain's operation, Denver mail volume soared by two million items. In late April, the *Wray Rattler* reckoned "most everybody in town has received one or more of them," and, it predicted, "scarcely a man or a woman in the country will escape receiving one of these letters, and strange as it may seem the young and the old are falling for it." Authorities considered prosecuting the participants for misusing the mail, but realizing that it would be difficult to jail half the population of Denver, along with a good many other Coloradans, officials gave up the idea. Instead, they sold lots of stamps. By mid-June, when the craze had subsided, postal workers had collected more than $20,000 in overtime.[34]

Sports also gave Coloradans an opportunity to forget their woes. By installing lights in 1930 at Denver's Merchants Park, the Denver Bears baseball team temporarily boosted its attendance from the 400 to 500 who came to afternoon games, to night crowds that sometimes exceeded 5,000. As the novelty of under-the-lights play declined and the Depression deepened, attendance fell. Not wanting to waste money sending their team to

Denver, Omaha promoters in 1931 hired Denverites and gave them uniforms so they could play the Bears. Only 75 spectators watched. The Bears revived in 1932, but in 1933 other Western League members, tired of losing money in Colorado, forced both the Bears and the Pueblo Braves out of the league. That killed professional baseball in Colorado for the rest of the decade.

Semi-pro, amateur, and touring teams took center stage after 1933. The Colorado Springs Orioles, the Coors Brewers, M & O Cigars, Joe's Cave [a Denver bar], the Denver Athletic Club, and the Pueblo Peppers gave fans a run for their money. Some of the best baseball came from African-Americans from local organizations such as Denver's White Elephants and from touring clubs such as the Ethiopian Clowns and the Negro National League All-Star team. In 1936 the All-Stars, blessed with pitcher Satchel Paige, easily won the *Denver Post* baseball tournament. Coloradans also enjoyed watching the formidable House of David team from Benton Harbor, Michigan, whose players let their hair grow long.[35]

Softball flourished, with thousands participating and tens of thousands watching. Fort Collins initiated night games in late May 1932 with a contest between the Tilley Grocers and the Northern Barbers. Holyoke lit its fairgrounds for a softball game for the first time on August 31, 1933, and soon after offered night football. Estimates from Denver put the number of fans watching softball games in 1933 as high as 300,000. In the Wray area alone, a dozen teams, including the Beer Mugs and the Rinky Dinks, played during the summer of 1935.[36]

Having lost professional baseball, Denver paid more attention to basketball. Backed by William N. Haraway, president of the local Piggly-Wiggly stores, the Denver team, sometimes dubbed the Pigs and sometimes the Grocers, emerged as a major Amateur Athletic Union (AAU) power during the 1930s. Hosting the AAU national tournament in 1935, Denver saw its Pigs slaughtered by Kansas City, and the team proved pokey again in 1936. But in 1937 more than 7,000 fans watched the team, by then renamed the Safeways, win the AAU championship by defeating the Phillips 66ers at the Denver Auditorium. In 1938 the Safeways suffered a double setback, losing the AAU tournament and the sponsorship of Safeway, which axed basketball to express its displeasure at the tax Colorado imposed on chain stores. Renamed the Nuggets at the suggestion of *Denver Post* sports writer Ray McGovern, the team won both the Missouri Valley League and the AAU championships in 1939. Coach Jack McCracken, who, along with Robert "Ace" F. Gruenig, was consistently among the team's top players, had won, said the *Post*, "an everlasting place in the hearts of Denver sports lovers."[37]

Earl (Dutch) Clark set a similar high standard for football players. Playing for Colorado College in the late 1920s, he helped the Colorado Springs school earn enough money to build a new stadium. Once, in a game against the University of Denver, he was responsible for the only scores for both teams. Bill Barker and Jackie Lewin explain in their book *Denver*: "In

his own end zone during the second quarter, Dutch failed to get a punt away, and D.U. downed him to lead two to nothing. In the fourth quarter he kicked a 35-yard field goal. Final score: C.C. 3, D.U. 2." Adept at baseball, basketball, bowling, golf, and pocket billiards, Clark stuck with football in the 1930s as a coach and as a professional player.[38]

Colorado College downplayed football in the 1930s after a couple of players died from broken necks. The public's gaze shifted to larger schools, especially to the University of Colorado, where quarterback William Lam helped win games in the mid-1930s, and to the University of Denver, where guard Alex Drobnitch thrilled fans. Even more adept at grabbing the football and the headlines was Byron "Whizzer" White, who became Colorado's all-American boy hero. Born in Fort Collins in 1917, White grew up in nearby Wellington, where his father was once mayor. His mother, lacking much schooling herself, insisted that Byron and his brother get a good education. "I'd rather see you win one medal for scholarship than win 40 football games," she told them.[39]

Byron did both. Described by Frank Potts, a CU coach, as "the perfect combination of brains, strength, and coordination," White emerged as a star quarterback in his junior year. One of his greatest moments came on Thanksgiving in 1936 when he ran 102 yards for a touchdown against the University of Denver. The 1937–1938 season, White's last as an undergraduate, culminated in CU's being invited to the 1938 Cotton Bowl in Fort Worth, the first bowl invitation ever extended to a Colorado team. White, a top scholar, missed some practice so he could compete for a Rhodes scholarship to Oxford. CU lost the game to Rice by 14 points, but White won both the scholarship and a $15,800-a-year professional contract with the Pittsburgh Pirates (later named the Steelers). Asked to comment on Byron's salary, Dutch Clark remarked, "For $15,000 I would play football on crutches." White also went to Oxford, later became an attorney, and in 1962 was appointed to the U.S. Supreme Court by President John F. Kennedy.[40]

Football got thousands of Coloradans outdoors. Nearly 28,000 watched the 1936 CU vs. DU game in Denver's Hilltop Stadium. But watching others play did not give many people exercise. Skiing did. Already popular in the 1910s and 1920s, the sport gained the momentum in the 1930s that would make it a top Colorado industry by the 1960s. The road-building campaign made the mountains more accessible. Hunger for tourist dollars in Hot Sulphur Springs, Steamboat Springs, and Aspen also spurred the sport. In the 1920s Denverites slushed around on Genesee Mountain 20 miles west of the city, thinking, said *The Denver Post*, that it might become "a miniature St. Moritz." By the late 1930s skiers were routinely tackling serious slopes at Berthoud Pass, the state's most popular area, and at newly developed Winter Park to the north of Berthoud.[41]

In early 1937, George E. Cranmer, Denver's manager of Parks and Improvements, told *Denver Post* reporter Ernest H. Mitchell that Colorado had been missing a bet: "Concentrating on summer tourist business we have completely overlooked the possibilities offered by our mountains during the winter." A few tourist dollars were being harvested at Berthoud, but with more than 25,000 skiers in 1937–1938, it was considered over-crowded. Cranmer proposed creating a "winter playground that would be the world's best" at the west portal of the Moffat Tunnel.[42]

Accessible by highway and by railroad, the spectacular slopes brought praise from Otto E. Schneibs, a top European skier. The Forest Service cleared trails; Cranmer scraped up federal and state money and cajoled volunteers to do some of the work. On January 9, 1938, the Denver and Salt Lake Railroad started running special ski trains to West Portal. Soon thousands of enthusiasts were enjoying what came to be known as Winter Park. Like Berthoud it boasted a ski tow, a luxury also enjoyed by Glen Cove, 23 miles west of Colorado Springs on Pikes Peak.[43]

Hot Sulphur Springs and Steamboat Springs also went after tourist money. Both had long sports-skiing traditions, thanks, in part, to the Norwegian Carl Howelsen, who in 1913 helped promote jumping contests at Hot Sulphur. The next year he made skiing more pleasant for people in Steamboat by teaching them to bind their skis to their boots, thereby saving them the chore of chasing detached skis down the slopes. In the 1930s both towns staged well-established ski festivals.[44]

Aspen did little to capitalize on its potential until the late 1930s. Frank Willoughby, writing in the *Aspen Times*, reported, "Until the winter months of 1936–1937 there had been aroused no appreciable interest in the sport of skiing in the town of Aspen. The total number of skiers was small, and the

general proficiency of what skiers there were was practically insignificant." Promoter Tom Flynn interested local people in skiing. Andre Roch, a Swiss expert, mapped out runs and jump sites. Local enthusiasts raised money to finance clearing of the runs and volunteered to do some of the work. Frank Willoughby of the Aspen Ski Club credited Aspen's women, who outnumbered men in the club, for much of the work that went into finishing Roch Run in the summer of 1937. A 1938 Works Progress Administration grant, followed by help from the National Youth Administration, fostered a process that would make Aspen one of the nation's top ski spots.[45]

Ski tows and lifts made the sport more attractive. Berthoud, Winter Park, and Glen Cove all had tows by the late 1930s. At Loveland Pass a 4.5-horsepower motor powered a 1,000-foot rope tow. The Pioneer ski area 20 miles north of Gunnison claimed the state's first chair lift (1939). Aspen skiers rode a boat tow, an eight-passenger sled that slowly took them up Ajax Mountain; a similar device was rigged up at Steamboat. The Gunnison Ski Club defeated gravity with the help of the Denver and Rio Grande Railroad, which ran a ski train to the top of Marshall Pass. There skiers

Federal funds helped make Winter Park one of Colorado's most visited ski areas by the late 1930s. (Colorado Historical Society)

Walter Walker (1883–1956) pictured on his "dash" to Washington, D.C., in early December 1932. (Colorado Historical Society)

disembarked to ski down the pass, where they caught the train again and returned to the top.[46]

In 1937–1938 nearly 5,000 skiers enjoyed the Routt National Forest, many of them using Howelsen Hill at Steamboat. Hot Sulphur Springs, served that season by seven ski trains from Denver, counted 3,300 visitors. Wolf Creek Pass in the southwest also had a good 1938 season because highway crews kept roads open, allowing 3,200 to reach it. At Aspen and Highland Basin more than 6,000 skied, Engineer Mountain in the San Juan National Forest reported 650, and Monarch Pass hosted 900. Compared to the 10.4 million skier visits tallied in the 1991–1992 season, the 1930s numbers were small, but the groundwork for a flourishing sport was well established.[47]

George Cranmer's faith in skiing as a fountain of revenue rested on the transportation revolution Colorado experienced in the 1930s. The tortoise-like trip Walter Walker made from Grand Junction to Washington, D.C., in 1932 illustrates the slowness of travel at the start of the decade. Walker had been defeated for a short term in the U.S. Senate by Karl Schuyler in November, but tardy returns held up Schuyler's official certification. Until Schuyler was certified, Walker had a right to the seat. Thinking that they might need his vote, Democrats asked him to hurry to Washington in early December. Driven by his son Preston, it took Walker the night of December 4 to cover 387 miles from Grand Junction to Denver. He flew the rest of the way, a journey that consumed another 27 hours.

Forty-two hours after he left Grand Junction, he arrived in Washington to be sworn in to the Senate, where he served for less than a day.[48]

At the start of the decade air transportation appeared to be the answer to the state's transportation woes. Stories of speed records and of airplanes able to carry 11 passengers dazzled newspaper readers. In 1933, Denver restaurateur Albert A. McVittie sponsored a contest that promised eight winners an airplane trip aboard a chartered plane to the Century of Progress World's Fair in Chicago. *The Denver Post* touted the airplane as having "all the comforts and conveniences, a wide aisle between high backed wicker seats, ample head room, individual ventilators. Everything for comfort is at hand, even to ice water and the morning paper. The trip will be made in eight hours."[49]

High hopes nose-dived as Coloradans lowered their aviation expectations during the early and mid-1930s. The number of airplanes in the state plunged from 91 in 1930 to 56 in 1935 before starting a gradual climb to 143 in 1940. The Western Slope, which had once thought that airplanes

The hope of large-scale air transportation in Colorado proved to be pie in the sky in the 1930s. (Colorado Historical Society)

The Denver Zephyr could take passengers from Denver's Union Station to Chicago in less than 16 hours. (Colorado Historical Society)

would rescue it from its isolation, saw little progress in the decade. Commercial service along the Front Range was hobbled by Post Office practice. By using its airmail subsidies to control airlines, the bureaucrats kept Denver from having direct flights to the East until 1937. Denver travelers either had to go south to Albuquerque or north to Cheyenne to connect with eastbound flights. A loosening of Post Office rules allowed United Airlines to directly serve Denver with one daily flight to, and another from, the East in mid-May 1937. Travelers could reach Chicago in little more than five hours; Salt Lake City was only three hours and 11 minutes from Denver. Yet, progress was slow. In late 1938 United offered only two daily flights to the East.[50]

High-speed streamlined trains had a far greater impact on Colorado in the 1930s than did airplanes. Diesel-powered electric train engines slowly replaced steam, especially on passenger runs. The monster steam engines, although capable of speeds greater than 100 miles per hour, had to stop occasionally to take on coal and water and to dispose of ash. Diesels could run for hours without pausing, an advantage that insured that on average they would be faster than steam.[51]

Burlington's Zephyr, named for the west wind, gave Colorado a taste of the future on May 26, 1934, when it dispatched a three-car passenger diesel on a test run from Denver to Chicago. The tracks were carefully inspected; more than 2,000 men were stationed along the 1,015.4-mile route to prevent interference from side traffic. At 5:05 A.M. the Zephyr, carrying assorted bigwigs, 30 company officials, 20 reporters, and a mule named Zeph as a mascot, whistled out of Union Station. At 7:10 P.M. it arrived in Chicago — 13 hours, 4 minutes, and 58 seconds after leaving Denver. At its best the train hit 112.5 miles per hour; for 200 miles it averaged more than 90 miles per hour. The fastest steam run, 37 years earlier, had taken more than 18 hours.[52]

It took the Burlington two years to put the Zephyr into regular service in Colorado. By then it had set even more impressive records — a 12-car train raced from Denver to Chicago in 12 hours and 12 minutes in October 1936, hitting 116 miles per hour between Akron and Brush. On November 8, 1936, the Denver Zephyr began scheduled runs to Chicago. A trip that once consumed 24 hours could, by the end of the 1930s, easily be made overnight. Other railroads also sought speed. The Santa Fe sent a fast diesel through Trinidad in mid-October 1935 on a record-breaking 39-hour, 34-minute run from Los Angeles to Chicago. The Rock Island competed with its Rock Island Rocket. When the Union Pacific gave Coloradans a glimpse of its streamlined aluminum train in March 1934, the *Rocky Mountain News* likened it to a huge yellow caterpillar and reported that as the creature whizzed through northeastern Colorado, horses ran from it and dogs howled.[53]

George Cranmer had visions of easterners rushing off to Winter Park for a ski weekend, although it is unlikely that many made the 30-hour round-trip from Chicago to Denver to ski for half a day or less. Summer tourists were far more important to Colorado in the 1930s than winter visitors. Most traveled by automobile; many were in-staters seeing their own backyard. In 1930 the number of visitors at Rocky Mountain National Park, the state's premier outdoor attraction, dipped compared to 1929, but in 1931 the count rose, and it continued to soar until 1938, when nearly 660,000 entered the park.[54]

Western Colorado tourism, small compared to the activity along the Front Range, also increased. On March 17, 1932, Herbert Hoover made the Great Sand Dunes in the San Luis Valley a national monument; on March 2, 1933, he did the same for the Black Canyon of the Gunnison. Initially, neither drew large numbers: Black Canyon reckoned 16,041 in 1939, and the Sand Dunes tallied 11,700. Mesa Verde did better. On July 3, 1938, 658 people tramped through the ruins, which, according to Park Superintendent Jesse L. Nussbaum, was the largest crowd to visit since the park's creation in 1906. In 1939 Mesa Verde totaled 32,246 visitors; Colorado National Monument drew 37,130.[55]

Opened on July 4, 1891, Pueblo's Mineral Palace, despite its imposing facade, had so badly deteriorated that it was closed in 1935. The WPA considered restoring it in 1938 but gave up the idea. The contractor who finished tearing it down in 1943 paid the city $633.33 for the salvage. (Pueblo Library District)

Many sightseers, including Franklin Roosevelt in July 1938, stopped at the Royal Gorge. Others enjoyed the view from Pikes Peak. Film star Shirley Temple built a snowman on the mountain in mid-June 1938. Young women danced their summers away at Steamboat Springs's Perry-Mansfield Dancing Camp; swimmers enjoyed the pools at Salida and at Steamboat, Glenwood, and Eldorado springs. People in Denver took their cousins from Illinois to Echo Lake and to the top of Mount Evans. The flatlanders picked up rocks to take home. They also pocketed tax tokens that were used to pay the state sales tax on small purchases. A penny would buy five, so as souvenirs they were a bargain. Produced by Cañon City penitentiary inmates, the nickel-sized aluminum disks inspired one of the best headlines of the decade: "Thugs Make Slugs."[56]

Denver, Colorado Springs, and Pueblo also offered new attractions and old. In Pueblo visitors could tour the steelworks or, before it closed in 1935, walk through the crumbling, unheated Mineral Palace, a vast building with 25 interior domes in a style described as "modernized Egyptian." There statues of King Coal and the Silver Queen still reigned, unaware that in reality both had been dethroned. In Denver the state Capitol attracted tourists, who had something new to see in 1940 when Allen True completed murals accompanied by Thomas Hornsby Ferril's poetry celebrating water in the West. At the Colorado Museum of Natural History in Denver's City

Artists elaborately decorated the Mineral Palace's ceiling. (Pueblo Library District)

Park, children and adults marveled at the nine-foot-tall mammoth discovered near Platteville in 1932. In 1938 museum experts and Works Progress Administration laborers mounted an even more impressive display, a 75-foot-long, 150-million-year-old dinosaur.[57]

Pikes Peak area tourists, if they had time to spare after seeing the Cave of the Winds and the Garden of the Gods, often visited the Cheyenne Mountain Zoo, one of millionaire Spencer Penrose's hobbies. Afterward they could drive up Cheyenne Mountain to another of Penrose's projects, the Shrine of the Sun (1937), a 103-foot memorial tower honoring humorist

Spencer Penrose planned to build a monument to himself on Cheyenne Mountain, but, as historian Marshall Sprague reports, friends convinced him to dedicate the shrine to the memory of Will Rogers. (Local History Collection, Pikes Peak Regional Library)

Will Rogers, who died in 1935. There Penrose's remains were laid to rest after his death on December 7, 1939. There, too, sculptor Jo Davidson placed a bust of Will Rogers, and muralist Randall Davey portrayed Penrose and his wife, Julie.[58]

Art lovers had even better cause to visit Colorado Springs after the 1936 completion of the Colorado Springs Fine Arts Center. The center reflected the generosity and drive of three women: long-time art patron Julie V. L. Penrose; Alice Bemis Taylor, a collector of southwestern art; and Elizabeth S. Hare, an energetic socialite. Hare had helped found the Fountain Valley School, a boys' academy south of Colorado Springs, and had

Anne Evans (1871–1941), a strong-willed woman, used her clout and connections to make a success of the Central City Opera. (Denver Public Library, Western History Department)

hired Boardman Robinson to teach art there. The chemistry for the fine arts center proved right: Robinson pushed for a museum, Taylor gave $400,000, and Penrose also supported it. John Gaw Meem of Santa Fe, a nationally renowned architect, designed the massive building, which echoed in cold gray concrete the warm brown adobe pueblos of New Mexico.

To inaugurate the center, Hare organized a week of entertainment, including modern dance by Martha Graham. Historian Marshall Sprague describes the scene: "Miss Graham's unique dancing was utterly new west of New York, and when she began gallumphing barefoot around the stage interpreting 'Frontier' and 'Quest' and 'Sportive Tragedy' most of the audience slumped into a stunned uncomprehending stupor." That Colorado was not the place for the avant-garde was also demonstrated in Denver when bandleader Benny Goodman bombed out at Elitch Gardens' Trocadero ballroom in 1935. Swing, even when played by Gene Krupa, Jess Stacey, Bunny Berrigan, and Jack Lacey, did not move Denver's guys and gals. Goodman remembered the engagement as "the loneliest two weeks of our lives. We could have caused a bigger flurry playing cards instead of music up on the bandstand. The folks wanted waltzes and the like, and darned if the boys were going to dish it out." A few weeks later Los Angeles gave Goodman a friendlier welcome.[59]

Anne Evans, a Denver civic leader, proved in 1931 that she understood Coloradans' tastes better than either Hare or Goodman did. Central City, once awash in gold and people, had, like most mining towns, faded by

1930. Unlike many other places, it retained many substantial buildings, including the Teller Opera House (1878). Moreover, it was close enough to Denver to be easily reached on a summer day. Evans and other members of the Denver Civic Theater board grasped the possibilities. Ida Kruse McFarlane, whose father had built the theater, arranged to have it donated to the University of Denver. Evans and other wealthy Denverites restored it. Actress Lillian Gish initiated a decade-long banquet of culture by appearing in *Camille* in 1932. Muriell Sibell Wolle, an artist and ghost-town devotee, remembered opening night: "The moment one stepped into the opera house one felt that he [*sic*] was living in 1878 for everyone was wearing clothes of that year, and when the curtain rose the effect was tremendous, for the actors' costumes and the setting of the play were of the same period." Wolle praised director Robert Edmond Jones: "The production was such a feast of color, rhythm, and music that by the end of the first act my companion and I were aesthetically drunk." By recruiting top talent — Metropolitan Opera star Gladys Swarthout, actor Walter Huston, actress Ruth Gordon — the Opera House Association not only promoted culture, it also helped save Central City.[60]

Summer plays at Central City, winter skiing at Berthoud Pass, jaunts to Pikes Peak and Manitou Springs: hundreds of recreational and cultural opportunities presented themselves to Coloradans with time and money. At times, however, many people simply stayed home and read a book. They had a rich menu to choose from: mysteries by Rex Stout and Dashiell Hammett, westerns by Zane Grey, best-sellers such as Pearl Buck's *The Good Earth* (1932), Hervey Allen's *Anthony Adverse* (1933), and Margaret Mitchell's *Gone With the Wind* (1936). If readers fancied a Colorado author or a Colorado setting, they had at least a few dozen writers from which to pick.

Thomas Hornsby Ferril distilled the state's mountains, rivers, cities, and people into poetry. Born in Denver in 1896, he graduated from Colorado College, after which he became a newspaper reporter and later a press agent for Great Western Sugar Company. His poem "This Foreman" won national acclaim in 1927, and in 1934 his collection titled *Westering* moved Ruth Lechlitner, reviewer for the *New York Herald Tribune*, to compare him favorably with Robert Frost and Carl Sandburg: "He is in some ways a better technician than Sandburg; he can take a much larger canvas, work with a fuller, less mincing stroke of the brush than Frost." Forced to spend his days praising sugar beets, Ferril never matched Frost's or Sandburg's output, but his diamonds sparkled.[61]

Hope Williams Sykes and Anne Ellis also depended upon the quality of their work, rather than on its quantity, to assure them top rank among Colorado authors. In *Second Hoeing* (1935), Sykes told the story of Hannah Schreissmiller, a German-Russian farm worker. With similar realism, Anne Ellis in *The Life of an Ordinary Woman* chronicled the harshness of her childhood and early adulthood on the mining frontier. In 1931 she wrote a second autobiographical work *'Plain Anne Ellis,'* followed by *Sunshine*

Thomas Hornsby Ferril (1896–1988) penned press releases for Great Western Sugar and poetry for posterity. With his wife Helen, he published the Rocky Mountain Herald, *a weekly paper peppered with polished prose and legal notices. (Denver Public Library, Western History Department)*

Preferred (1934). Despite the praise she received, she was unable to get other books published. Suffering from asthma and nearly penniless, she borrowed money in the spring of 1938 to return to Colorado, where the University of Colorado awarded her an honorary master's degree. CU's president George Norlin invited her to stay with his family during the summer, a gentle ending to a difficult life. Ellis, at age 63, died in August.[62]

John Fante, an Italian-American born in Denver in 1909, also trod the road of realism. Although he left the state early in the Depression, he used it as a setting for his first novel, *Wait Until Spring, Bandini* (1938), for his collection of short stories *Dago Red* (1940), and for his posthumous *1933 Was a Bad Year* (1989). His literary skills and his insights into Italian-American life brought him acclaim but not much cash, so he turned to writing screenplays. After he died in obscurity in 1983, he was rediscovered; *Bandini* was made into a movie, and several of his other works were republished.[63]

Dalton Trumbo followed a similar path, gathering more fame along the way. Born in Montrose in 1905, he moved as a youth to Grand Junction, where he attended high school and worked as a reporter for Walter Walker's *Daily Sentinel*. When his father was fired from his job as a salesman at Benge's Shoe Store in 1924, Dalton was forced to leave the University of Colorado and move with his family to Los Angeles. His first novel, *Eclipse* (1935), chronicled the fall of John Andrew, a man honored in Shale City until the failure of his bank stripped him of friends and dignity. Setting

Anne Ellis died of an asthma attack in Denver in August 1938 at age 63. Her ashes were placed in the Bonanza (southwest of Poncha Springs) cemetery. (Denver Public Library, Western History Department)

the scene for his exposé of small-town hypocrisy and small-mindedness, Trumbo told of farmers "drooling mud from the corners of their mouths," and of Stumpy Telsa, a local madam, "the wealthiest woman in town." Coloradans knew that Shale City was Grand Junction, and folks in Grand Junction, as they read *Eclipse,* recognized themselves. It was not the kind of publicity the chamber of commerce appreciated.[64]

Was Trumbo complimenting Shale City in *The Remarkable Andrew* (1941), in which he described its citizens as "honest, hard working, tolerant and remarkably sane"? Or was he parodying boosterism: "The air mail planes droning westward from New York, droning eastward from San Francisco, stop at the Municipal Airport to pick up messages which the residents of Shale City send each day to the four corners of the earth." Perhaps it made no difference to many of his former acquaintances in Grand Junction, who 40 years after Trumbo cast a shadow on them, still spoke disparagingly of him. Despite his fame as author of *Johnny Got His Gun* (1939) and as an Oscar-winning screenwriter, they found it difficult to forgive him.[65]

William McLeod Raine, an Englishman who settled in Denver in 1898, wrote he-man, shoot-em-up westerns, escapism more palatable to most readers than Trumbo's satiric realism. Top gun among Colorado writers of

William McLeod Raine (1871–1954) wrote westerns and advocated liberal causes. (Denver Public Library, Western History Department)

his era, he churned out adventures almost as fast as jackrabbits breed. "Any man," he said, "who writes a novel should be respected for it not so much for the literary value of it, but for the physical labor involved in producing it." By that yardstick Raine deserved a heap of respect. During the 1930s he produced 20 westerns, bringing his novel total to 65 by late 1940.[66]

Clem Yore, an Estes Park resident in his later years, drew upon his background as a Texas Ranger, stage driver, and cowpuncher to spin western yarns such as *Dusty Dan Delaney* (1930) and *Trigger Slim* (1934). Of *The Six-Gun Code* (1932), *Rocky Mountain News* reviewer Aurelita Sweet-Harrison wrote, "This is the sort of book that makes a great appeal to boys and Easterners." Courtney Riley Cooper, once Buffalo Bill's press agent and once city editor of *The Denver Post*, appealed to the same audience. Author of more than 500 short stories and many western novels, he hanged himself in New York City in 1940, allegedly miffed at FBI director J. Edgar Hoover for ignoring reports Cooper made on Nazi spies in Mexico.[67]

A few authors wrote both fiction and non-fiction. Gene Fowler, a former Denverite, entertained readers with *Timberline: A Story of Bonfils and Tammen* (1932), an account of *The Denver Post*'s publishers as irreverent as it was popular. Historical purists questioned Fowler's accuracy, but no one could doubt his speed — he wrote 145,000 words of the book in under 70 days. In his novel *Salute to Yesterday* (1937), Fowler used Denver as a backdrop for characters such as Captain James Job Trolley, who wished to have his tombstone proclaim, "There Is No God." Less given to hilarity,

Frank Waters penned two novels in the 1930s: *The Wild Earth's Nobility* (1935) and *Below Grass Roots* (1937). He also drew upon his family's experiences in Colorado Springs and Cripple Creek to write a biography, *Midas of the Rockies: The Story of Stratton and Cripple Creek* (1937).[68]

Horace Tabor, the nineteenth-century silver king, gave historical romancers more fodder for their typewriters than did Winfield Scott Stratton, Cripple Creek's leading millionaire. George F. Willison, a Denver-born East High graduate, mined Tabor and other colorful characters in *Here They Dug the Gold* (1931); David Karsner in *Silver Dollar: The Story of the Tabors* (1932) struck a profitable vein by portraying both Tabor and his family. Lewis Gandy hauled out more ore in 1934 with *The Tabors: A Footnote of Western History*. Hollywood also tried to hit Tabor pay dirt by cranking out *Silver Dollar* (1932), starring Edward G. Robinson as Horace and Bebe Daniels as his wife, Baby Doe.[69]

Tabor's rags-to-riches and riches-to-rags story sold well in the 1930s partly because it reflected the national experience of prosperity followed by penury. In Colorado the Tabor saga struck a particularly responsive chord because the reclusive Baby Doe Tabor (née Elizabeth McCourt), faithful to Horace's memory, still clung to the Matchless mine near Leadville. John C. Polly, a *Rocky Mountain News* reporter, visited her there in September 1932. Asked whether she had read Karsner's *Silver Dollar*, she replied, "I know the book contains untruths and I won't read it. . . . There is a story to be told sometime — if it is told correctly." Asked whether she were lonely, she answered, "How could that be, for I have God." But she did worry about the loss of two of her front teeth: "Perhaps I lost the teeth when the mine boiler exploded, or when I fainted and fell."[70]

Baby Doe died, at age 81, sometime in late February or early March 1935. Her frozen body was found in her shack at the Matchless on March 7. Her diary recounted visits from spirits. January 1934: "A great vision and I talked to a spirit." February 1934: "The devil attacked me." March 1934: "Oh, terrible, No food left. On my hands and knees. Need bread. Cold. Suffered alone. Awful blizzard. I saw purple near the ceiling." April 1934: "A vision of death, death in purple."[71]

Like Baby Doe, Coloradans hoped that perseverance and luck would triumph over bad times. They also continued to seek political solutions. In 1934 the Leadville Chamber of Commerce sent Roosevelt an ashtray made from Matchless mine silver as a "token of appreciation . . . for his interest in silver." Invited to attend the annual sowbelly dinner of the Colorado Mining Association in early January 1935, the president declined. Coloradans did not mind much; their faith in FDR remained strong in 1934 and through the election of 1936. At the end of the decade, however, the wheel of fortune again favored Republicans. By 1940 the Depression was almost dead in Colorado, and so were the Democrats and the New Deal.[72]

TWELVE

Decade's End

The New Deal was a godsend to many unemployed workers. It did a lot. The best friend we ever had, President Roosevelt. Yeah, he was the best friend we ever had.

Thomas Nother
retired Denver carpenter
November 25, 1981[1]

As I see it, the New Deal has been the worst fraud ever perpetrated on the American people.

Edwin C. Johnson
U.S. Senator
Rocky Mountain News
October 23, 1944

Herb Holloway's distress call was picked up in Sterling in mid-evening, April 27, 1937. Enveloped in a dust storm, which kept him from landing his Boeing transport plane at Cheyenne, he flew blindly across northeastern Colorado. Sterling's mayor, C. O. Boggs, alerted the town by sounding the fire siren. Heeding the advice of bandmaster L. E. Smith, nearly 1,000 drivers sped to the airport, where they lit the runway with their car headlights. As Holloway passed over at 8:25 P.M., he saw the lights, the first glimpse of the ground he and the three others on board had had in hours. After circling for 25 minutes, he safely landed. "Where are we?" he asked.[2]

Coloradans also wondered where they were in the late 1930s. They wanted to believe that their self-reliance and ingenuity had pulled them through the Depression, just as those virtues had saved Holloway, but they were not certain. Fortune-tellers at county fairs could not foresee the bountiful harvests of the early 1940s, nor did their crystal balls foretell the full employment of World War II. Blessed with hindsight and armed with statistics, economists knew that 1937 was better than 1932. Pueblo's Colorado Fuel and Iron Corporation (CF&I) emerged from three years of bankruptcy in 1936 and in 1937 made 541,867 tons of steel, not far below its 1929–1930 production of 600,000 tons. Farmers battled grasshoppers in 1937, but the year proved one of their best in the decade in terms of income.[3]

The respite was brief. The national economy soured in 1938, a recession some blamed on Social Security taxes, which drained money from consumers' paychecks. CF&I's orders declined, and by 1939 its great steelworks was producing at less than half capacity. Farmers got rain in 1938, and the grasshoppers ate less. Nevertheless, low prices wrecked balance sheets,

Teller Ammons (1896–1973), at left, with E. R. Pearson of the Ford Motor Company and Denver's mayor Benjamin F. Stapleton (right) in front of the state Capitol, May 1937. (Colorado Historical Society)

which showed farmers' income nearly 20 percent below 1937 levels. As the economy seesawed, Colorado suffered political convulsions.[4]

Teller Ammons, who succeeded Edwin C. Johnson as governor in early 1937, was, at age 39, one of the youngest men ever elected to the post. His father, Elias, governor from 1913 to 1915, muddled through the 1914 Ludlow Massacre, in which state troopers attacked striking coal miners, sparking a fire that killed two women and 11 children. Teller rose from the ashes of his father's administration, becoming a lawyer, a state senator from Denver, and Denver's city attorney. As governor, however, he was almost as jinxed as his father. He beat his Republican rival, Charles M. Armstrong, by more than 50,000 votes in November 1936. After that, Ammons, a man remembered as well meaning but unable to work miracles, went downhill.[5]

Ed Johnson wisely escaped to the U.S. Senate early in 1937, leaving the governorship to Lieutenant Governor Ray H. Talbot for a little more than a week. When Ammons took over in mid-January, he found the state treasury $1 million in the red. Distressing in itself, the deficit reflected even deeper problems. By earmarking funds for particular purposes — gas taxes to highways; liquor and sales taxes to pensioners — voters starved the governor and hobbled the legislature. To conquer the fiscal labyrinth of more than 200 different funds, Ammons desperately needed FDR's skills: foxlike slyness and a lionlike roar. He had neither. His formal power was limited by the state constitution; his political clout rested on divided Democrats. As to slyness, consider his 1938 blunder: when criticized for sharing a "raw" story with a men's group in Trinidad, he snapped at his detractors, "Kiss my foot." Fred E. Winsor, editor of the Republican-inclined Trinidad *Chronicle-News,* seized the opportunity to reply, "If your feet are no cleaner than your tongue, Mr. Governor, I would be exposing myself to physical as well as moral leprosy, by such indulgence."[6]

Ammons's foot went unkissed. So did his plans to fix state government and finance. In 1933, Johnson had persuaded the legislature to consolidate 44 state agencies into a five-member executive council. The move simplified administration but left responsibility fractured. Proposals to save money by combining some of the state's 63 counties, 20 of which tallied fewer than 4,000 people in 1930, met angry opposition. "The whole plan," said the *Aspen Times* in early 1938, "is just a round-about way for the political despots of the eastern slope to obtain control of the entire state." Catcalls also overwhelmed Ammons's designs to revamp the state bureaucracy. In 1938, Griffenhagen and Associates, a national research firm, drafted a reorganization plan, but lawmakers shelved it.[7]

Griffenhagen urged Colorado to stop earmarking revenue for specific purposes. That reform alone would have made Ammons a success. As it was, the underfunded General Fund often could not meet state obligations. Even a modest income tax passed in 1937, a property tax increase, and a service tax were insufficient. State agencies ran on credit. By late 1938, State Treasurer Homer F. Bedford was so low on funds that he had to lay off tax examiners. Creditors clamored for their money while other businessmen yelled that they were being taxed to death. A group of them, led by the luggage manufacturer Maurice B. Shwayder, marched on the Capitol on December 14, 1937, demanding to meet with Ammons. Told that the governor could not be found, one of them vented his frustration: "You fellows have gone to sleep up here, and the state's in a hell of a mess."[8]

The mess gave newspapers good copy, the best of it early in Ammons's term. Shortly before Johnson vacated his suite in the Capitol, a private detective, Jack H. Gilmore, connived with Denver attorney Erl H. Ellis and *Denver Post* reporter Walden E. Sweet to hide microphones in the governor's office. Connecting the microphones through telephone lines to Gilmore's apartment, the trio employed a stenographer and a dictaphone machine to record Ammons's conversations. Tipped off by an informant, Denver district attorney John A. Carroll hoped to snare the eavesdroppers. His plan derailed when Ammons's secretary inadvertently revealed that the governor knew of the bug. Ellis and his associates quickly turned their records over to Carroll and demanded that he investigate state government. "The urge had come upon me to be a reformer," Ellis explained. "I had sold myself on the idea that people had the right to honest government and it was my duty to tell them that they were far from getting it."[9]

Carroll considered it his duty to prosecute Ellis, Gilmore, and Sweet. Making a case proved difficult, not only because they claimed to be good citizens nobly engaged in ferreting out political weasels, but also because there was no specific law against bugging an office. When the legal dust settled, Gilmore and Sweet posted bonds to insure their future good behavior. Ellis not only forswore chicanery, he was also barred from practicing law, a restriction lifted after 18 months. Grand jurors who reviewed the purloined conversations and investigated state government concluded that "the condition of the Colorado legislature was one of subserviency, inefficiency and special privilege."[10]

A whiff of scandal clung to Ammons like cheap cologne. In a private letter, Aubrey A. Graves, editor of the *Rocky Mountain News*, insisted that Ammons was a man "of blameless record . . . and although the microphone spies listened unknown to him into his most private conversations for weeks, he emerged unscathed, save for the ordinary sort of political deals that every politician discusses and takes part in." Graves viewed the imbroglio as "a fight between two not particularly holy political factions, in which one side tried to play outside the rules of decent, human or even political conduct and the attempt backfired." Many voters did not pause for such rational analysis. They smelled a mess and, not asking who made it, decided to get a new governor. Even the *Rocky Mountain News*, normally friendly to Democrats, rejected Ammons in 1938. Ralph L. Carr, a Republican attorney, won the endorsement of business and of large-circulation newspapers, including the *News* and *The Denver Post*.[11]

Carr, like Ammons a Colorado native, was born in 1887 in Rosita (Custer County), a fading former boom town. A journalist and then a lawyer, he moved from Cripple Creek to Victor to Trinidad to Antonito, where he served as the Conejos County attorney. Herbert Hoover appointed him U.S. attorney for Colorado in 1929, a patronage post he lost in 1933. Then he practiced law in Denver. Having never held a statewide elective office, he avoided the tainted title of politician. Republicans liked him because he was one of them. Independents and some Democrats appreciated that he belonged to the post-Hoover breed of moderate Republicans willing to tolerate Democratic work and relief programs. "Those on relief and on WPA," he promised, "need have no fears. They will be taken care of regardless of what party is in power." In November 1938, Carr beat Ammons by more than 55,000 votes.[12]

Providing a pint of relief while scraping up cash for state institutions almost proved Carr's undoing. Facing a budget some $2.5 million out of balance in early 1939, he told the Lions Club in Denver, "I am not an alarmist, but when you see the state's penal institutions and hospitals without funds to pay salaries and buy groceries for their inmates, it is a bad situation." To save money he cut expenses. Pursuing fiscal flexibility, he cajoled the legislature in 1939 into diverting 65 percent of income-tax

Ralph Carr with children who are probably victims of polio. Tuberculosis declined in the 1930s, but infantile paralysis remained a scourge. (Colorado Historical Society)

revenue from education to the General Fund. Full employment in the early 1940s plugged the welfare drain and filled state coffers with income and sales taxes. Educators squawked, but to most people Carr was a hero — a pudgy, bespectacled Sir Lancelot of the ledger books.[13]

Business liked and supported Carr; organized labor did neither. On the federal level, New Deal Democrats brought meat to labor's table, enacting, among other measures, the National Labor Relations Act (1935), which protected workers' rights to join unions. During most of the 1930s, Colorado's unions generally backed Democrats: Edward Costigan and Josephine Roche with enthusiasm, Ed Johnson with reservations. Abetted by federal legislation, the Colorado State Federation of Labor (CSFL) pressured the legislature into rethinking, although by no means abandoning, the state's anti-labor heritage. Lawmakers limited the use of convict labor and, for a time, curtailed anti-union injunctions. CSFL also helped outlaw "yellow dog" contracts, agreements that employers extracted from prospective employees to keep them from joining unions.[14]

Labor's meager legislative gains were perhaps all it could get. Unions had little power in Colorado before the Depression; early twentieth-century radicals such as Big Bill Haywood were feared, hated, and, when possible, destroyed. Hammered by hard times, workers lost their jobs and quit their unions. Ed Ready, a Denver carpenter, recalled, "It was rough. My tools didn't come out of the closet for two years and a half." The United Brotherhood of Carpenters and Joiners saw local after local disband — Durango and Walsenburg went under in 1931, Leadville and Longmont in 1932, Silverton in 1933. Only four locals sent delegates to the union's 1933 state convention. Not until 1937 did splintered carpenters piece together another statewide meeting.[15]

Labor had itself to blame for some of its problems. In 1935 national tensions between craft and industrial unions prompted John L. Lewis, head of the United Mine Workers, to create the Committee for Industrial Organization (CIO) within the American Federation of Labor (AFL) and in 1938 to bolt from the AFL entirely by establishing the Congress for Industrial Organization (CIO). Colorado's union members, numbering only around 20,000, tried to stay out of the fray. Led by CSFL president Frank Hefferly, they ignored AFL chief William Green's orders to boot out CIO affiliates. In 1938, Green, once dismissed as a "creampuff" by Hefferly, demonstrated his backbone by seizing control of CSFL and ousting Hefferly. The AFL victory stripped CSFL of 10,000 members.[16]

No time was a good time for the state's anemic labor movement to forget solidarity, but in the late 1930s, unity was crucial. An improving economy enhanced labor's chances of striking successfully. Earlier in the decade, with employers courting bankruptcy and with replacement workers easy to get, strikes made little sense. In the three years from 1931 to 1933 there were only 11, involving fewer than 1,000 workers. In 1934 the number of strikes rose to 12 but fell to 8 in 1935. As the Depression temporarily lifted in 1937, strikes mushroomed to 17; in 1938, a down economic year, they declined to 11. In 1939, the worst year for work stoppages in the 1930s, there were 17, accounting for more than 75,000 lost work days. One strike, at Silverton's Shenandoah-Dives mine, saw the CIO defeated; another, at the Green Mountain Dam construction site 16 miles south of Kremmling, saw the AFL triumphant.[17]

Silverton Miners' Union No. 26, a CIO affiliate, struck Shenandoah-Dives on Sunday morning, July 26, 1939, asking for a 12-hour cut in the work week to 44 hours and demanding that the company permit fuller unionization. Idle miners bolstered their spirits by sponsoring picnics and dances. When they ran out of money, they unsuccessfully tried to get San Juan County to put them on relief. As the strike wore on, some miners cooled on it. Merchants also grumbled at the CIO, blaming it for their

declining sales. But Adolphus S. Embree, the CIO organizer, insisted that the work stoppage continue — until a mob convinced him to step aside.[18]

Hundreds, perhaps even 1,000, angry townspeople besieged the Union Hall late in the evening of August 28, demanding that Embree leave town. The *Silverton Standard* praised Sheriff Fred Patterson and the town's police chief Frank Salfisberg for "rare tact in keeping the insistant [*sic*] group orderly." The lawmen "persuaded Embree and Charles Yates, local union secretary, that their safety called for them to leave Silverton. They left with the officers for Ridgway shortly before midnight." The anti-strike miners' faction promptly ended the walkout, and 14 of them formed a new union, unaffiliated with the CIO. When Governor Carr visited in mid-September, he congratulated Silverton for settling its "labor difficulties without cost to the state."[19]

Carr had cause to thank the vigilantes. In Kremmling that summer, he had been compelled to spend $1,000 a day for nearly a month to keep uneasy peace in the wake of a strike at the Green Mountain Dam site. On July 12 the AFL unions struck the Warner Construction Company, which was building Green Mountain Dam, a component of the Colorado–Big Thompson water diversion project. The State Industrial Commission ruled the action illegal, but the unions went ahead anyway, complaining of

The 1939 strike at Silverton's Shenandoah-Dives mine saw CIO officials run out of town. (Photo by Russell Lee, September 1940, FSA, Library of Congress)

cockroach-ridden company boardinghouses that dished up maggot-infested chow. They also charged that Warner misclassified workers to keep their pay low. Most of all, the AFL wanted Warner to hire only union members, a demand for a closed shop that the company rejected.[20]

Businessmen fumed at the AFL for preventing non-union laborers, many local men, from crossing the picket lines to get work. As in Silverton, townspeople, aided by local lawmen, broke the strike. On Tuesday morning, August 1, a delegation of 20 businessmen told J. A. Walther, the AFL representative, that "it would be to the public interest for him to move his office out of the community." He left. That afternoon some 40 carloads of Kremmling men went to the dam site and ran the picketers off. Deputized by Sheriff John H. Lee of Summit County, the "back-to-workers" won control of the area, making their headquarters in a tavern known as the Bucket of Blood. On Wednesday, August 2, strikers clashed with strikebreakers. In the meantime, union partisans from Denver, described by Kremmling's *Middle Park Times* as "500 Mexicans, Negroes, and hard cases," rushed to Green Mountain to reinforce their beleaguered comrades.[21]

George Harbac, a union representative, described the scene at Henney, a hamlet near the dam site, where AFL men from Denver tried to cross a bridge on August 2:

> We walked to about seventy-five feet of the bridge. Paul Heeney [*sic*], rancher, who owns and runs Heeneyville, pulls up his gun. The sheriff [John Lee] tells him not to shoot. Heeney says it is a private road and he'll shoot anyone he wants. . . . A man told us the bridge was loaded with dynamite. We did not believe him and we started to walk forward. When we were within thirty feet of the bridge, it blew up.

According to Harbac, that triggered an attack on the union men. "They [the anti-union forces] were firing like out of machine guns. Tiny [Thomas Kellerhaus] was shot through the eye and some fellows tried to get him picked up off the ground. Art Morrow was shot through the chest and the arm. After the men were hurt, we turned around and started back."[22]

The *Middle Park Times* blamed the violence on the Denver mob, which the paper, revising its earlier estimate, described as "200 men armed with clubs and firearms, actively engaged in blocking state highways, cutting telephone lines, dynamiting power lines, attempting to force their way into private property against the orders of officers of the law, threatening to destroy private property and human lives." Whoever was at fault, AFL sympathizers suffered the most. By August 2, six union men had been shot, and one had had his head gashed. The *Middle Park Times,* fearing that bagging only six of the AFLers might reflect badly on local marksmen, made a bet: "We are willing to wager that any one of 100 of these deputies can hit a running buck deer at 300 yards, and therefore should have no difficulty in nicking a man-sized skunk at half that distance."[23]

While mayhem ruled in Summit and Grand counties, Governor Carr vacationed with former president Herbert Hoover in Glenwood Springs. Initially hesitant to declare martial law, Carr did so on the evening of August 2, signing a declaration drafted by Byron G. Rogers, Colorado's attorney general. National Guardsmen, commanded by Adjutant General Harold H. Richardson, rushed to Kremmling, arriving early on August 4. Armed with machine guns and backed by two tanks, militiamen disarmed strikers and non-strikers. Warner resumed work unhampered by pickets.[24]

At first it appeared that the National Guard had vanquished the AFL. But in the end the AFL won. With the help of federal mediators and the assistance of Father J.W.R. Maguire of Chicago, a mediator with access to one of the Warner owners, the AFL convinced Warner to accept a closed union shop in return for a three-and-a-half year "no strike" pledge and the AFL's promise to let local men join the unions. Maguire explained, "Warner Brothers, the contractors, have always employed union labor but they were under great pressure from forces in Colorado which were opposed to unions and which were anxious to prevent the signing of a contract." The Kremmling *Middle Park Times* damned the dam agreement: "It is unfair, illegal, and definitely un-American." Secretary of the Interior Harold Ickes, on the other hand, sided with the AFL. Reminding Coloradans that the federal government was financing the project, he noted that "the proposition that non-urban labor should have first call on the jobs appears unfair to me in the face of great unemployment in labor in the larger cities."[25]

Colorado National Guardsmen equipped with tanks restored order in Kremmling, August 1939. (Colorado Historical Society)

Carr sailed through the choppy summer of 1939 without taking on much water. Labor criticized him for calling out the Guard, but most voters applauded him. In 1940, John Carroll, the heir to Edward Costigan's and Josephine Roche's New Dealism, was defeated in the Democratic gubernatorial primary by George E. Saunders, a protégé of Ed Johnson's. In November, Carr beat Saunders by more than 50,000 votes.[26]

Democrats could not shrug off Carr's re-election. More than a tribute to his personal popularity, his victory represented a Republican trend on the way to becoming an avalanche. In 1933, 1935, and 1937, Democrats controlled both houses of the General Assembly. In 1939 they lost the state House of Representatives, and in 1943 their state Senate majority evaporated. In 1933 there had been only 20 Republicans in the 100-member Assembly; in 1943 there were only 21 Democrats.[27]

U.S. congressional elections also went against Colorado Democrats. After the death of John A. Martin of Pueblo in 1939, William E. Bundy, a Democrat, served out the rest of Martin's term, but Bundy was replaced as the Third District's congressman in 1940 by J. Edgar Chenoweth, a Republican. In the northeast a Republican, William S. Hill, ousted Democrat Fred Cummings in 1940. Lawrence Lewis of Denver, one of the most strongly anti-Roosevelt Democrats in Congress, retained his seat until he died in 1943. He was succeeded by a Republican, Dean M. Gillespie. In the west, Edward T. Taylor, the granddad of Democrats, won his seventeenth consecutive term in 1940. Upon his death on September 3, 1941, he was followed by a Republican, Robert F. Rockwell.[28]

Fortunately for the Democrats, neither of the state's U.S. Senate seats was open to contest in 1940. Senator Ed Johnson trod the trail he blazed as governor, when he first distanced himself from the New Deal. Often he voted against Roosevelt's programs, and in 1944 he declared, "As I see it, the New Deal has been the worst fraud ever perpetrated on the American people." When Carr challenged Johnson for the U.S. Senate in 1942, Big Ed reminded voters that Carr had welcomed Japanese-American citizens to Colorado after the outbreak of World War II. The role of anti-Japanese sentiment in Johnson's 1942 victory is as unclear as the part anti-Hispanic prejudice, stirred by his 1936 state blockade, played in his initial election to the Senate. Bigotry may have brought him some, perhaps all, of the votes by which he beat Carr. Certainly Johnson's narrow 3,642-vote edge rested more on his folksy charm and his conservative positions than on his tenuous ties with FDR. Alva B. Adams, who like Johnson often voted against Roosevelt, was returned to the U.S. Senate in 1938, despite FDR's failure to endorse him. On his death in 1941 he was succeeded by Eugene D. Millikin, a Republican.[29]

Roosevelt shunned Colorado in 1940 when he again sought the presidency. Carr's popularity may have convinced the president that the state was lost to the Democrats. He could have guessed as much by reading the *Rocky Mountain News*, which viewed his unprecedented bid for a third term as unacceptable, indeed as un-American. In "Why We Oppose Roosevelt," the *News* editorialized, "Because one-man rule is contrary to the whole of democracy. Because one-man rule is sweeping the world and we are not immune. Because a third term is a long step toward one-man rule." A majority of Coloradans agreed as they gave Wendell Willkie, the Republican nominee, nearly 15,000 more votes than FDR in 1940. Roosevelt survived the snub, winning without Colorado's help.[30]

The New Deal political revolution in Colorado was, on a scale of 10, at best a 2. In the early 1930s conservative-to-moderate Democrats held sway. In the late 1930s and early 1940s, Republicans returned: some, moderates such as Carr; others, conservatives such as Millikin, described by journalist John Gunther as "among the most extreme reactionaries in the Senate." Costigan, a true New Dealer, proved to be a supernova — bright, brief, memorable, and rare. Ammons, although on good terms with the Costiganite John Carroll, was, said *Rocky Mountain News* editor Aubrey Graves, bossed by Benjamin F. Stapleton, Denver's conservative Democratic mayor. Party labels confused observers. The Republican Carr was at least a foot, and perhaps a yard, to the left of the Democrat Billy Adams. Senators Johnson and Adams, as well as Denver's congressman Lawrence Lewis, all Democrats, were, from FDR's standpoint, little better than Republicans.[31]

The feebleness of the political revolution was matched by the paleness of the economic revolution. In *Inside U.S.A.* (1947), Gunther portrayed Colorado in the mid-1940s, basing his assessment in part on the politics of the preceding 15 years. After noting that "there are tories [conservatives] in . . . Denver who make Hoover seem like an anarchist," Gunther considered the wellsprings of power: the bankers on Denver's Seventeenth Street, the Colorado Fuel and Iron Corporation, the beet-sugar companies, all strongly protective of their interests.[32]

Business understood what government could do for it. The Moffat Tunnel, completed in 1927 at the property taxpayers' expense, was conceived as a boon to the Denver and Salt Lake Railroad. The Dotsero cutoff, financed by the Reconstruction Finance Corporation (RFC) in the early 1930s, benefited the Denver and Rio Grande Railroad. The Colorado National Bank survived the panic of 1932–1933, thanks to Reconstruction Finance loans; many smaller banks failed. Senator Edward Costigan came to the aid of the Boettchers and other sugar company stockholders through the Jones-Costigan Sugar Act. It not only supported domestic prices, but also protected sugar from foreign competition, with the result that consumers nationwide paid more.[33]

By raising the price of silver and gold, FDR did little for small-scale gold panners but much for large mining companies. Farm Security Administration resettlement schemes saved only a few poor farmers. Agricultural Adjustment Administration payments and Farm Credit Administration loans helped growers with capital hold on to it, as did massive water projects such as Colorado–Big Thompson and the John Martin Dam. By pouring money into the state for the Federal Emergency

Relief Administration (FERA) without getting an appropriate match from Colorado, the federal government relieved local taxpayers of relief burdens. From almost every large New Deal grant program, Colorado received more than its per capita share. Throughout the 1930s the New Deal helped shift tax dollars from the East and the South to the West: Connecticut's and Virginia's taxes helped pay for Colorado's roads and dams.[34]

Lorena Hickok, Harry Hopkins's investigator, reported in 1934 that FERA was "in the position of subsidizing John D. Rockefeller." Not only at Rockefeller's Colorado Fuel and Iron in Pueblo but throughout the state, business profited from the New Deal. Hickok mused, "What we really did, I guess, was to subsidize the Great Western Sugar company by carrying practically all of the Mexican labor and a good many farmers, too, on relief last winter [1933–1934]."[35]

Not only did the New Deal help maintain a cheap labor pool; it also helped quiet potential unrest. Roy Howard, head of Scripps-Howard, which owned the *Rocky Mountain News,* wrote Claude Boettcher in 1936: "I am convinced that not only the interests of the masses, but the interests of men like you and me — call us capitalists, if you please — will be best served by a continuance of the present Democratic administration, even with all its flagrant weaknesses." Symbolically, two of Denver's best-known Public Works Administration (PWA) projects, Phipps Auditorium at the Colorado Museum of Natural History and Boettcher School for Crippled Children, eventually bore the names of the city's two most prominent capitalists.[36]

Business leaders had little objection to Hoover's Reconstruction Finance Corporation; they welcomed Costigan's sugar legislation, they accepted the PWA, and they raised no great objection to the Civilian Conservation Corps. They took occasional shots at the Works Progress Administration, although usually they bore it as a necessary evil.

But businessmen fiercely resisted New Deal attempts to rearrange the social order by advancing the cause of labor. Alfred B. Trott, head of Denver's Daniels and Fisher department store, complained to Roy Howard about the *Rocky Mountain News*'s pro-labor stance, suggesting that big advertisers would shun the paper. Howard responded that Scripps-Howard favored "establishing the rights of labor on a basis at least equal to those enjoyed in other English speaking democracies. . . . I need not tell you that we are living in a trying and dangerous period."[37]

Behind the scenes, Howard tried to moderate the *News*'s approach — the department stores were, after all, big advertisers. He wrote to editor Aubrey Graves that "Denver is made up of a large percentage of 'economic royalists.' Those who are not in this class are — or I believe the great majority are — conservative, or they are at least not radical or leftist." Howard suggested that Graves "recognize the nature of your audience, and dish up your product accordingly." Seeing scant support for labor, Democrats in the General Assembly did little for the unions. When Republicans took command of both houses in 1943, they passed the Labor Peace

Act, a measure John Gunther described as wiping "out every labor gain since the Ludlow Massacre in 1914; it set a record in the nation for antilabor legislation."[38]

As intense as their resistance to change was, at times the "interests" gave ground. Sentiment for pensions was so strong and senior citizens so well organized that wise politicians such as Ed Johnson embraced the cause. Even the powerful pensioners, however, were partially defeated, as the state rarely came up with the $45 monthly payments. Josephine A. Roche's fight for a progressive state income tax in 1934 helped her earn the title of "radical." Colorado sputtered along on gasoline, liquor, sales, and property taxes — revenue sources that proportionately hit the poor and the middle class harder than the rich.

When the General Assembly, prodded by voters, passed an income tax in 1937, they set the top rate at 6 percent for individuals and 4 percent for corporations. Aubrey Graves told Roy Howard that under the old system, Frederick Bonfils, publisher of *The Denver Post* until his death in 1933, "had a $750,000 [annual] income" and "paid one-tenth of one percent of his income to support state and local government." Graves also explained to Howard that " 'the 17th street boys' who lobbied for it, as against another proposed income tax bill which would have hit wealth harder, told our reporters they were well satisfied."[39]

An aroused middle class could get its way sometimes. Those on the lowest rungs of the socioeconomic ladder were less able to change things. African-Americans remained segregated in Denver in 1940, as they were in 1930; their proportion of the state population remained at approximately 2 percent in 1940. Hispanos also fared poorly. Federal legislation in 1937 curtailed child farm-labor, and by 1940 average wages for farm workers had risen by 6.4 percent over 1937. But, as historian Sarah Deutsch points out, restrictions on child labor deprived families of income. "Wages rose slightly after 1937, but each spring 78 percent of beet families found themselves living on store credit, 11 percent on relief, and 4 percent on advances from the grower."[40]

The failure of the New Deal to do as much as it might have for African-Americans and Hispanos reflects the attitudes shared by most whites. New Deal paternalism may have been better than unadulterated racism, but it left much to be desired. Lorena Hickok railed against child labor and damned the exploitation of beet workers. Nonetheless, she described Hispanic laborers to Harry Hopkins as "illiterate peons, very low grade mentally." When a delegation of African-Americans visited WPA chief Paul Shriver in 1941 asking for good construction jobs at the Denver Ordnance Plant, Shriver responded, "Negroes and Mexicans have one chance in a thousand [to be employed]."[41]

The success of entrepreneurs in getting the New Deal to finance their recovery while resisting its feeble efforts to rearrange their society rested on their ability to control both the Democratic and Republican parties within the state. Forced to change mounts on occasion, they demonstrated consummate horsemanship. Their task was made easier by splits among the Democrats. John Carroll recalled, "We went to the same church, but we did not sit in the same pew." Businessmen could almost always find a popular Democrat, like Ed Johnson, to their liking.[42]

The sons and grandsons of the empire builders had learned time-proven formulas for western success from their fathers and grandfathers. Nineteenth-century subsidies for railroads and silver paved the way for 1930s subsidies for highways and sugar. For common folk, western self-reliance meant avoiding the dole and fending for oneself; for the Boettchers and their friends, it meant getting everything they could from Washington. Savoring those parts of Roosevelt's program that helped them, they shunned seeds of social change.

That triumph of conservatism and capitalism stands as one of the great ironies in the state's history. Far from driving the economic royalists from the temple, Franklin Roosevelt rebuilt Colorado's temple of capitalism and then sold it back to the former owners for a prayer. Harold Ickes saw what was happening in 1939 when he urged anti-union farmers to be fair to the AFL at Green Mountain: "When the dam is built and there is water on the land, the water users will have a benefit out of all proportion to the wages that workers can earn." The water users liked it that way, and if they had free rein, as did the mine owners in Silverton, they would have kept it that way.[43]

To admit that the New Deal helped business and maintained the old social order in Colorado is not to suggest that it did not benefit ordinary people. When C. E. Luker of Eastlake asked God to bless FDR for saving "us farmers' lives" and when Thomas Nother, a carpenter, concluded "the New Deal was a godsend to many unemployed workers," they spoke for thousands of other ordinary people who considered Roosevelt their friend. Welfare and work programs sustained tens of thousands until business revival brought private jobs. Pensions and Social Security made it easier for the middle class to grow old gracefully and comfortably.

Modern highways, sewage treatment facilities, schools, flood control projects, forest trails, outdoor amphitheaters, better-managed and conserved agricultural and grazing lands, new airports, hospitals, and public buildings helped finish a state that at the start of the 1930s was not long removed from frontier primitivism. The water diversion and storage projects, controversial in their time and still subject to debate, may not have been as wise as they originally appeared, but much of eastern Colorado's development since 1930 has depended upon Colorado–Big Thompson, Fryingpan-Arkansas, and other water wonders that followed the federally financed diversion and storage schemes of the 1930s.[44]

The New Deal and, more important, defense spending revived Colorado's industry, mining, and agriculture. Although the notion of plutocrats feasting at Harry Hopkins's table upset Lorena Hickok's stomach, the meal, it might be argued, ended pleasantly. Colorado Fuel and Iron Corporation and Great Western Sugar, for all their faults, provided jobs. For a

time, the possessors of great wealth enjoyed it; later much of it passed into public hands. Whether spurred by inheritance taxes or moved by the obligations of nobility, which John Gunther defined as "conscience money," many of the rich established foundations: Boettcher, Bonfils, Penrose, and Phipps, among them. Their contributions — to schools, hospitals, churches, theaters, museums, orchestras, libraries, zoos — served, albeit unequally, the high, the middle, and the low.[45]

By giving the state an infrastructure of highways, reservoirs, and clean drinking water, by restoring its farms and protecting its grazing land, by sustaining its mining industry, the New Deal positioned Colorado to boom during and after World War II. By advancing the principle of federal-state responsibility for economic welfare, New Dealers redefined federal-state relations and reoriented the Democratic and Republican parties. Just as the federal government broadened its role in relation to Colorado, the state expanded its responsibilities. In the early 1930s Billy Adams saw relief as largely a county duty; by the late 1930s many Coloradans not only admitted the state's role in relief, but through the income tax, broadened its financing of education. Carr diverted almost two-thirds of that money to the General Fund, but the idea of state attention to pre-college education remained.

"War in Europe means more prosperity for thousands of Colorado stockmen and farmers," Kremmling's *Middle Park Times* happily reported

Construction at Lowry Field gave Denver's economy a boost in 1940. (Colorado Historical Society)

As Colorado's molybdenum production soared from less than 2 million pounds in 1932 to more than 25 million pounds in 1941, Climax, north of Leadville, boomed. (Photo by Marion Post Wolcott, September 1941, FSA, Library of Congress)

on September 7, 1939, a few days after Germany's invasion of Poland embroiled Europe in war. William C. Sweinhart, the state's agricultural director, predicted that war demand would soon soak up the 14 million bushels of surplus wheat stored in local grain elevators, as well as tons of lard, pork, and corn previously without a good market. Lawrence M. Pexton, manager of the Denver Union Stockyards, forecast that packinghouses would soon operate around the clock, slaughtering animals to feed European armies.[46]

The horror of World War II hit home on December 7, 1941, as the Japanese attack on Pearl Harbor pushed the United States into declaring war. Aboard the *Arizona,* one of the U.S. ships sunk that day, were brothers Norman, age 20, and Francis, age 22, sons of Clara May Morse of Lamar. Both were among the 1,117 fatalities. Clara wrote in her diary, "I'll never sing before breakfast again, for this is what I did this morning even when my dear ones were giving their lives I was singing."[47]

With the tragedy of war came full economic recovery. By 1942 Colorado farm income stood at more than $253 million, nearly 20 percent above its level in prosperous 1929. In 1943 Colorado Fuel and Iron made more than 50 percent more steel than it had in 1929; in 1944 the plant was running at 111-percent capacity making forgings for 155-millimeter shells. Able to market the profitable property, the Rockefellers sold CF&I in 1945.[48]

Franklin Roosevelt, accompanied by his terrier, Fala, made his last visit to Colorado in late April 1943. In Denver he toured Lowry Field, the Denver Ordnance Plant, and Fitzsimons Hospital, where wounded soldiers cheered him and "he saluted them." At Camp Carson, near Colorado Springs, he watched a test firing of a bazooka and saw the Eighty-ninth Infantry in action. A week after he left, the newspapers, constrained by wartime secrecy, reported his defense-centered trip. With their sons and daughters at war, Coloradans no longer thought about brain trusts, economic royalists, or the New Deal. A new trial faced them; a new triumph awaited them.[49]

Appendix 1: Population Statistics

Table 1. Population Change: Colorado and Selected Counties, 1930–1940

	1930	1940	Increase/Decrease Number	Increase/Decrease Percent
Colorado	1,035,791	1,123,296	87,505	8.4
County				
Adams	20,245	22,481	2,236	11.0
Arapahoe	22,647	32,150	9,503	42.0
Baca	10,570	6,207	-4,363	-41.3
Boulder	32,456	37,438	4,982	15.4
Denver	287,861	322,412	34,551	12.0
El Paso	49,570	54,025	4,455	9.0
Jefferson	21,810	30,725	8,915	40.9
Kit Carson	9,725	7,512	-2,213	-22.8
Lake	4,899	6,883	1,984	40.5
Larimer	33,137	35,539	2,402	7.2
Las Animas	36,008	32,369	-3,639	-10.1
Mesa	25,908	33,791	7,883	30.4
Pueblo	66,038	68,870	2,832	4.3
Weld	65,097	63,747	-1,350	-2.1

Source: Colorado State Year Book, 1941–1942, p. 18.

Table 2. Population: Colorado and Selected Towns, 1900, 1930, 1940, 1990

	1900	1930	1940	1990
Colorado	539,700	1,035,791	1,123,296	3,294,394
City				
Alamosa	1,141	5,107	5,613	7,579
Boulder	6,150	11,223	12,958	83,312
Cañon City	3,775	5,938	6,690	12,687
Colorado Springs	21,085	33,237	36,789	281,140
Denver	133,859	287,861	322,412	467,610
Durango	3,317	5,400	5,887	12,430
Englewood	—	7,980	9,680	29,387
Fort Collins	3,053	11,489	12,251	87,758
Grand Junction	3,503	10,247	12,479	29,034
Greeley	3,023	12,203	15,995	60,536
La Junta	2,513	7,193	7,040	7,637
Longmont	2,201	6,029	7,406	51,555
Loveland	1,091	5,506	6,145	37,352

Table 2 *(continued)*

	1900	1930	1940	1990
Pueblo	28,157	50,096	52,162	98,640
Sterling	998	7,195	7,411	10,362
Trinidad	5,345	11,732	13,223	8,580
Walsenburg	1,033	5,503	5,855	3,300

Source: Colorado State Year Book, 1941–1942, p. 25; U.S. Dept. of Commerce, Bureau of the Census, 1990 Census of Population: General Population Characteristics, Colorado, Table 1

Appendix 2: Economic Statistics

Table 1. Passenger Cars and Tourism, 1929–1940

Year	Passenger Cars in Colorado	Visitors to Rocky Mountain National Park	Visitors to Mesa Verde National Park
1929	273,960	274,408	14,517
1930	276,847	255,874	16,656
1931	276,376	265,663	18,003
1932	255,854	282,980	15,760
1933	239,058	291,934	16,185
1934	246,373	365,392	21,474
1935	256,148	367,568	21,835
1936	284,131	550,496	25,571
1937	304,419	651,899	28,171
1938	301,838	659,802	30,911
1939	312,847	609,029	32,246
1940	321,810	627,847	36,443

Source: Colorado State Year Book, 1941–1942, pp. 375, 481.

Table 2. Mineral Production Value, 1910–1940, Amounts in Millions

Year	Gold	Silver	Lead	Zinc	Coal	Petroleum	Molybdenum
1910	$20.5	$4.6	$3.3	$4.2	$17.0	$0.26	$0.00
1920	7.6	5.9	3.7	4.0	42.8	0.20	0.00
1930	4.5	1.7	2.2	3.5	21.5	1.50	2.60
1940	12.9	6.9	1.1	0.6	16.6	1.50	15.9

Source: LeRoy Hafen, Colorado and Its People, II: 691–693.

Table 3. Building Permits, 20 Leading Colorado Cities, 1929–1940

Year	Value	Year	Value
1929	$21,575,638	1935	$ 7,176,981
1930	11,707,791	1936	11,473,160
1931	9,127,502	1937	12,395,231
1932	4,363,398	1938	10,786,042
1933	2,782,412	1939	15,987,668
1934	3,747,310	1940	17,564,059

Source: LeRoy Hafen, Colorado and Its People, I: 637.

Table 4. Bank Clearings, Principal Cities, Selected Years

Year	Denver	Pueblo	Colorado Springs
1929	$2,027,274,024	$90,395,740	$71,753,636
1930	1,694,207,214	79,301,192	61,740,665
1931	1,342,832,980	62,042,177	51,016,097
1932	960,057,246	36,266,401	34,477,507
1933	896,617,504	21,986,583	25,341,507
1934	1,088,005,002	26,846,585	25,381,311
1940	1,627,431,420	35,558,367	31,244,067

Source: Colorado State Year Book, 1941–1942, p. 166.

Table 5. Estimated Number of Millionaires in Colorado Based on Number of People Reporting Incomes $50,000 or More, 1929–1938

Year	Estimated # of Millionaires
1929	181
1930	110
1931	64
1932	29
1933	35
1934	44
1935	63
1936	117
1937	107
1938	62

Source: Colorado State Year Book, 1941–1942, p. 310.

Table 6. Highway Disbursements for Construction, Maintenance, Administration, 1929–1940, Amounts in Millions

Year	Highway Disbursements
1929	$5.8
1930	7.1
1931	10.1
1932	6.3
1933	7.7
1934	10.4
1935	7.6
1936	16.1
1937	22.1
1938	17.0
1939	12.2
1940	8.0

Source: Colorado State Year Book, 1941–1942, p. 363.

Table 7. Total Value Mining, Manufacturing, Agriculture, 1929 and 1939

Year	Mining	Manufacturing	Agriculture
1929	$55,331,911	$286,732,996	$159,177,950
1939	64,144,557	221,642,666	125,318,443

Source: LeRoy Hafen, *Colorado and Its People,* I: 635.

Table 8. Federal Non-Repayable Expenditures in Colorado, 1933–1939

Federal Emergency Relief Administration	$40,345,338
Agricultural Adjustment Administration	41,806,752
Civilian Conservation Corps	42,764,170
Bureau of Public Roads	28,780,718
Public Works Administration	23,120,754
Works Progress Administration	75,219,110
Veterans Administration	41,053,284
Total Non-Repayable	$375,101,905

Source: Don Reading, "A Statistical Analysis of New Deal Economic Programs," p. 165.
Note: Total is greater than the sum of the listed programs because not all programs have been listed. Text sometimes gives different amounts because different years are included.

Appendix 3: Election Statistics, 1928–1940

I. President of the United States: State and County Data

	Colorado	Denver	El Paso	Mesa	Pueblo
1928					
Herbert Hoover(R)	253,872	73,605	16,243	6,446	15,576
Alfred Smith(D)	133,131	41,524	5,069	3,260	7,915
1932					
F. D. Roosevelt(D)	250,877	73,032	11,353	6,604	15,332
Herbert Hoover(R)	189,617	59,372	12,017	4,388	10,414
1936					
F. D. Roosevelt(D)	295,021	99,340	15,719	7,839	18,685
Alfred Landon(R)	181,267	50,743	11,007	3,675	10,071
1940					
Wendell Willkie(R)	279,576	81,388	16,766	7,049	14,198
F. D. Roosevelt(D)	265,554	91,069	13,320	7,712	18,805

II. Governor of Colorado

1928 General		1930 General	
William H. Adams(D)	240,160	William H. Adams(D)	197,067
William L. Boatright(R)	144,167	Robert F. Rockwell(R)	124,157

1932 Primary — Democratic		1932 Primary — Republican	
Ed C. Johnson	87,700	James D. Parriott	77,430
E. V. Holland	30,308	Warren F. Bleecker	35,574

1932 General		1934 Primary — Democratic	
Ed C. Johnson(D)	257,188	Ed C. Johnson	76,240
James D. Parriott(R)	183,258	Josephine Roche	63,107

1934 General		1936 Primary — Democratic	
Ed C. Johnson(D)	237,026	Teller Ammons	58,043
Nate C. Warren(R)	162,791	Ray H. Talbot	38,378
		Moses E. Smith	39,620

1936 General		1938 Primary — Democratic	
Teller Ammons(D)	263,311	Teller Ammons	67,992
Chas. M. Armstrong (R)	210,614	George J. Knapp	40,948

1938 General		1940 Primary — Democratic	
Ralph L. Carr(R)	255,159	George E. Saunders	75,130
Teller Ammons(D)	199,562	John A. Carroll	50,787

1940 General	
Ralph L. Carr(R)	296,671
George E. Saunders(D)	245,292

III. United States Senators From Colorado

1928 General
No senatorial election. Republican incumbents Lawrence Phipps and Charles Waterman remained in office.

1930 Primary — Democratic		1930 Primary — Republican	
Edward P. Costigan	24,698	George H. Shaw	63,112
Morrison Shafroth	15,819	William Hodges	49,043
James Marsh	7,337		

1930 General		1932 Primary — Democratic	
Edward P. Costigan(D)	180,028	Alva B. Adams	65,701
George H. Shaw(R)	137,487	John T. Barnett	58,938

1932 Primary — Republican		1932 General (6 year term)	
Karl C. Schuyler	66,179	Alva B. Adams(D)	226,516
Nate C. Warren	47,080	Karl C. Schuyler(R)	198,519

1932 General (Short Term)		1936 Primary — Democratic	
Karl C. Schuyler(R)	207,540	Ed C. Johnson	94,922
Walter Walker(D)	206,475	William E. Sweet	44,672

1936 General		1938 General	
Ed C. Johnson(D)	299,376	Alva B. Adams(D)	262,806
Raymond L. Sauter(R)	166,308	Archibald Lee(R)	181,297

IV. United States Representatives From Colorado

Colorado's four congressional districts from 1928 to 1940 were First (Denver County); Second (northeastern Colorado, including the counties of Adams, Arapahoe, Boulder, Cheyenne, Clear Creek, Douglas, Elbert, Gilpin, Jefferson, Kit Carson, Larimer, Lincoln, Logan, Morgan, Phillips, Sedgwick, Washington, Weld, Yuma); Third (southeastern and southern Colorado, including the counties of Alamosa, Baca, Bent, Conejos, Costilla, Crowley, Custer, El Paso, Fremont, Huerfano, Kiowa, Las Animas, Mineral, Otero, Prowers, Pueblo, Rio Grande, Saguache, Teller); Fourth (western Colorado, including the counties of Archuleta, Chaffee, Delta, Dolores, Eagle, Garfield, Grand, Gunnison, Hinsdale, Jackson, Lake, La Plata, Mesa, Moffat, Montezuma, Montrose, Ouray, Park, Pitkin, Rio Blanco, Routt, San Juan, San Miguel, Summit).

First District (Denver)

1928		1930	
William R. Eaton(R)	63,258	William R. Eaton(R)	39,907
S. Harrison White(D)	44,713	Lawrence Lewis(D)	38,152

1932		1934	
Lawrence Lewis(D)	70,826	Lawrence Lewis(D)	59,744
William R. Eaton(R)	56,601	William R. Eaton(R)	34,073

1936		1938	
Lawrence Lewis(D)	100,704	Lawrence Lewis(D)	83,517
Harry Zimmerhackel(R)	41,574	William I. Reilly(R)	42,758

1940	
Lawrence Lewis(D)	110,078
James D. Parriott(R)	59,427

Second District (Northeast)

1928		1930	
Charles B. Timberlake(R)	62,375	Charles B. Timberlake(R)	55,099
Earl E. House(D)	31,480	Dr. O. E. Webb(D)	37,760

1932			1934		
Fred Cummings(D)	63,399		Fred Cummings(D)	64,719	
George Bradfield (R)	56,516		George Bradfield(R)	49,142	

1936			1938		
Fred Cummings(D)	66,420		Fred Cummings(D)	65,448	
George Bradfield(R)	57,145		William S. Hill(R)	60,259	

1940		
William S. Hill(R)	76,859	
Fred Cummings(D)	66,662	

Third District (Southeast and South)

1928			1930		
Guy U. Hardy(R)	64,116		Guy U. Hardy(R)	55,170	
Harry A. McIntyre(D)	34,670		Guy M. Weybright(D)	35,744	

1932			1934		
John A. Martin(D)	59,882		John A. Martin(D)	73,281	
Guy U. Hardy(R)	57,793		W. O. Peterson(R)	39,753	

1936			1938		
John A. Martin(D)	74,013		John A. Martin(D)	72,736	
J. Arthur Phelps(R)	48,871		Henry Leonard(R)	54,007	

1940		
J. Edgar Chenoweth(R)	70,842	
Byron G. Rogers(D)	65,269	

Fourth District (West)

1928			1930		
Edward T. Taylor(D)	30,142		Edward T. Taylor(D)	34,536	
William P. Dale(R)	21,089		Webster Whinnery(R)	17,051	

1932			1934		
Edward T. Taylor(D)	40,736		Edward T. Taylor(D)	39,747	
Richard C. Callen(R)	20,993		Harry McDevitt(R)	17,234	

1936			1938		
Edward T. Taylor(D)	42,010		Edward T. Taylor(D)	43,596	
John S. Woody(R)	22,175		John S. Woody(R)	24,805	

1940		
Edward T. Taylor(D)	44,095	
Paul W. Crawford(R)	30,126	

Notes

All citations involving Record Groups (RG) are from the National Archives, Washington, D.C., with the exception of a few, which are designated as NARS, Denver Branch. The following abbreviations have been used in the notes: CHS, Colorado Historical Society; CSA, Colorado State Archives; *CSYB, Year Book of the State of Colorado; DP, The Denver Post;* DPLWHD, Denver Public Library Western History Department; *RMN, Rocky Mountain News.*

Works are given a full citation in first reference in each chapter, even if they have been cited in an earlier chapter. After the first full reference, only the author's last name and a shortened title is given.

Preface

1. *RMN,* January 21, 1935. I am indebted to one of my students in my history of Denver class for discovering the Hill story. It and about five other pieces of information used in this book were discovered by class members.

2. Frank Cross, "Revolution in Colorado," *The Nation* (February 7, 1934): 153.

3. George Carlson interview with David McComb, March 20, 1975, CHS; *Lamar Daily News,* April 10, 1935; *RMN,* October 23, 1944, as quoted in James F. Wickens, *Colorado in the Great Depression* (New York: Garland Publishing, 1979), p. 397.

4. Robert G. Athearn, *The Mythic West in Twentieth-Century America* (Lawrence: University Press of Kansas, 1986), p. 99.

5. Ibid., p. 103.

Chapter 1. The Year of Discontent: 1932

1. Agent 57 Report, January 22, 1931, Adjutant General File, Box 26843, William H. Adams Papers, CSA.

2. *RMN,* June 11, 1932. The *Colorado Springs Gazette,* July 12, 1932, compared the fright to the Salem witch-hunts of the 1690s, an astute insight into paranoia in troubled times.

3. Agent 57 Report, July 11, 1931, Adjutant General File, Box 26843, Adams Papers, CSA.

4. *Colorado Springs Gazette,* July 2, July 3, July 15, and July 21, 1932; *DP,* September 12, 1934; *Cañon City Daily Record,* January 6 and February 3, 1934.

5. *RMN,* June 11, 1932; Mrs. John Whisnand to Edwin C. Johnson, December 3, 1931, and Johnson to Whisnand, December 4, 1931, State Board of Health File, Box 26843, Adams Papers, CSA.

6. *DP,* July 3, 1932.

7. Kenneth S. Davis, "FDR and Biography," *The American Scholar* 53 (Winter 1983–1984): 103. Anna Carlson interview with Stephen J. Leonard, November 30, 1991. For a consideration of Hoover, see J. Joseph Huthmacher and Warren I. Susman, eds., *Herbert Hoover and the Crisis of American Capitalism* (Cambridge, Mass.: Schenkman Publishing, 1973).

Chapter 2. Farewell to the 1920s

1. *Pueblo Chieftain,* November 4, 1928; *DP,* November 4, 1928.

2. *Daily Sentinel* (Grand Junction), November 1, 1928; *RMN*, November 15, 1928.

3. *DP*, November 4, 1928; *Colorado Springs Gazette*, November 5, 1928; *Chronicle-News* (Trinidad), November 2, 1928.

4. *Daily Democrat* (La Junta), November 8, 1928.

5. *DP*, November 7, 1928; *RMN*, December 18, 1928.

6. *RMN*, November 8, 1928; *Pueblo Chieftain*, January 1, 1929.

7. *Pueblo Chieftain*, January 2, 1929; *Del Norte Prospector*, September 22, 1933.

8. *Pueblo Chieftain*, January 1, 1930.

9. *Chronicle-News* (Trinidad), January 14, 1929.

10. *Durango Herald-Democrat*, October 10, 1929; *CSYB, 1935–1936*, pp. 221–224, gives a good summary of natural-gas history in Colorado. *CSYB, 1930*, p. 288, does the same for radio. See *RMN*, November 11, 1928, for list of stations, including wavelength revisions.

11. *Julesburg Grit-Advocate*, November 28, 1928; *Colorado Springs Gazette*, November 7, 1929; *Steamboat Pilot*, November 8, 1929; *Chaffee County Republican*, January 21, 1927.

12. *RMN*, November 13, 1928; Marshall Sprague, *Newport in the Rockies: The Life and Good Times of Colorado Springs* (Chicago: Swallow Press, 1971), pp. 237–241.

13. *RMN*, November 13, 1928; Paul S. Taylor, *Mexican Labor in the United States: Volume I* (Berkeley: University of California Press, 1930; reprint New York: Arno Press, 1970), p. 144.

14. *CSYB, 1935–1936*, p. 298.

15. *CSYB, 1930*, p. 298; "A Survey of Civic Conditions of Colorado Cities Having a Population of 2,000 or More," *Colorado Municipalities* 5 (January 1929): 9.

16. *RMN*, October 5, 1929.

17. *DP*, October 22, 1929. For a summary on the Fleagle gang, see *DP*, October 15, 1930; *Durango Herald-Democrat*, October 14, 1929. On the Denver airport, see *RMN*, October 17–19, 1929.

18. For a general account of the smashup, see William E. Leuchtenburg, *The Perils of Prosperity, 1914–1932* (Chicago: University of Chicago Press, 1958), pp. 241–268. Also see *DP*, October 29, 1929.

19. E. Warren Willard interviews with David McComb, February 20 and February 27, 1975, CHS.

20. *Daily Sentinel* (Grand Junction), October 25, 1929.

21. *Chronicle-News* (Trinidad), October 26 and November 7, 1929; *Durango Herald-Democrat*, November 2, 1929; *Steamboat Pilot*, November 8, 1929.

22. *CSYB, 1930*, p. 297; *Daily Democrat* (La Junta), October 28, 1929; *Colorado Springs Gazette*, November 10, 1929.

23. *Montrose Daily Press*, October 21, 1929.

Chapter 3. Good-Bye to Good Times: 1930–1932

1. Jenette Beresford to Charles Boettcher, May 12, 1932, Box 8, Charles Boettcher Papers, CHS.

2. *Pueblo Chieftain*, January 1, 1930; *DP*, January 1, 1930; *RMN*, January 1, 1930.

3. *CSYB, 1935–1936*, p. 62; *RMN*, October 17, 1930, and January 1, 1931; *Pueblo Chieftain*, January 1, 1930.

4. *RMN*, January 1, 1931; *South Side Monitor* (Denver), October 31, 1930, gives a good description of the Mayan.

5. *CSYB, 1941–1942*, p. 136.

6. *Herald-Democrat* (Leadville), January 1, 1931.

7. *Summit County Journal* (Breckenridge), July 21, 1931; Charles Thomas to J. H. Taylor, December 12, 1932, Charles Thomas Papers, CHS. The Bimetallic Association papers are at CHS.

8. *Chronicle-News* (Trinidad), December 14, 1930.

9. *Chronicle-News* (Trinidad), September 4 and November 3, 1930.

10. James F. Wickens, *Colorado in the Great Depression* (New York: Garland Publishing, 1979), p. 409, gives a summary of agricultural income. *Julesburg Grit-Advocate,* October 30, 1930.

11. *RMN,* March 15, 1928.

12. Josephine Roche radio speech, February 16, 1932, quoted in Marjorie Hornbein, "Josephine Roche: Social Worker and Coal Operator," *The Colorado Magazine* 53 (Summer 1976): 243.

13. *Time,* March 17, 1930, noted, "A Phipps speech empties the Senate Press Gallery." See William Sweet Papers at CHS for information on Phipps's ties with the KKK.

14. Walter F. O'Brien to Morrison Shafroth, September 6, 1930, Morrison Shafroth Papers, Box 24, DPLWHD.

15. Edward P. Costigan to Edward Keating, November 14, 1930, Edward Keating Papers, University of Colorado at Boulder.

16. Fred Greenbaum, *Fighting Progressive: A Biography of Edward P. Costigan* (Washington, D.C.: Public Affairs Press, 1971), p. 125. See also *Congressional Record,* 72nd Congress, 1st Session, February 3, 1932, p. 3, 307.

17. *Steamboat Pilot,* October 23, 1931; Thurman Arnold, "The Crash — and What It Meant," in Isabel Layton, ed., *The Aspirin Age, 1919–1941* (New York: Simon and Schuster, 1949), p. 222.

18. *Fort Collins Express-Courier,* April 5, 1932; *RMN,* June 6, 1932; *Colorado Springs Gazette,* July 26, 1932.

19. *RMN,* October 19, 1929; *CSYB, 1935–1936,* p. 355; *Herald-Democrat* (Leadville), July 8, 1932.

20. James F. Wickens, *Colorado in the Great Depression,* p. 22; *Colorado Labor Advocate* (Denver), December 11, 1930, and January 15, 1931.

21. *Herald-Democrat* (Leadville), September 16, 1931.

22. *Aspen Times,* December 12, 1930; *Gunnison News-Champion,* January 1, 1931; *Colorado Springs Gazette,* May 1, 1932.

23. *Herald-Democrat* (Leadville), September 24, 1931; *Colorado Labor Advocate* (Denver), September 24, 1931.

24. *Fort Collins Express-Courier,* April 6, 1932; *Herald-Democrat* (Leadville), September 24, 1931; Charles Boettcher to Sidney W. Sinsheimer, June 24, 1931, Box 6, Boettcher Papers, CHS.

25. *Colorado Springs Gazette,* July 24, 1932; *Las Animas Leader,* September 27, 1932; *County Seat News-Tribune* (Kiowa), October 28, 1932.

26. *Monte Vista Journal,* August 3 and September 13, 1932.

27. *Daily Sentinel* (Grand Junction), August 31, 1931; *Colorado Springs Gazette,* September 2, 1932.

28. *Colorado Springs Gazette,* July 17 and July 24, 1932; *RMN,* October 24, 1932; *Fort Collins Express-Courier,* August 24, 1932.

29. *Colorado Municipalities* 8 (October 1932): 184; *Herald-Democrat* (Leadville), July 31, 1931; *CSYB, 1935–1936,* p. 245; Irving P. Johnson to William H. Adams, June 2, 1932, Box 26843, William H. Adams Papers, CSA.

30. *Democrat-Herald* (Springfield), June 9, 1932; *Holyoke Enterprise,* September 1, 1932; *Fort Collins Express-Courier,* January 22, 1933; *Durango Herald-Democrat,* July 26, 1932; *Bent County Democrat* (Las Animas), July 15, 1932.

31. *Monte Vista Journal,* August 16, 1932; *Brighton Blade,* June 7, 1932.

32. *Colorado Springs Gazette,* July 3, 1932; *Durango Herald-Democrat,* November 2, 1932; *Montrose Daily Press,* September 22, 1932.

33. *Steamboat Pilot,* April 1, 1932; *Montrose Daily Press,* October 31, 1932.

34. *Summit County Journal* (Breckenridge), January 22, 1932.

35. Michael McGiffert, *The Higher Learning in Colorado: An Historical Study, 1860–1940* (Denver: Sage Books, 1964), p. 199; *Durango Herald-Democrat,* August 13 and August 31, 1932; Beryl McAdow, *From Crested Peaks: The Story of Adams State College of Colorado* (Denver: Big Mountain Press, 1961), p. 65; *RMN,* June 29, 1939.

36. Harold Stansell, *Regis: On the Crest of the West* (Denver: Regis Educational Corporation, 1977), p.105; Wallace B. Turner, *Colorado Woman's College: The First Seventy-Five Years* (Boulder, Colo.: Johnson Publishing, 1962), pp. 117–118,125; Allen Dupont Breck, *From the Rockies to the World: A Companion to the History of the University of Denver, 1864–1989* (Denver: University of Denver, 1989), pp. 117–120.

37. *CSYB, 1935–1936,* Louise Hill to Nathaniel P. Hill, August 2 and September 29, 1931, and October 16 and August 2, 1930, Louise Hill Papers, Box 9, CHS.

38. Louise Hill to Nathaniel P. Hill, October 23, 1933, Box 9, Hill Papers, CHS. Donald C. Reading, "A Statistical Analysis of New Deal Economic Programs in the Forty-Eight States" (Ph.D. diss., Utah State University, 1972), p. 350. Reading's figures are from Abner Horwitz and Caryle P. Stallings, "Inter-regional Differentials in Per Capita Real Income Changes," *Studies in Income and Wealth,* vol. 21, National Bureau of Economic Research (Princeton, N.J.: Princeton University Press, 1946), pp. 195–265. They are based on 1947–1949 prices.

39. Louise Hill to Crawford Hill, Jr., March 30, 1936, and April 22, 1935, and Louise Hill to Nathaniel P. Hill, July 17, 1931, Box 9, Hill Papers, CHS.

40. *Cañon City Daily Record,* December 29, 1933; *Colorado Springs Gazette,* June 26, July 1, July 3, and July 11, 1932.

41. *Cañon City Daily Record,* January 6, 1934, and February 3, 1934.

42. *Gunnison News-Champion,* December 29, 1932.

43. *Holyoke Enterprise,* March 1, 1934; *Colorado Springs Gazette,* June 23, 1932.

44. *Del Norte Prospector,* January 1, 1932, and June 23, 1933; *Monte Vista Journal,* January 26 and September 30, 1932; *Daily Sentinel* (Grand Junction), February 1, 1932.

45. *Herald-Democrat* (Leadville), May 11, 1932; Carrie Rollan to Edwin C. Johnson, May 20, 1934, Box 26879, Edwin C. Johnson Papers, CSA; Fred A. Rosenstock, "The Denver I Remember," in Robert Mutchler, ed., *The Denver Westerners 1973 Brand Book* (Boulder, Colo.: Johnson Publishing, 1974), p. 418.

46. Jenette Beresford to Charles Boettcher, May 12, 1932, Box 8, Boettcher Papers, CHS.

Chapter 4. Breakdown and the Rise of Roosevelt

1. *Colorado Labor Advocate* (Denver), September 11, 1930.

2. *Colorado Springs Gazette,* July 13, 1932; McFall Kerbey, "Colorado, A Barrier That Became a Goal," *The National Geographic* 62 (July 1932): 51; *Congressional Record,* 72nd Congress, 1st Session, February 3, 1932, p. 3,306.

3. Edgar M. Wahlberg, *Voices in the Darkness: A Memoir* (Boulder, Colo.: Roberts Rinehart, 1983), pp. 43–63, 94.

4. *Herald-Democrat* (Leadville), August 19, 1931; *Gunnison News-Champion,* January 7, 1932; *Fort Collins Express-Courier,* September 1, 1932; *Bent County Democrat* (Las Animas), October 14, 1932; *Monte Vista Journal,* February 12, 1932; *Cañon City Daily Record,* November 10, 1932.

5. Bernard Mergen, "Denver and the War on Unemployment," *The Colorado Magazine* 47 (Fall 1970): 328; *RMN,* January 1, 1932, on Red Rocks.

6. *Herald-Democrat* (Leadville), December 11, 1931; "City News Briefs," *Colorado Municipalities* 7 (August 1931): 142; *RMN,* November 25, 1931; *Fort Collins Express-Courier,* June 16, 1932; *Brighton Blade,* July 19, 1932; *Boulder Daily Camera,* January 4, 1933.

7. *Colorado Statesman* (Denver), September 3, 1932; *DP,* June 1, 1932.

8. *Summit County Journal* (Breckenridge), May 20, 1932; Thomas C. Coltman to William H. Adams, June 2, 1932, RFC File, Box 26850, William H. Adams Papers, CSA.

9. Mark S. Foster, *Henry M. Porter: Rocky Mountain Empire Builder* (Niwot: University Press of Colorado, 1991), p. 136; *RMN,* February 7, 1932; Mark S. Foster, *The Denver Bears: From Sandlots to Sellouts* (Boulder, Colo.: Pruett Publishing, 1983), p. 49.

10. King Shwayder interviews with David McComb, April 17, 1974, and May 10, 1974, CHS; Farrington R. Carpenter, *Confessions of a Maverick* (Denver: Colorado Historical Society, 1984), p. 146. The bull story is from a May 21, 1959, interview of Carpenter by Vi Ward at CHS.

11. *Monte Vista Journal,* September 13, 1932; *Fort Morgan Times,* August 31, 1932; *Colorado Springs Gazette,* February 23, 1932; *Colorado Labor Advocate* (Denver), April 28, 1932.

12. Adonias Garcia to William H. Adams, January 18, 1932, Box 26843, Adams Papers, CSA; *Daily Sentinel* (Grand Junction), July 4, 1932; *Fort Collins Express-Courier,* November 3, 1932; Gertrude M. Hollingsworth to William H. Adams, March 8, 1932, State Board of Health File, Box 26843, Adams Papers, CSA.

13. *Fort Collins Express-Courier,* May 19, 1932; M.L.K. Phillips to William H. Adams, October 17, 1932, and William C. Danks to Phillips, October 19, 1932, Adjutant General File, Box 26843, Adams Papers, CSA.

14. Bernard Mergen, "Denver and the War on Unemployment," p. 330, says that the Unemployed Citizens League "eventually had twenty-five locals, a few of which were organized by blacks and Mexican-Americans." *RMN,* August 26, 1932.

15. *Fort Collins Express-Courier,* June 8, 1932.

16. *Florence Daily Citizen,* November 2, 1932.

17. *Herald-Democrat* (Leadville), August 15, 1932; *RMN,* September 2, 1932.

18. Bill Stone to Edgar Wahlberg, March 13, 1931, Socialism File, Box 2, Edgar Wahlberg Papers, Auraria Library, Denver; Manuel L. Chait, "The Development of American Communism With Particular Emphasis on Colorado" (master's thesis, University of Denver, 1959); Frank Palmer, *Chameleon on Plaid: A Tale of Two Lives* (Holland, Mich.: n.p., 1973).

19. Agent 57 Reports and "Bulletin, Adjutant General of Colorado on Subversive Movements," Box 26843, Adams Papers, CSA.

20. Fritz Cansler to O. T. Jackson, August 10, 1931, Adjutant General File, Box 26843, Adams Papers, CSA.

21. Samuel E. Carey to Lewis N. Scherf, March 3, 1932, Adjutant General File, Box 26843, Adams Papers, CSA. Walter White to T. T. McKinney, August 22, 1932, and White to George D. Begole, August 22, 1932, NAACP Branch Files–Denver, Library of Congress.

22. Robert B. Girvan, "Carle Whitehead and the Socialist Party in Colorado 1930–1955," (masters thesis, University of Denver, 1967). National Socialist Labor Party Papers are at CHS.

23. *Boulder Daily Camera,* October 13, 1932; *RMN,* October 14, 1932.

24. *DP,* November 5, 1932.

25. Richard D. Lamm and Duane A. Smith, *Pioneers and Politicians: 10 Colorado Governors in Profile* (Boulder, Colo.: Pruett Publishing, 1984), pp. 124–135, gives a good portrait of Edwin Johnson. On Kountze, see Thomas J. Noel, *Growing Through History With Colorado: The Colorado National Banks, The First 125 Years, 1862–1987*, (Denver: Colorado National Banks and the Colorado Studies Center, University of Colorado at Denver, 1987), p. 80.

26. *Democrat-Herald* (Springfield), October 20, 1932.

27. *RMN,* September 16, 1932.

28. *RMN, September 2* and November 3, 1932; *Holyoke Enterprise,* October 20, 1932. FDR also stopped in Akron late in September. See *Sterling Farm Journal, September 29, 1932.*

29. *Weld County News* (Greeley), November 11, 1932.

Chapter 5. Fear, Relief, and Politics: 1933–1936

1. Louie Bunelen to Franklin Roosevelt, July 12, 1933, RG69, Federal Emergency Relief Administration (FERA), State Series, Colorado, 460.

2. *RMN,* March 3 and March 5, 1933.

3. *RMN,* March 15, 1933; *Holyoke Enterprise,* March 16, 1933; *Fort Collins Express-Courier,* January 1, 1935; Thomas J. Noel, *Growing Through History With Colorado: The Colorado National Banks, The First 125 Years, 1862–1987* (Denver: Colorado National Banks, 1987), pp. 75–84; Robert S. Pulcipher, ed., *The Pioneer Western Bank — First of Denver: 1860–1980* (Denver: First Interstate Bank of Denver, 1984), pp. 154–158.

4. *RMN,* May 3, 1933, and June 25, 1934.

5. "Silver Triumphant," *Time,* January 1, 1934; John A. Brennan, *Silver and the First New Deal* (Reno: University of Nevada Press, 1969) details the fight for silver. Also see William D. Leuchtenburg, *Franklin D. Roosevelt and the New Deal, 1932–1940* (New York: Harper and Row, 1963), p. 83.

6. *RMN,* April 7, 1933.

7. *RMN,* December 2, 1934.

8. John E. Gross to Harry Hopkins, February 18, 1935, RG69, FERA, Colorado-Connecticut, 401.

9. J. P. Soderstrum to John S. Wynce, RG69, Civil Works Administration (CWA), State Series, labeled California but has Colorado material, Box 10. See issues of *Colorado Municipalities* 1934–1935 for numerous CWA and FERA projects.

10. Arthur E. Burns and Edward A. Williams, *Federal Work, Security, and Relief Programs* (New York: DaCapo Press, 1941; reprint 1971), p. 131.

11. Vance Cherbonnier to Elizabeth Wickenden, May 7, 1934, and O. H. Lull to Wickenden, May 21, 1934, RG69, FERA, Administrative Central Files, 1933–1936, Transient Division, Colorado, 406–420.

12. John F. Bauman and Thomas H. Coode, *In the Eye of the Great Depression: New Deal Reporters and the Agony of the American People* (DeKalb: Northern Illinois Press, 1988), p. 186; Charles E. Johnson to Morris Lewis, April 30, 1934, RG69, FERA, as cited in note 11.

13. Rev. John R. Mulroy to Harry Hopkins, February 10, 1934, and Aubrey Williams to Mulroy, February 12, 1934, RG69, FERA, State Series, Colorado, 400.

14. L. G. Trueheart, "Report on the Failure of the Horse Creek Dam," undated report, RG69, WPA Central Files, State Series, 1935–1940, Colorado, 651.107.

15. William Dumm to Lawrence Lewis, May 5, 1934, Estelle K. Sudler to Bruce McClure, May 25, 1934, and Helen Fischer to Harry Hopkins, April 29, 1935, RG69, FERA, State Series, Colorado, 460.

16. Edwin C. Johnson to Harry Hopkins, December 20, 1933, RG69, FERA, State Series, Colorado, 400.

17. Harry Hopkins to Edwin C. Johnson, December 20, 1933, RG69, FERA, State Series, Colorado, 400; *RMN*, December 19, 1933; Frank Cross, "Revolution in Colorado," *The Nation* (February 7, 1934): 153; Edgar M. Wahlberg, *Voices in the Darkness: A Memoir* (Boulder, Colo.: Roberts Rinehart, 1983), p. 73.

18. *RMN*, March 2, 1935, and August 16, 1937; *Greeley Daily Tribune*, January 1, 1939; *CSYB, 1939–1940*, p. 176.

19. Pierce Williams to Harry Hopkins, August 11, 1933, RG69, FERA, State Series, Colorado, 406.

20. County Statistics in State Wide Social Welfare Survey, comp., "The Administration of County Poor Relief in Colorado," typescript dated October 24, 1934, in CHS manuscript collection. Medical report in Alice E. van Diest to Harvey T. Sethman, October 9, 1933, RG69, FERA, 400. Grace Blair to Harry Hopkins, December 12, 1933, and Helen Fischer to Harry Hopkins, April 29, 1935, RG69, FERA, State Series, Colorado, 460; Lorena Hickok to Harry Hopkins, June 24, 1934, RG69, FERA, Central Files, 3/1933–11/1935, Field Reports, R. O. Carte–J. M. Jordan.

21. Richard M. Broad, Jr., to Pierce Williams, August 11, 1933, RG69, FERA, State Series, Colorado, 406; Richard Broad to Harry Hopkins, July 22, 1933, RG69, FERA, State Series, Colorado, 400.

22. *RMN*, January 24, 1934; T. J. Edmonds to Harry Hopkins, January 20, 1934, FERA, State Series, Colorado, 406.

23. John A. Carroll interview with Stephen J. Leonard, February 27, 1976; *RMN*, May 24 and August 19, 1934.

24. *RMN*, September 7 and September 9, 1934; Edward Costigan, KOA radio address, August 24, 1934, Box 46, Edward P. Costigan Papers, University of Colorado at Boulder.

25. *DP*, September 12, 1934.

26. *RMN*, April 20, 1975.

27. Pierce Williams to Harry Hopkins, October 9, 1933, RG69, FERA, State Series, Colorado, 406.

28. "Relief Cold Weather," *Time*, November 12, 1934, p. 17; Memo of telephone conversation between Aubrey Williams and Casper Shawver, October 31, 1934, RG69, FERA, Central Files, 1933–1936, State Series, Colorado, 400.

29. Memo of telephone conversation between Ed Johnson and Aubrey Williams, ca. November 9, 1934, RG69, FERA, State Series, Colorado, 400; Benjamin Glassberg to Harry Hopkins, March 8, 1935, RG69, FERA, State Series, Colorado 406.1; Alice E. van Diest to Aubrey Williams, January 5, 1936, RG69, FERA, State Series, Colorado, 403.

30. *Daily Sentinel* (Grand Junction), January 1, 1935; *RMN*, March 15, 1933; Leuchtenburg, *Franklin D. Roosevelt*, p. 124.

31. Memorandum from Mr. Gill to Mr. Fox, December 14, 1935, RG69, FERA, State Series, Colorado, 400. See *RMN*, April 4, 1934, for a good article on the Costigan-Johnson split.

32. Fred Greenbaum, *Fighting Progressive: A Biography of Edward P. Costigan* (Washington, D.C.: Public Affairs Press, 1971), pp. 176–177, says that Johnson had promised not to oppose Costigan in the primary election.

33. *DP*, April 10, 1936.

34. Edwin C. Johnson to Worth Allen, April 13, 1936, Box 26915, Edwin C. Johnson Papers, CSA; *DP*, June 2, 1970.

35. *RMN*, January 18, 1939, and April 20, 1975; *DP*, January 19, 1939; *RMN*, April 20, 1975. William C. Ferril gives a summary of Costigan and politics in *Rocky Mountain Herald* (Denver), January 21, 1939.

36. Benjamin Glassberg to Harry Hopkins, March 8, 1935, RG69, FERA, State Series, Colorado, 406.1; John A. Martin to Harry Hopkins, October 25, 1934, RG69, FERA, State Series, Colorado, 400.

Chapter 6. The Civilian Conservation Corps

1. Vic M. to Ma and Sis, undated letter, ca. June 1, 1933, in RG35, Civilian Conservation Corps (CCC), Division of Selection, State Procedural Records, Colorado.

2. Report, "What Civilian Conservation Corps Have Meant to Las Animas County," RG35, as cited in note 1. My assumption is that Vic M. was from Las Animas County because his name was included in the report from that county.

3. *RMN*, April 2, 1933; "1930 Employment 1980," p. 3 (leaflet in CCC file, DPLWHD). Wayne Aspinall interview with David McComb, June 11, 1974, CHS.

4. Robert B. Parham, "The Civilian Conservation Corps in Colorado" (master's thesis, University of Colorado at Boulder, 1981), pp. 41, 140, 143; Bernard Valdez, quoted in "1930 Employment 1980." The CCC changed age and other requirements on occasion.

5. *DP*, March 30, 1958, and October 31, 1938; *CSYB, 1941–1942*, p. 489.

6. Parham, "CCC in Colorado," pp. 169–176, lists camps; C. N. Alleger and L. A. Gleyre, comps., *History of the Civilian Conservation Corps in Colorado, Littleton District–Grand Junction District; That the Work of Young America May Be Recorded* (Denver: Press of the Western Newspaper Union, ca. 1936) tells of out-of-staters at various camps.

7. Vic M. to Ma and Sis, as cited in note 1. C. W. Buchholtz, *Rocky Mountain National Park: A History* (Boulder: Colorado Associated University Press, 1983), pp. 184–187.

8. James C. Reddoch, Camp Reports: Buffalo Creek, December 18, 1934; Delta, August 12, 1937; Idaho Springs, September 27, 1940, RG35, CCC, Camp Inspection Records, Colorado, 1933–1942.

9. Vic M. to Ma and Sis, as cited in note 1. Vallecito Report, September 24, 1940; Norwood Report, June 4, 1938; Delta Report, August 12, 1937, RG35, CCC, Inspection Records, Colorado, 1933–1942.

10. Alice D. Morrison to Norma Queen, June 6, 1934, W. G. Runge to Queen, June 6, 1934, and "CCC Enrollment Procedures, December 21, 1936," RG35, CCC, Division of Selection, State Procedural Records, Colorado.

11. Camp Inspection Reports, CCC Company 3899, Camp F-71-C, Gunnison, Colorado, May 7, 1941, RG35, CCC, Inspection Records, Colorado, 1933–1942.

12. *Sterling Advocate*, May 10, 1935; *Elk Mountain Pilot* (Crested Butte), July 29, 1937; *Montrose Daily Press*, January 2, 1935; Parham, "CCC in Colorado," p. 103; *Craig Empire Courier*, December 14, 1938; *DP*, October 31, 1938.

13. Richard Lowitt, *The New Deal and the West* (Bloomington: Indiana University Press, 1984), pp. 65–72.

14. *Daily Sentinel* (Grand Junction), December 13, 1933, and January 1, 1935. In 1934, $500,000 was spent on Colorado National Monument projects, making it among Colorado's largest recipients of federal funds. Parham, "CCC in Colorado," p. 79; *Pueblo Star-Journal*, January 3, 1937; *Boulder Daily Camera*, January 1, 1935; Rev. James Sunderland, S. J., interview with Stephen J. Leonard, July 5, 1992; *DP*, November 24, 1937.

15. Stephen J. Leonard and Thomas J. Noel, *Denver Mining Camp to Metropolis* (Niwot: University Press of Colorado, 1990), p. 213; *DP*, June 9, 1941; *RMN*, January 1, 1932, March 4, 1941, June 26, 1941, and April 22, 1984. As the theater cost an estimated $1 million, it is good that Cranmer had Uncle Sam's pockets to pick.

16. *Chronicle-News* (Trinidad), March 16, 1936; C. N. Alleger and L. A. Gleyre, comps., *History of the Civilian Conservation Corps*, p. 87; *Denver Catholic Register*, December 29, 1938.

17. *DP*, March 28, 1937; Thomas Lyons, ed., *1930 Employment 1980* (Boulder: Colorado Humanities Program, ca. 1980), p. 182 (leaflet in DPLWHD's CCC file has the same title). Rev. John F. Brady, S.J., interview with Stephen J. Leonard, July 5, 1992.

18. W. E. Runge to Norma Queen, June 6, 1934, RG35, CCC, Division of Selection, State Procedural Records, Colorado; Warwick Downing to Harry C. Dunham, May 15, 1935, Box 8935, Denver Records, CSA.

19. *DP*, June 21, 1933; George Carlson interview with David McComb, March 20, 1975, CHS; George Begole to Oscar Chapman, December 27, 1934, Box 8945, Denver Records, CSA.

20. E. L. Creager to John R. Hermann, August 26, 1938, RG35, CCC, Camp Inspection Reports, Colorado; *Eastern Colorado Plainsman* (Hugo), April 21, 1939.

21. *CSYB, 1941–1942*, p. 464; Lyons, *1930 Employment 1980*, p. 184; *DP*, April 19, 1936.

Chapter 7. Blockade

1. *DP*, April 19 and April 20, 1936.

2. Paul S. Taylor, *Mexican Labor in the United States: Volume I* (Berkeley: University of California Press, 1930; reprint New York: Arno Press, 1970), pp. 221, 222, 228; J. M. Wilson to Edwin C. Johnson, April 27, 1936, Box 26916, Edwin C. Johnson Papers, CSA.

3. *Colorado Labor Advocate* (Denver), May 19, 1932.

4. *Colorado Labor Advocate* (Denver), May 12, 1932; *Weld County News* (Greeley), June 2, 1932; *Brighton Blade*, May 26, 1932.

5. *Brighton Blade*, May 20, 1932; *Fort Collins Express-Courier*, May 11, 1932; *Daily Democrat* (La Junta), June 25, 1932; Abraham Hoffman, *Unwanted Mexican Americans in the Great Depression: Repatriation Pressures, 1929–1939* (Tucson: University of Arizona Press, 1974), p. 119, reproduces a map created by Paul Taylor that shows that 8,439 Mexicans were repatriated from Colorado between 1930–1932.

6. Bureau of Public Welfare, "Resume of Relief Picture . . . as of Oct. 1935," a report in Denver Mayor Welfare File, Box 8985, CSA; *DP*, April 19, 1936; O. Edgar Abbott to Harry Hopkins, October 28, 1934, RG69, FERA, Central Files, 1933–1936, State Series, Colorado, Complaints.

7. *Cañon City Daily Record*, March 25, March 27, and May 7, 1935; *Chronicle-News* (Trinidad), March 27 and March 29, 1935; *Lamar Daily News*, May 11 and May 14, 1935.

8. *DP*, April 19, 1936. Johnson may have taken a cue from Florida's blockade in the autumn of 1935 and the Los Angeles Police Department's bum blockade of early 1936. See David Scholtz to Edwin C. Johnson, February 29, 1936, Box 26915, Johnson Papers, CSA.

9. *DP*, April 19–20, 1936.

10. *Durango Herald-Democrat*, April 21, 1936; *DP*, April 20–21, 1936.

11. *RMN*, April 26, 1936; *DP*, April 20, 1936; T. R. Mahan to Edwin C. Johnson, April 24, 1936, Box 26916, Johnson Papers, CSA.

12. *DP*, April 23, 1936.

13. *Greeley Daily Tribune*, April 27, 1936; Edwin C. Johnson to Edgar Wahlberg, May 4, 1936, and David Chavez, Jr., to Johnson, April 25, 1936, Box 26916, Johnson Papers, CSA; *Durango Herald-Democrat*, April 27, 1936.

14. Mrs. George A. Ullery to Edwin C. Johnson, undated letter, and W. C. Springer to Johnson, May 18, 1936, Johnson Papers, Box 26916, CSA; *Durango Herald-Democrat*, April 28, 1936.

15. *DP*, April 29, 1936; *Lamar Daily News*, April 30, 1936; John W. Lohman to Edwin C. Johnson, May 14, 1936, Box 26916, Johnson Papers, CSA. Sarah Deutsch, in her detailed study, *No Separate Refuge: Culture, Class and Gender on an Anglo-Hispanic Frontier in the American Southwest, 1880–1940* (New York: Oxford University Press, 1987), p. 166, notes that before the blockade, some Spanish-American groups in Colorado had "asked the

governor for protection against the importance of alien labor" but "as the blockade continued, and stories of Spanish Americans suffering harassment surfaced, more conservative Hispanic groups . . . joined the radical Spanish Speaking Workers League in protest."

16. *RMN*, September 7, 1936.

Chapter 8. Work Programs and Pump-Priming

1. Ray H. Talbot to Paul D. Shriver, April 2, 1942, RG69, Works Progress Administration (WPA), State Central Files, Colorado, 651.1.

2. *RMN*, October 13, 1936.

3. Ibid.

4. *DP*, October 28, 1936; *Colorado Springs Gazette*, October 29, 1936; *Pueblo Chieftain*, October 13, 1936; *RMN*, October 13, 1936.

5. *CSYB, 1939–1940*, p. 345; *RMN*, October 13, 1936.

6. James F. Wickens, *Colorado in the Great Depression* (New York: Garland Publishing, 1979), p. 170.

7. O. Otto Moore, *Mile High Harbor* (Denver: Associated Publishers, 1947), pp. 78–87, 215; Donald C. Reading, "A Statistical Analysis of New Deal Economic Programs in the Forty-Eight States, 1933–1939" (Ph.D. diss., Utah State University, 1972), pp. 94–95.

8. *DP*, June 28, 1935; *The Taxpayer's Review*, November 8, 1940, in DPLWHD clips; *Colorado Labor Advocate* (Denver), May 13, 1937; *RMN*, February 20, 1938, and April 28, 1939; C. P. Sauter to Franklin Roosevelt, March 5, 1939, RG69, WPA, State Central Files, Colorado, 641; *RMN*, September 15, 1992.

9. Arthur E. Burns and Edward A. Williams, *Federal Work, Security, and Relief Programs* (New York: DaCapo Press, 1941; reprint 1971), pp. 71, 137, indicate that the WPA local match on a national basis rose from 11.6 percent in 1935 to 28.5 percent in 1940. The PWA local match dropped from 45 percent in 1933–1934 to 30 percent after 1935.

10. Wickens, *Colorado in the Great Depression*, pp. 283, 285.

11. Paul D. Shriver to Edwin C. Johnson, August 15, 1935, RG69, WPA, State Central Files, Colorado, 610; *DP*, June 27, 1935, and August 16, 1937. The *Fort Morgan County Herald*, June 27, 1940, reported that starting March 6, 1939, affidavits of citizenship were required for WPA employment and that in 1940, affidavits stating that the applicant was neither a Nazi nor a Communist were required.

12. Paul D. Shriver to Harry Hopkins, June 13, 1935, RG69, WPA, State Central Files, Colorado, 610; Malcolm B. Catlin to David L. Bryant, RG69, WPA, State Central Files, General, September 1936–March 1939, Region V, 131.5; L. L. Ecker to Harry Hopkins, January 28, 1936, RG69, WPA, State Central Files, Colorado, 610; Clinton P. Anderson to Robert H. Hinckley, October 25, 1935, RG69, WPA, Central Files, General, 1935–1944, California-Wyoming, 1935–1938, 132.5; *RMN*, April 23, 1938, and March 28, 1943.

13. *DP*, March 14, 1938; Donald D. Wall interview with Stephen J. Leonard, October 15, 1992.

14. *RMN*, May 11, 1941, and March 28, 1943.

15. Margaret Reef interview with Helen Christy, October 1, 1979, DPLWHD; *RMN*, December 6, December 9, and December 12, 1937; *DP*, November 20, 1938; *Colorado Springs Gazette*, May 8, 1937.

16. *RMN*, February 4, 1934, and April 23, 1935; *DP*, March 1, 1936. Gladys Caldwell later became Gladys Caldwell Fisher.

17. Charles Tribble interview with Helen Christy, September 24, 1979, DPLWHD.

18. Forbes Watson to Edward B. Rowan, undated memo, ca. September 25, 1939, and Edward B. Rowan to Boardman Robinson, October 17, 1939, RG121, Records Concern-

ing Federal Art Activities, Textual Records of the Section of Fine Arts, Public Buildings Administration and Its Predecessors, Case Files Concerning Embellishments of Federal Buildings, 1934–1943, Colorado, Box 11, Entry 133. Hereafter cited as RG121, Embellishment File.

19. Edward B. Rowan to Victor Higgins, March 22, 1943 (includes clip from *Rocky Ford Daily Gazette-Topic,* February 23, 1943), Edward B. Rowan to Ernest Blumenschein, May 3, 1938, and Ernest Blumenschein to Edward B. Rowan, April 1938, RG121, Embellishment File.

20. Edward B. Rowan to George Vander Sluis, November 25, 1941, RG121, Embellishment File.

21. Gus C. Flake to Edward B. Rowan, July 15, 1942, RG121, Embellishment File.

22. Boardman Robinson to Hallie Flanagan, July 7, 1937, and Karon Tillman to J. Howard Miller, January 30, 1939, RG69, WPA, State Central Files, Colorado, 651.312; Miller to Flanagan, October 15, 1935, RG69, WPA, Federal Theater Project (FTP), Correspondence of the National Office with Regional Offices, 1935–1939, California-Oregon.

23. Text of *Me Third,* RG69, WPA, FTP, Play Scripts, 1936–1939.

24. FTP Region V Report, July 1936, RG69, WPA, FTP, Regional Reports, 1935–1939, Region V, Box 100.

25. W. J. Nixon to Hallie Flanagan, March 29, 1939, and Jay du Von to Mr. Wright, March 3, 1939, RG69, WPA, State Central Files, Colorado, 651.312; *DP,* December 26, 1938.

26. Report, Federal Music Project (FMP), Colorado Springs, December 31, 1936, RG69, FMP, Reports and Summaries, 1936–1939; Report, FMP, Denver Units, July 1, 1937, to November 1, 1937, RG69, WPA, State Central Files, Colorado, 651.311; James Michael Bailey, "Notes of Turmoil: Sixty Years of Denver's Symphony Orchestras," *Colorado Heritage* (Autumn 1992): 39.

27. Henry Alsberg to Morris M. Cleavenger, May 24, 1939, RG69, WPA, State Central Files, Colorado, 651.3172. Notes by Anthony Venneri on introductory pages of a copy to the *Guide* in S. J. Leonard's files.

28. The guide, renamed *The WPA Guide to 1930s Colorado,* with a new introduction by Thomas J. Noel, was published in 1987 by the University Press of Kansas. See pp. vii, xvii–xviii, 86. For Ferril's blast at *Ghost Towns,* see *New York Herald Tribune,* May 11, 1947. For Willison's connection with Ferril, see *RMN,* August 1, 1972, which reports on Willison's death at age 76. Also see Jerre G. Mangione, *The Dream and the Deal: The Federal Writer's Project, 1935–1943* (Philadelphia: University of Pennsylvania Press, 1983), p. 338. Mangione says that Ferril objected to the *Guide's* unkind portrayal of the Great Western Sugar Company's treatment of Spanish-American sugar-beet workers. Mangione may be wrong: the treatment of Great Western on pp. 66–67 and 200–201 is not particularly damning.

29. Margaret Reef interview with Helen Christy, October 1, 1979, DPLWHD; Phil Goodstein interview with Stephen J. Leonard, March 8, 1993; Colorado WPA Division of Information, "Women at Work in Colorado" (pamphlet in clipping collection, DPLWHD); *RMN,* December 4, 1937; *DP,* October 16, 1935.

30. Amer Lehman to Orren H. Lull, December 7, 1938, RG119, NYA, Records of the Deputy Executive Director, Testimonial Letters, 1936, Box 1; *CSYB, 1939–1940,* p. 364, gives $16.96 as average pay per month in 1939. For Coloradans' strong ties to the national administration of NYA, see Wickens, *Colorado in the Great Depression,* p. 315. On Amer Lehman, see his interview with David McComb, January 25, 1974, CHS.

31. *RMN,* December 3, 1937, and February 20, 1938; *Montrose Daily Press,* August 24, 1939. Pay varied. Urban unskilled received $55 a month in 1937. Region V, Report on Colorado, by Alice S. Clements, April 18, 1936, RG69, WPA, Central Files, 1935–1944, California-Wyoming 1935-1938, 132.5; Estanislado Valverde to F. C. Harrington, September 21, 1939, WPA, State Central Files, Colorado, 642.

32. Paul D. Shriver to David K. Niles, July 23, 1937; affidavit, April 8, 1940, from WPA workers in Springfield, Colorado, to Mrs. Franklin D. Roosevelt, RG69, WPA, State Central Files, Colorado, Complaints, 641.

33. Mary F. Adams to Paul D. Shriver, May 24, 1938, and Alfred Edgar Smith to Paul D. Shriver, June 8, 1938, RG69, WPA, State Central Files, Colorado, 641; Mary Chase to Herbert Little, July 24, 1941, RG119, NYA, Correspondence of the Director with State Officials Concerning Publicity; "Sugar Beet Conference in Colorado as of March 19, 29, 1937," RG69, WPA, State Central Files, Colorado, 640.

34. Edward T. Taylor to Harry Hopkins, January 9, 1936, and E. L. Lopez to Harry Hopkins, April 12, 1936, RG69, WPA, State Central Files, Colorado, Complaints, 641.

35. *RMN,* July 21, 1938.

36. John E. Hill to Franklin Roosevelt, October 22, 1936, RG69, WPA, State Central Files, Colorado, Complaints, 641; *Greeley Daily Tribune,* April 27, 1936.

37. *DP,* August 3, 1938, November 24, 1938, May 16, 1939, and July 16, 1940; *RMN,* July 16, 1940; Region V Reports, November 19, 1937, and July 27, 1938, RG69, WPA, Central Files, 1935–1944, 131.5; Phil Goodstein interview with Stephen J. Leonard, March 8, 1993.

38. Ray H. Talbot to Paul D. Shriver, April 2, 1942, RG69, WPA, State Central Files, Colorado, 651.1; Ralph C. Taylor, *A Guide to Historic Pueblo* (Pueblo, Colo.: Pueblo Metropolitan Museum, 1978), p. 19; *Cañon City Daily Record,* June 17, 1937; *Pueblo Chieftain,* January 2, 1938, November 28, 1939, and December 31, 1939; *Colorado Labor Advocate* (Denver), May 28, 1936.

39. *RMN,* December 15, 1937, and December 16, 1937; *Colorado Springs Gazette,* January 1, 1938; *Daily Sentinel* (Grand Junction), January 1, 1938, January 1, 1939, and January 1, 1940.

40. "Works Progress Administration of Colorado," *Colorado Municipalities* 12 (January-February 1936): 7; Testimonials concerning WPA benefits, 1938, RG69, WPA, Central Files, Colorado, 620.

41. *Pueblo Chieftain,* January 28, 1938; *Greeley Daily Tribune,* January 3, 1938; *Lamar Daily News,* January 30, 1939; *DP,* May 20, 1938; *Limon Leader,* November 6, 1939; *Pueblo Chieftain,* January 20, 1974; *RMN,* December 8, 1937, January 3, 1938, and November 6, 1938.

42. *Lamar Daily News,* January 30, 1939; *RMN,* December 8, 1937; also see WPA clipping file at DPLWHD.

43. *Fort Morgan County Herald,* June 14, 1937; *Pueblo Chieftain,* January 3, 1937; *DP,* October 24, 1938; "Report on the Denver Police Department," Benjamin Stapleton Papers, Box 4, CSA; *DP,* June 21, 1936, August 25, 1937, and October 4, 1938; *RMN,* December 6, 1937.

44. Frederick S. Allen et al., *The University of Colorado, 1876–1976* (New York: Harcourt Brace Jovanovich, 1976), pp. 109–110; *DP,* August 25, 1937; Beryl McAdow, *From Crested Peaks: The Story of Adams State College of Colorado* (Denver: Big Mountain Press, 1961), pp. 51–52; *Fort Morgan County Herald,* June 14, 1937; *Pueblo Chieftain,* January 3, 1937.

45. *RMN,* January 25, 1934, and May 18, 1938; "Moffat Water Tunnel Celebration," pamphlet in Box 4, Benjamin Stapleton Papers, CHS.

46. *Colorado Springs Gazette,* January 11, 1938; *Pueblo Star-Journal and The Sunday Chieftain,* December 29, 1935.

47. Daniel Tyler, *The Last Water Hole in the West: The Colorado—Big Thompson Project and the Northern Colorado Water Conservancy District* (Niwot: University Press of Colorado, 1992); *RMN,* July 26, 1937.

48. James Earl Sherow, *Watering the Valley: Development Along the High Plains Arkansas River, 1870–1950* (Lawrence: University Press of Kansas, 1990) contains much material on the 1930s. Sherow notes that under pressure from the federal government, water users managed to cooperate. The same thing happened with Colorado–Big Thompson, as

Daniel Tyler shows. *Pueblo Chieftain,* January 3, 1937, and December 31, 1939; *CSYB, 1941–1942,* p. 75.

49. Franklin Roosevelt to Harry Hopkins, October 2, 1937, RG69, WPA, State Central Files, Colorado, 1935–1944, 651.107; *CSYB, 1941–1942,* p. 74; *RMN,* May 18, 1938.

50. Edward N. Chapman, M.D., "The Menace to Life and Health From Improper Sewage Disposal in Colorado," *Colorado Municipalities* 10 (February 1934): 99–105.

51. *Pueblo Chieftain,* January 5, 1934; Chapman, "The Menace," pp. 99–105.

52. Report No. 5, "Status of Completed Non Federal Alloted Projects, " Region 5, Colorado, RG135, PWA, available in Civil Records Section, NARS; *RMN,* November 8, 1937; *DP,* October 30, 1938; B. V. Howe, "Progress in Sewage Treatment in Colorado," *Colorado Municipalities* 16 (November 1940): 182–185.

53. Federal Emergency Administration of Public Works, "Alphabetical Index to Non-Federal Projects, February 8, 1939," RG135, PWA, available in files of Civil Records Section, NARS; *Eastern Colorado Plainsman* (Hugo), April 7, 1939.

54. *RMN,* December 12, 1937; *Eastern Colorado Plainsman* (Hugo), April 21, 1939.

55. DPLWHD has a good collection of old highway maps, which show the extent of paving and winter conditions; Hansen quoted in Tyler, *Last Water Hole,* p. 65.

56. Robert G. Athearn, *The Denver and Rio Grande Western Railroad: Rebel of the Rockies* (Lincoln: University of Nebraska Press, 1977) amply covers the Rio Grande during the Depression.

57. *RMN,* January 25, 1937; *Montrose Daily Press,* December 12, 1937; *Eastern Colorado Plainsman* (Hugo), April 21 and August 4, 1939; *CSYB, 1941–1942,* p. 481.

58. *RMN,* November 21, 1937; *DP,* June 22, 1938; *Arriba Record,* October 13, 1939.

59. *DP,* January 1, 1940, and January 30, May 26, June 3, and December 4, 1942; *RMN,* December 5, 1942, and March 28, 1943.

60. Sherow, *Watering the Valley,* pp. 166–172.

61. All figures from Reading, "A Statistical Analysis," 20, 51, 56, 62, 71, 81, 95, 101, 105.

62. Memo of Harry Hopkins's telephone conversation with Paul Shriver, January 27, 1936, RG69, WPA, State Central Files, Colorado, 610; *CSYB, 1939–1940,* pp. 317–318; Reading, "A Statistical Analysis," pp. 377–378.

63. "WPA Administrators of Region #5 Conference, October 22, 1937, Washington, D.C.," RG69, WPA.

Chapter 9. Down on the Farm

1. *RMN,* September 7, 1936.

2. *RMN,* March 28, 1931, and December 5, 1982.

3. *Daily Sentinel* (Grand Junction), March 26, 1935. Untiedt eventually finished high school. He died in Denver in December 1977. See *DP,* December 30, 1977.

4. Robert B. Rogerson, *The Last of the Rogersons: 95 Years of Colorado Pioneer History — Horse, Cattle, and Sheep Lore* (no imprint), p. 106.

5. *Fort Collins Express-Courier,* January 1, 1934; H. D. Brindle to C. F. Lane, August 21, 1936, RG96, Records of the Farmers Home Administration (FHA), Rehabilitation Administration, Region 10, Office of Director, General Correspondence, 1935–1943, Box 32, NARS, Denver Branch; Hatfield Chilson interview with David McComb, April 4, 1975, CHS; *Pueblo Chieftain,* December 29, 1935.

6. Alvin T. Steinel, *History of Agriculture in Colorado* (Fort Collins, Colo.: State Board of Agriculture, 1926), p. 254, quoting *Colorado Farmer,* October 7, 1886; *Fort Collins Express-Courier,* June 17, 1932. County population comparisons may be found in *CSYB, 1941–1942,* p. 18.

7. U.S. Department of Agriculture, Weather Bureau, *Climatological Data,* May 1932; Louisa Arps, *Denver in Slices* (Denver: Sage Books, 1959), pp. 74–87, treats Cherry Creek floods, including that of August 3, 1933.

8. *Climatological Data,* May through October 1934.

9. *Lamar Daily News,* April 23, 1935, April 27,1936, and May 10, 1935.

10. *Democrat-Herald* (Springfield), May 9 and May 16, 1935.

11. *Wray Rattler,* June 6 and June 13, 1935; James E. Mills, "A History of Brush, Colorado" (master's thesis, University of Colorado at Boulder, 1964), pp. 82–83; *DP,* May 31, 1935; *RMN,* June 2, 1935.

12. *Wray Rattler,* June 13, 1935. A 1930 Colorado State Highway map shows Launchman Creek; the 1990 Colorado Department of Highways map shows it as Landsman Creek north of Burlington.

13. *Climatological Data,* May 1935; Ralph Baird to Harry Hopkins, July 25, 1935, RG69, WPA, State Central Files, Colorado, 651.104.

14. *Fort Collins Express-Courier,* January 1, 1937; *RMN,* June 30, 1937; "1930 Employment 1980" pamphlet, DPLWHD.

15. *RMN,* July 5, July 16, July 18–19, and July 26, 1937.

16. *CSYB, 1939–1940,* p. 92.

17. R. Douglas Hurt, *The Dust Bowl: An Agricultural and Social History* (Chicago: Nelson-Hall, 1981), p. 11; *Chronicle-News* (Trinidad), April 16, 1935.

18. *DP,* April 12, 1935; *Climatological Data* often included special reports on dust in monthly bulletins for 1935 and 1936.

19. Charles Boettcher to John C. Morgan, April 15, 1936, Box 7, Charles Boettcher Papers, CHS; *Democrat-Herald* (Springfield), April 18, 1935; *Chronicle-News* (Trinidad), April 16, 1935; *Durango Herald-Democrat,* April 17, 1935.

20. Hurt, *Dust Bowl,* pp. 3, 34. Robert E. Geiger, an Associated Press journalist, gave the Dust Bowl its name in April 1935. For one of Geiger's reports covering southeastern Colorado, see *Chronicle-News* (Trinidad), April 16, 1935.

21. Fred M. Betz, Sr., interview with David McComb, November 1, 1974, CHS; *Democrat-Herald* (Springfield), April 25, 1935; *Lamar Daily News,* April 30, 1935; *Chronicle-News* (Trinidad), April 16, 1935; Rev. John F. Brady interview with Stephen J. Leonard, July 5, 1992.

22. Mayme Stagner, "Resettlement — A Story of Faith and Courage, A Tape Recording Made by Mrs. Mayme (Bert) Stagner, April 8, 1981," *San Luis Valley Historian* 21, no. 2 (1989): 6.

23. Ibid., p. 10.

24. *Climatological Data,* February and April 1936.

25. Hurt, *Dust Bowl,* p. 53; Vance Johnson, *Heaven's Tableland: The Dust Bowl Story* (New York: Farrar, Straus, 1947), p. 184; *Chronicle-News* (Trinidad), April 16, 1935.

26. *Lamar Daily News,* April 10, 1935; Thomas Harper, "The Development of a High Plains Community: A History of Baca County" (master's thesis, University of Denver, 1964), p. 111.

27. Richard Lowitt, *The New Deal and the West* (Bloomington: Indiana University Press, 1984), p. 96.

28. Lorena Hickok to Harry Hopkins, June 17, 1934, quoted in Lowitt, *The New Deal and the West,* p. 22; Rogerson, *Last of the Rogersons,* p. 108.

29. Paul Bonnifield, *The Dust Bowl: Men, Dirt, and Depression* (Albuquerque: University of New Mexico Press, 1979), pp. 156–162. For a more positive view of SCS, see Johnson, *Heaven's Tableland,* pp. 220–231, and Lowitt, *The New Deal and the West,* pp. 58–61.

30. *Daily Sentinel* (Grand Junction), January 1, 1940; *La Junta Tribune,* July 28, 1938.

31. *Lamar Daily News,* January 15, 1935.

32. *DP,* September 21, 1934.

33. "Pledge of Cooperation," August 1, 1940, RG96, Farmers Home Administration, Reha-
bilitation Loan Cases, 1934–1944, Colorado, Alamosa County, NARS, Denver Branch.
FSA was eventually reorganized, so its papers wound up in Home Administration files.
The NARS collection at the Denver Branch deserves scholarly attention.

34. *CSYB, 1962–1964,* p. 501.

35. *Greeley Daily Tribune,* January 7, 1938; typescript copy of Connie Will letter published
in the *Crow Valley News,* July 27, 1939, in RG96, Farmers Home Administration, Region
10, Office of the Director, General Correspondence, 1935–1943, Box 16, Clippings,
163-01, 20/25/6:6, NARS, Denver Branch.

36. Stagner, "Resettlement — A Story," p. 15.

37. *RMN,* August 19, 1938; *Daily Sentinel* (Grand Junction), January 1, 1940. Wheat prices
are summarized in U.S. Department of Agriculture, Agricultural Marketing Service,
Division of Agricultural Statistics and Colorado State Planning Commission, *Colorado
Agricultural Statistics 1940* (Denver: Colorado State Planning Commission, ca. 1941), p.
98.

38. James F. Wickens, *Colorado in the Great Depression* (New York: Garland Publishing, 1979),
p. 409; Everett S. Lee et al., *Population Redistribution and Economic Growth, United States,
1870–1950: I, Methodological Considerations and Reference Tables* (Philadelphia, Pa.: The
American Philosophical Society, 1957), p. 253; *Holyoke Enterprise,* January 18, 1934.

39. Harper, "The Development of a High Plains Community," p. 263; Stagner, "Resettlement — A Story," p. 14.

40. Donald Worster, *Dustbowl: The Southern Plains in the 1930s* (New York: Oxford University
Press, 1979), p. 230.

Chapter 10. An Album of FSA Photographs

1. Roy Emerson Stryker and Nancy Wood, *In This Proud Land: America 1935–1943 as Seen
in the FSA Photographs* (Greenwich, Conn.: New York Graphic Society, 1973), p. 14. In
James C. Anderson, ed., *Roy Stryker: The Humane Propagandist* (Louisville, Ky.: University of Louisville, 1977), p. 6, Calvin Kytle explains that he wrote a chapter for a
proposed book on Stryker. That book was never finished, but the Kytle chapter,
"without Roy's knowledge but with his presumed approval . . . turned up under his
byline as the lead essay in a handsome volume of FSA photographers called *In This
Proud Land.*" One might assume, therefore, that some of what appears to be Stryker's
prose is actually Kytle's.

2. Stryker and Wood, *In This Proud Land,* p. 11. Thomas Munro co-authored the text with
Tugwell and Stryker.

3. William E. Leuchtenburg, *Franklin D. Roosevelt and the New Deal, 1932–1940* (New York:
Harper and Row, 1963), p. 32, discusses the "brains trust," which eventually came to
be called the "brain trust." Originally it consisted of Tugwell, Raymond Moley, and
Adolph Berle, Jr.

4. Stryker and Wood, *In this Proud Land,* pp. 9, 11.

5. Carl Fleischhauer and Beverly W. Brannan, eds., *Documenting America, 1935–1943*
(Berkeley: University of California Press, 1988), pp. 330–342, covers the arrangement of
the collection and estimates its size.

6. Roy Stryker to Arthur Rothstein, July 31, 1936, in Roy E. Stryker Papers, microfilm
edition, available in Prints and Photographs Division of the Library of Congress.
Hereafter cited as Stryker Papers.

7. Arthur Rothstein interview with Richard Doud, reprinted in Arthur Rothstein, *Arthur Rothstein: Words and Pictures* (New York: American Photographic Book Publishing, 1979), p. 11; Roy Stryker to Arthur Rothstein, April 29, 1936, Stryker Papers.

8. Arthur Rothstein to Roy Stryker, September 23, 1939, Stryker Papers.

9. The picture caption in the Library of Congress FSA-OWI File (LC-USF-34-28372-D) gives the spelling as Bahain, but Bill Ganzel in *Dust Bowl Descent* (Lincoln: University of Nebraska Press, 1984), p. 50, gives it as "Bihain," which is likely correct because Ganzel photographed the Bihains' son B. D. (Don) standing against a cottonwood holding corn. Rothstein, *Arthur Rothstein*, p. 55, provides technical information regarding the photo: "Linhof 9x12 cm, with Double Protar 15 cm lens. Panatomic film exposed 1/2 sec. at f/16."

10. Arthur Rothstein to Roy Stryker, October 4, 1939, Stryker Papers.

11. Roy Stryker to Dorothea Lange, September 7, 1939, Stryker Papers.

12. Russell Lee to Roy Stryker, September 7, 1940, and Stryker to Lee, undated letter, ca. September 1940, Stryker Papers.

13. Roy Stryker to Marion Post, July 14, 1938, Stryker Papers.

14. Paul Hendrickson, *Looking for the Light: The Hidden Life and Art of Marion Post Wolcott* (New York: Alfred A. Knopf, 1992), pp. 198–199; Marion Post Wolcott to Roy Stryker, September 9, 1941, Stryker Papers.

15. F. Jack Hurley, *Portrait of a Decade: Roy Stryker and the Development of Documentary Photography in the Thirties* (Baton Rouge: Louisiana State University Press, 1972), p. 166.

16. Hendrickson, *Looking for the Light*, p. 206.

Chapter 11. Life Goes On

1. The creature may have been an axolotl, a type of salamander. See *RMN*, October 31, 1982.

2. Colorado State Planning Commission, *Colorado: A Guide to the Highest State* (Denver: Colorado State Planning Commission, 1941; reprinted by the University Press of Kansas in 1987 as *The WPA Guide to 1930s Colorado*, with a new introduction by Thomas J. Noel), pp. xl–xli, lists holidays. Hereafter cited as *WPA Guide*. *RMN*, December 2, 1935; *Pueblo Star-Journal and The Sunday Chieftain*, January 1, 1939.

3. *Durango Herald-Democrat*, March 21, 1932; *Fort Collins Express-Courier*, January 1, 1937, (reports that the bonus payments, previously denied, were made to veterans in mid-1936); *Pueblo Chieftain*, November 30, 1939; *Pueblo Star-Journal and The Sunday Chieftain*, December 2, 1934; *RMN*, May 9, 1938.

4. *RMN*, March 1, 1935; *Greeley Daily Tribune*, January 1, 1939; *RMN*, November 27, 1939; *Colorado Springs Gazette*, July 20, 1939.

5. *RMN*, November 23, 1978; Robert Perkin, *The First Hundred Years: An Informal History of Denver and the Rocky Mountain News* (Garden City, N.Y.: Doubleday, 1959), pp. 534–535; "George C. Cox," *Colorado Municipalities* 16 (March 1940): 37.

6. *RMN*, June 2, 1991, on Miller; March 24, 1938, on Whiteman; and November 27, 1939, on Gash; Joan Reese, "Two Gentlemen of Note: George Morrison, Paul Whiteman, and Their Jazz," *Colorado Heritage* 2 (1986): 2–13; Louise Hill to Mrs. N. P. Hill, September 27, 1939, Box 9, Louise Hill Papers, CHS. Hill used a derogatory term for African-Americans.

7. *RMN*, August 17, 1932. Ironically the Pike feature portraying blacks as happy-go-lucky appeared on the morning of the Washington Park race riot.

8. *RMN*, August 18, 1932; *Colorado Springs Gazette*, April 5, 1935, and January 1, 1938; R. W. [unidentified except for initials on copy of letter] to Dr. T. T. McKinney [President, Denver branch NAACP], August 31, 1932, NAACP Papers, Branch Files, Box G28, Library of Congress.

9. *DP,* February 14, 1933; *New York Times,* February 13, February 14, February 20, and February 26, 1933. Hereafter abbreviated *NYT.*

10. *NYT,* March 2, 1933; *RMN,* March 3, 1933.

11. *NYT,* February 1, February 10, and October 27, 1934; Bill Barker and Jackie Lewin, *Denver!* (Gordon City: Doubleday & Co., Inc., 1972), pp. 127–129.

12. *NYT,* March 19, 1933; *RMN,* March 3, 1933.

13. *RMN,* January 1, 1931, treats big crime stories of 1930, which included the case of Pearl O'Loughlin, accused of murdering her child. For more, see Lee T. Casey, ed., *Denver Murders* (New York: Duell, Sloan and Pearce, 1946), pp. 167–190. *DP,* February 1, February 4, February 15, and February 18–23, 1931, covers Merritt, and the *Daily Sentinel* (Grand Junction), September 9, 1931, contains additional information. The *Daily Courier* (Alamosa), April 23, 1936, tells of Wettengel; *RMN,* July 16, 1938, treats Trinidad.

14. Russell Nye, *The Unembarassed Muse: The Popular Arts in America* (New York: The Dial Press, 1970), pp. 226, 229, 236, tells of Chester Gould's " 'Dick Tracy' . . . the first appearance in the comics of real violence." Perry Mason, born full-grown in Gardner's *The Case of the Velvet Claws* (1933), brought dollars to Colorado when Raymond Burr, TV's Perry Mason, taped episodes in Denver in the 1980s and 1990s. On Denver's last legal public hanging, see William M. King, *Going to Meet a Man: Denver's Last Legal Public Execution, 27 July 1886* (Niwot: University Press of Colorado, 1990), pp. 116–145.

15. *Daily Sentinel* (Grand Junction), January 2, 1931; *DP,* January 31, 1931.

16. *RMN,* January 17, 1977, gives details on Ives.

17. *RMN,* November 26, 1933.

18. *RMN,* October 21, 1934.

19. *RMN,* June 23, 1934; Richard Lowitt and Maurine Beasley, eds., *One Third of a Nation: Lorena Hickok Reports on the Great Depression* (Urbana: University of Illinois Press, 1981), pp. xxiv, 285. The Hickok letter is dated June 23, 1934.

20. *DP,* April 4, 1949.

21. *RMN,* January 7, 1939.

22. J. Percy H. Johnson, ed., *N. W. Ayer & Son's Directory of Newspapers and Periodicals . . . 1940* (Philadelphia, Pa.: N. W. Ayer & Son, 1940) gives circulation data for newspapers.

23. Bill Hosokowa's *Thunder in the Rockies: The Incredible Denver Post* (New York: William Morrow, 1976), pp. 152–166; *RMN,* August 26, 1932.

24. John Gunther, *Inside U.S.A.* (New York: Harper and Brothers, 1947), p. 225, for the Bonfils funeral story, which Gunther quotes from *Saturday Evening Post,* December 23, 1944.

25. *Pueblo Star-Journal and The Sunday Chieftain,* February 2, 1936.

26. Roy Howard to Charles Lounsbury, January 18, 1934, Box 89, Roy Howard Papers, Library of Congress; Perkin, *The First Hundred Years,* pp. 529–550.

27. *RMN,* March 16, 1937; *CSYB, 1931,* p. 326; *CSYB, 1939–1940,* p. 463.

28. James Thurber, *The Beast in Me and Other Animals* (New York: Avon Books, 1948), p. 151; Nye, *The Unembarassed Muse,* pp. 390–406.

29. *CSYB, 1940–1941,* p. 258; *Daily Sentinel* (Grand Junction), January 1, 1931; *Sterling Farm Journal,* November 29, 1938.

30. Ralph J. Batschelet, *The Flick and I* (Smithtown, N.Y.: Exposition Press, ca. 1981), pp. 13–16.

31. Leslie Halliwell, *The Filmgoer's Companion* (New York: Hill and Wang, 1967), pp. 123, 124, 510, 741; *Fort Collins Express-Courier,* January 2, 1938. Morris graduated from Colorado State College (later CSU) in Fort Collins in 1935. On his Berlin Olympic victory and subsequent winning of the Sullivan Memorial Trophy, see *Time,* January 11, 1937.

32. *DP,* June 19, 1987; *RMN,* June 19, 1987.

33. *Pueblo Star-Journal and The Sunday Chieftain,* February 2, 1936; *Pueblo Chieftain,* February 4, 1936.

34. *NYT,* April 28, May 16, and June 17, 1935; *RMN,* April 26–28, 1935; *Wray Rattler,* May 2, 1935; Jay du Von, "Chain-Letter Madness," *The Nation* 140 (June 12, 1935): 682.

35. Mark S. Foster, *The Denver Bears: From Sandlots to Sellouts* (Boulder, Colo.: Pruett Publishing, 1983), pp. 42–50, deftly covers baseball. *RMN,* June 27, 1938; *DP,* May 28, 1939; *Colorado Springs Gazette,* July 29, 1939.

36. *Fort Collins Express-Courier,* May 23, 1932; *Holyoke Enterprise,* September 28, 1933; *Wray Rattler,* July 18, 1935; Foster, *The Denver Bears,* p. 47.

37. Adolph Grundman, "Denver, The Basketball Capital of the United States" (unpublished paper presented at the Conference of the North American Society for Sport History, Banff, Canada, May 18, 1990), p. 9; *DP,* March 20, 1939.

38. *RMN,* October 31, 1934; *DP,* August 31, 1953; Barker and Lewin, *Denver!,* p. 132.

39. J. Juan Reid, *Colorado College: The First Century, 1874–1974* (Colorado Springs: The Colorado College, 1979), p. 122.

40. *DP,* March 7, 1965; *RMN,* March 24, 1938. On White's resignation in 1993, see *RMN,* March 21, 1993.

41. *RMN,* July 1, 1935; *DP,* December 1, 1929.

42. *DP,* March 27, 1937; *Glenwood Post,* May 5, 1938.

43. *RMN,* December 11, 1937, and December 18, 1938; *DP,* February 26 and September 11, 1939; *Colorado Springs Gazette and Telegraph,* May 29, 1938.

44. *Westerns Nyheter* (Denver), December 21, 1939; *DP,* February 2, 1933.

45. *Aspen Times,* November 4, 1937, January 20, 1938, April 6, 1939, February 1, 1940; *Westerns Nyheter* (Denver), December 21, 1939; *Daily Sentinel* (Grand Junction), January 1, 1939.

46. Abbott Fay, *Ski Tracks in the Rockies: A Century of Colorado Skiing* (Louisville, Colo.: Cordillera Press, 1984), pp. 25–26; Duane Vandenbusche and Duane A. Smith, *A Land Alone: Colorado's Western Slope* (Boulder, Colo.: Pruett Publishing, 1981), p. 247.

47. *Glenwood Post,* May 5, 1938; *RMN,* May 16, 1993.

48. *NYT,* December 5, 1932; *RMN,* December 5–6, 1932. Interstate 70 and other highway improvements had reduced the Denver-to-Grand Junction–roadway distance to 248 miles in 1990, and the driving time to approximately 4.5 hours. Walker's route may have been indirect because of closed passes.

49. *DP,* March 19, 1933.

50. Vandenbusche and Smith, *A Land Alone,* p. 223; *Time,* May 10, 1937; *RMN,* May 16, 1937, and January 1, 1939.

51. David P. Morgan, *Diesels West! The Evolution of Power on the Burlington* (Milwaukee, Wis.: Kalmbach Publishing, 1963), p. 78.

52. Morgan, *Diesels West!,* pp. 47–50.

53. *Wray Rattler,* October 29, 1936; *Chronicle-News* (Trinidad), October 19, 1935; *RMN,* March 4, 1934, and July 12, 1937.

54. *CSYB, 1939–1940,* p. 62.

55. *CSYB, 1939–1940,* pp. 63–64; *Durango Herald-Democrat,* July 9, 1938.

56. *RMN,* June 13, 1938, on Shirley Temple. A good source on Colorado attractions in the 1930s is the *WPA Guide.* On the tax tokens, see *Aspen Times,* October 7, 1937, and June 16, 1938. In 1938 expectations were that two million tokens would be retained by tourists and that others would wind up as children's play money.

57. *WPA Guide,* pp. 187–188; *RMN,* March 10, 1935, and March 27, 1938. For the significance of the mammoth find that took place at a rail stop named Dent, see E. Steve Cassells, *The Archaeology of Colorado* (Boulder, Colo.: Johnson Books, 1983), pp. 39–50.

58. Marshall Sprague, *Newport in the Rockies: The Life and Good Times of Colorado Springs* (Chicago: The Swallow Press, 1971), pp. 269–271, 309.

59. Sprague, *Newport,* p. 305; *RMN,* July 23, 1951.

60. Muriell Sibell Wolle, *Stampede to Timberline: The Ghost Towns and Mining Camps of Colorado* (Chicago: The Swallow Press, 1974), p. 27; *WPA Guide,* p. 96. An amateur production had been given at the Opera House in 1931. See Caroline Bancroft, *Historic Central City* (Boulder, Colo.: Johnson Publishing, 1974), p. 31.

61. *New York Herald Tribune,* December 9, 1934; *DP,* October 29, 1988; *RMN,* February 6, 1977; November 13, 1988.

62. Anne Ellis, *The Life of an Ordinary Woman* (Lincoln: University of Nebraska Press, 1929; reprint 1980) includes a helpful introduction by Elliot West.

63. *RMN,* November 27, 1938; *DP,* July 18, 1989.

64. Dalton Trumbo, *Eclipse* (London: Lovat Dickson and Thompson, 1935), pp. 16–17.

65. Dalton Trumbo, *The Remarkable Andrew: Being the Chronicle of a Literal Man* (Philadelphia, Pa.: J. B. Lippincott, 1977), pp. 40–43.

66. *RMN,* October 28, 1933, and December 30, 1940; *Publisher's Weekly,* August 14, 1954, p. 625.

67. *RMN,* October 24, 1936; *Colorado Plainsman* (Hugo), October 4, 1940. Among 1930s novels set at least in part in Colorado are books by Willa Cather, G. A. Clevenger, Clyde Brion Davis, Peter Field, Dorothy Gardiner, Wallace Irwin, Horace Joseph, Upton Sinclair, Anne Stewart, and Clifford Sublette. Forbes Parkhill and Marian Castle, destined to write important novels later, were producing articles in the 1930s. Lenora Mattingly Weber wrote a number of books for teenagers during the 1930s, as did Nelly Graf and Frank Cheley. For a fairly complete listing of authors working in Colorado in the late 1930s, see Lorene L. Scott, comp., *Colorado Writers* (Denver: Denver Public Library, 1939). On poets of the 1930s, see Henry Harrison, ed., *Colorado Poets* (New York: Henry Harrison, 1935), which lists more than 50 versifiers. Compiled and edited by a quartet of luminaries — Eleanor Gehres, Maxine Benson, Stanley Cuba, and Sandra Dallas — *The Colorado Book,* a long-needed collection of fiction relating to Colorado, is slated for 1993 publication by Fulcrum Press.

68. H. Allen Smith, *The Life and Legend of Gene Fowler* (New York: William Morrow, 1977), p. 244. Like Fowler, Smith also worked in Denver.

69. Willison, who went to school with Thomas Hornsby Ferril, borrowed a line from Ferril's poem "Ghost Town" for the title of *Here They Dug the Gold.* See *RMN,* August 1, 1972.

70. *RMN,* September 8, 1932.

71. *RMN,* March 8 and March 15, 1935.

72. *DP,* December 14, 1934.

Chapter 12. Decade's End

1. Elizabeth Jameson, *Building Colorado: The United Brotherhood of Carpenters and Joiners of America in the Centennial State* (Denver: Egan Printing, 1984), p. 56, quoting interview of Thomas Nother, November 25, 1981.

2. *Sterling Farm Journal,* April 29, 1937.

3. H. Lee Scamehorn, *Mill and Mine: The CF&I in the Twentieth Century* (Lincoln: University of Nebraska Press, 1992), p. 145. When it emerged from bankruptcy, the Colorado Fuel and Iron Company dropped "Company" in favor of "Corporation" in its name.

4. Kenneth W. Rowe to Orren H. Lull, August 15, 1938, RG119, NYA, Records of the Deputy Executive Director, Correspondence with States, Box 5.

5. *DP,* January 20, 1973, obituary of Ammons gives his birthdate as December 3, 1895, but several Who's-Who-type publications give 1896.

6. *RMN,* May 13, 1938. The "lion and fox" analogy is borrowed from James MacGregor Burns, *Roosevelt: The Lion and the Fox* (New York: Harcourt, Brace and World, 1956), p. vii. Burns borrowed it from Machiavelli.

7. James F. Wickens, "Tightening the Colorado Purse Strings," *The Colorado Magazine* 46 (Fall 1969): 271–286; *Aspen Times,* March 31, 1938. Roy E. Brown, "Colorful Colorado: State of Varied Industries," in Thomas C. Donnelly, ed., *Rocky Mountain Politics* (Albuquerque: University of New Mexico Press, 1940), pp. 51–87, comments on politics.

8. *DP,* December 15, 1937; *RMN,* December 4, 1938. The deficits did not hit all funds; some agencies, depending on their funding source, were able to pay their bills.

9. Marjorie Hornbein, "For the Public Good: The Strange Case of Colorado's Eavesdroppers," *Colorado Heritage* 3 (1985): 33, 36.

10. Hornbein, "For the Public Good," p. 36.

11. Aubrey A. Graves to George B. Parker, December 3, 1937, Box 123, Roy Howard Papers, Library of Congress, hereafter cited as Howard Papers; *RMN,* November 6, 1938. In the same issue, the *News* advocated the retention of Senator Alva B. Adams and Representative Lawrence Lewis, both Democrats.

12. *RMN,* November 14, 1938.

13. *RMN,* April 12, 1939.

14. Harry Seligson and George E. Bardwell, *Labor-Management Relations in Colorado* (Denver: Sage Books, 1961), pp. 97–101, consider some of labor's legislative gains in the 1930s, as does Jameson in *Building Colorado,* pp. 55–57. For a general history of labor in Colorado, see Harold V. Knight, *Working in Colorado: A Brief History of the Colorado Labor Movement* (Boulder: University of Colorado Center for Labor Education and Research, 1971).

15. Jameson, *Building Colorado,* p. 48, quoting her interview of Samuel E. (Ed) Ready, April 13, 1982.

16. Ellen A. Slatkin, "A History of the Response of the Colorado State Federation of Labor to the Great Depression, 1929–1940" (master's thesis, University of Denver, 1984), p. 102, quoting *RMN,* August 14, 1937.

17. Seligson and Bardwell, *Labor-Management Relations,* p. 73.

18. *Silverton Standard,* August 4, August 11, August 18, and August 25, 1939.

19. *Colorado Labor Advocate* (Denver), August 30, 1939; *Silverton Standard,* September 1, September 8, and September 15, 1939. Hearings in October 1939 were extensively reported in the *Standard.*

20. *Middle Park Times* (Kremmling), August 3, 1939; Colorado Citizens Committee to Protect Civil Rights, "Green Mountain Facts," pp. 10–11. Pamphlet in the files of DPLWHD.

21. Daniel Tyler, *The Last Water Hole in the West: The Colorado–Big Thompson Project and the Northern Colorado Water Conservancy District* (Niwot: University Press of Colorado, 1992), pp. 107–112, covers the strike and events leading to it, including a CIO walkout on March 14, 1939. Tyler notes that the water district feared higher labor costs would drive up the cost of the project, for which they were borrowing from the federal government. The *Middle Park Times*'s warning about "Mexicans, Negroes" was likely hyperbole.

22. Colorado Citizens Committee, "Green Mountain Facts," pp. 9–10.

23. *Middle Park Times* (Kremmling), August 3 and August 10, 1939. The strike was extensively covered in Denver. See *RMN,* August 3, 1939.

24. Philip Fox, a 20-year-old guardsman, was accidentally shot and killed. *Middle Park Times* (Kremmling), August 31, 1939.

25. *Colorado Labor Advocate* (Denver), August 23, 1939, covers the negotiations ending the strike. Tyler, *Last Water Hole,* p. 122, quotes Ickes.

26. Saunders, sheriff of Larimer County (1932–1935) had been appointed by Johnson to fill the vacancy created by the resignation of James H. Carr as secretary of state in late 1935.

27. Seligson and Bardwell, *Labor-Management Relations*, p. 318, give a table detailing composition of the General Assembly from 1919 to 1959.

28. Taylor, born in Woodford, Illinois, June 19, 1858, was at the time of his death the only member of the House of Representatives born before the Civil War. As chairman of the House Appropriations Committee, he was among the most powerful people in Washington. His career in Colorado went back to 1881, when he served as the first principal of the Leadville High School. See *RMN*, February 23, 1937, August 8, 1939, and September 5, 1941.

29. James F. Wickens, *Colorado in the Great Depression* (New York: Garland Publishing, 1979), p. 397, quoting *RMN*, October 23, 1944; Bill Hosokowa, *Nisei: The Quiet Americans, The Story of a People, With a New Afterword* (Niwot: University Press of Colorado, 1992), pp. 225–226.

30. *RMN*, November 1, 1940.

31. John Gunther, *Inside U.S.A.* (New York: Harper and Brothers, 1947), p. 148.

32. Gunther, *Inside U.S.A.*, pp. 148, 220–221.

33. Thomas J. Noel, *Growing Through History With Colorado: The Colorado National Banks, The First 125 Years, 1862–1987* (Denver: Colorado National Banks and Colorado Studies Center, University of Colorado at Denver, 1987), pp. 77–85; Richard Lowitt, *The New Deal and the West* (Bloomington: Indiana University Press, 1984), pp. 22, 95–98, 246.

34. Donald C. Reading, "A Statistical Analysis of New Deal Economic Programs in the Forty-Eight States, 1933–1939" (Ph.D. diss., Utah State University, 1972), p. 139, shows that both Virginia and Connecticut, much larger states in terms of population, received, on a per capita basis, much less than Colorado.

35. Lorena Hickok to Harry Hopkins, June 17 and June 24, 1934, in Richard Lowitt and Maurine Beasley, eds., *One Third of a Nation: Lorena Hickok Reports on the Great Depression* (Urbana: University of Illinois Press, 1981), pp. 281, 291.

36. Roy Howard to Claude Boettcher, August 25, 1936, Box 111, Howard Papers.

37. Roy Howard to A. B. Trott, October 6, 1937, Box 123, Howard Papers.

38. Roy Howard to Aubrey A. Graves, June 10–11, 1937, Box 123, Howard Papers; Gunther, *Inside U.S.A.*, p. 222.

39. Aubrey A. Graves to Roy Howard, June 8, 1937, Box 123, Howard Papers.

40. Lowitt, *The New Deal and the West*, p. 96; Sarah Deutsch, *No Separate Refuge: Culture, Class, and Gender on an Anglo-Hispanic Frontier in the American Southwest 1880–1940* (New York: Oxford University Press, 1987), p. 179.

41. Lorena Hickok to Harry Hopkins, June 23, 1934, in Lowitt and Beasley, eds., *One Third of a Nation*, p. 287. Hickok did point out that Hispanic children were bright and noted that their parents' condition was likely due to years of miserable work. Nationally, the New Deal tried to improve the lot of African-Americans. See Anthony J. Badger, *The New Deal: The Depression Years, 1933–1940* (New York: Hill and Wang, 1989), pp. 207–208. For Shriver's remark, see *Colorado Statesman* (Denver), March 7, 1941.

42. John Carroll interview with Stephen J. Leonard, February 27, 1976, in Carroll Papers, Auraria Library, Denver.

43. Tyler, *Last Water Hole*, p. 112.

44. *RMN*, October 13, 1936. See note 1.

45. Gunther, *Inside U.S.A.*, p. 224; *RMN*, February 28, 1993, on Helen Bonfils's $50 million to performing arts in Denver. Among the Boettchers' donations to Colorado was the Governor's Mansion.

46. *Middle Park Times* (Kremmling), September 7, 1939.

47. Clark Secrest, "The Day Clara May Morse Died. Pearl Harbor and One Mother's Heartbreak," *Colorado Heritage* (Autumn 1991): 40.

48. Scamehorn, *Mill and Mine*, pp. 153–160.

49. *RMN*, April 30, 1943, and April 13, 1945.

Bibliography

The items listed below constitute only a small fraction of the material available on the 1930s. James F. Wickens gives an extensive bibliography in his *Colorado in the Great Depression* (1979); Badger, Oehlerts, Schlachter, and Wynar, cited below, are also valuable bibliographical sources.

Books

Allen, Frederick S., et al. *The University of Colorado, 1876–1976.* New York: Harcourt Brace Jovanovich, 1976.

Alleger, C. N. and L. A. Gleyre, comps. *History of the Civilian Conservation Corps in Colorado, Littleton District–Grand Junction District; That the Work of Young America May Be Recorded.* Denver: Press of the Western Newspaper Union, ca. 1936. This well-illustrated and detailed book covers the early years of the CCC. Some of the photographs in it are in the collection of the DPLWHD.

Amole, Gene. *Amole Again.* Denver: Denver Publishing, 1985. Amole, who grew up in Denver in the 1930s, sometimes writes of the decade in his *Rocky Mountain News* column. See also his *Morning* (Denver Publishing, 1983).

Anderson, James C., ed. *Roy Stryker: The Humane Propagandist.* Louisville, Ky.: University of Louisville, 1977.

Arps, Louisa. *Denver in Slices.* Denver: Sage Books, 1959.

Athearn, Robert G. *The Coloradans.* Albuquerque: University of New Mexico Press, 1976. This book devotes 23 pages to the Depression. Other texts tend to do less.

————. *The Denver and Rio Grande Western Railroad: Rebel of the Rockies.* Lincoln: University of Nebraska Press, 1977. This well-written and well-researched study devotes nearly 30 pages to the 1930s.

————. *The Mythic West in Twentieth-Century America.* Lawrence: University Press of Kansas, 1986. The University Press of Kansas, which has published such first-rate books as Rhonda Levine's *Class Struggle and the New Deal* (1988) and James Sherow's *Watering the Valley* (1990), deserves much credit for advancing western and New Deal studies.

Badger, Anthony J. *The New Deal: The Depression Years, 1933–1940.* New York: Hill and Wang, 1989. Excellent bibliographical essay on New Deal nationally, pp. 313–364. Includes material on blacks, women, Mexican-Americans.

Baldwin, Sidney. *Poverty and Politics: The Rise and Decline of the Farm Security Administration.* Chapel Hill: University of North Carolina Press, 1968.

Barker, Bill, and Jackie Lewin. *Denver! An Insider's Look at the High, Wide and Handsome City.* Garden City, N.Y.: Doubleday, 1972.

Batschelet, Ralph J. *The Flick and I.* Smithtown, N.Y.: Exposition Press, ca. 1981. Slim volume that tells of author's career managing Colorado movie theaters.

Bauman, John F., and Thomas H. Coode. *In the Eye of the Great Depression: New Deal Reporters and the Agony of the American People.* De Kalb: Northern Illinois Press, 1988.

Bean, Geraldine B. *Charles Boettcher: A Study in Pioneer Western Enterprise.* Boulder, Colo.: Westview Press, 1976.

Bluemel, Elinor. *The Golden Opportunity: The Story of the Unique Emily Griffith Opportunity School of Denver.* Boulder, Colo.: Johnson Publishing, 1965.

Bonnifield, Paul. *The Dust Bowl: Men, Dirt, and Depression.* Albuquerque: University of New Mexico Press, 1979. Bonnifield celebrates the triumph of people over adversity. For a somewhat different point of view, see James Sherow.

Braeman, John, et al., eds. *The New Deal: The State and Local Levels.* Columbus: Ohio State University Press, 1975. Contains a chapter by James Wickens, the best short summary of the New Deal in Colorado available.

Breck, Allen Dupont. *From the Rockies to the World: A Companion to the History of the University of Denver, 1864–1989.* Denver: University of Denver, 1989.

Brennan, John A. *Silver and the First New Deal.* Reno: University of Nevada Press, 1969.

Buchholtz, C. W. *Rocky Mountain National Park: A History.* Boulder: Colorado Associated University Press, 1983.

Burns, Arthur E., and Edward A. Williams *Federal Work, Security, and Relief Programs.* New York: DaCapo Press, 1941; reprint 1971. A good short summary of progams that includes useful tables.

Burns, James MacGregor. *Roosevelt: The Lion and the Fox.* New York: Harcourt, Brace and World, 1956.

Burroughs, John R. *Steamboat in the Rockies.* Fort Collins, Colo.: The Old Army Press, 1974.

Carpenter, Farrington R. *Confessions of a Maverick.* Denver: Colorado Historical Society, 1984. Carpenter covers his involvement with Harold Ickes.

Casey, Lee T., ed. *Denver Murders.* New York: Duell, Sloan and Pearce, 1945.

Cassells, E. Steve. *The Archaeology of Colorado.* Boulder, Colo.: Johnson Books, 1983.

Colorado Legislative Council. *Presidents and Speakers of the Colorado General Assembly: A Biographical Portrait From 1876.* Denver: Eastwood Printing, 1980.

Colorado Press Association, comp. *Who's Who in Colorado.* Boulder: Extension Division, University of Colorado, ca. 1938.

Colorado Springs Fine Arts Center. *Pikes Peak Vision: The Broadmoor Art Academy 1919–1945.* Colorado Springs, Colo.: Colorado Springs Fine Arts Center, 1989. Includes biographical information on many artists.

Colorado State Planning Commission. *Colorado: A Guide to the Highest State.* Denver: Colorado State Planning Commission, 1941, reprinted in 1987 by University Press of Kansas as *The WPA Guide to 1930s Colorado,* with a new introduction by Thomas J. Noel. The *Guide* is a gold mine of information, much relating to the 1930s.

Colorado State Planning Commission. *Year Book of the State of Colorado.* Denver: Colorado State Planning Commission, various dates. Full of statistics, the year books are basic, if sometimes boring, reading on the 1930s. At the start of the decade they were issued annually, but then shifted to a bi-annual schedule. Researchers should be aware that agricultural statistics are sometimes included in separate volumes.

Congdon, Don, ed. *The Thirties: A Time to Remember.* New York: Simon and Schuster, 1962.

Cook, Bruce. *Dalton Trumbo.* New York: Charles Scribner's Sons, 1977.

Curtis, James. *Mind's Eye, Mind's Truth: FSA Photography Reconsidered.* Philadelphia, Pa.: Temple University Press, 1989.

Deutsch, Sarah. *No Separate Refuge: Culture, Class, and Gender on an Anglo-Hispanic Frontier in the American Southwest 1880–1940.* New York: Oxford University Press, 1987. An important book with considerable material on Colorado.

Dixon, Penelope. *Photographers of the Farm Security Administration: An Annotated Bibliography, 1930–1980.* New York: Garland Publishing, 1983. More than 200 pages of bibliography, plus short biographical sketches of major FSA photographers.

Dodds, Joanne. *Pueblo: A Pictorial History.* Norfolk, Va.: Donning, 1982.

Donnelly, Thomas C., ed. *Rocky Mountain Politics.* Albuquerque: University of New Mexico Press, 1940.

Dorsett, Lyle W., and Michael McCarthy. *The Queen City: A History of Denver.* Boulder, Colo.: Pruett Publishing, 1986. Chapters 7 and 8 give detailed accounts of the 1930s in Denver, with considerable attention to George Cranmer.

Dubofsky, Melvin, ed. *The New Deal: Conflicting Interpretations and Shifting Perspectives.* New York: Garland Publishing, 1992.

Ellis, Anne. *The Life of an Ordinary Woman.* Lincoln: University of Nebraska Press, 1929; reprint 1980. Includes a useful introduction by Elliot West.

Ellis, Richard N., and Duane A. Smith. *Colorado: A History in Photographs.* Niwot: University Press of Colorado, 1991.

Fay, Abbott. *Famous Coloradans: 124 People Who Have Gained Nationwide Fame.* Paonia, Colo.: Mountaintop Books, 1990. Among the sketches of Coloradans are a number pertaining to the 1930s, including pieces on Arthur Carhart, Glenn Miller, George Morrison, Ted Mack, Damon Runyon, H. Allen Smith, William McLeod Raine, Lowell Thomas, and Dalton Trumbo.

————. *Mountain Academia: A History of Western State College of Colorado.* Boulder Colo.: Pruett Press, 1968.

————. *Ski Tracks in the Rockies: A Century of Colorado Skiing.* Louisville, Colo.: Cordillera Press, 1984.

Ferril, Thomas H. *Westering.* New Haven, Conn.: Yale University Press, 1934.

Fleischhauer, Carl, and Beverly W. Brannan, eds. *Documenting America: 1935–1943.* Berkeley: University of California Press, 1988. Among the best of the many FSA books, *Documenting America* has an excellent description of the FSA-OWI collection at the Library of Congress.

Follansbee, Robert. *Floods in Colorado.* Washington, D.C.: Government Printing Office, 1948.

Foster, Mark S. *The Denver Bears: From Sandlots to Sellouts.* Boulder, Colo.: Pruett Publishing, 1983.

————. *Henry M. Porter: Rocky Mountain Empire Builder.* Niwot: University Press of Colorado, 1991.

Ganzel, Bill. *Dust Bowl Descent.* Lincoln: University of Nebraska Press, 1984. Includes FSA photographs juxtaposed with more recent photos taken in the same area, often of the same people.

Garnsey, Morris E. *America's New Frontier: The Mountain West.* New York: Alfred A. Knopf, 1950.

Goodstein, Phil. *The Seamy Side of Denver.* Denver: New Social Publications, 1993. This work examines the Wettengel case and touches on gambling.

————. *South Denver Saga.* Denver: New Social Publications, 1991.

Greenbaum, Fred. *Fighting Progressive: A Biography of Edward P. Costigan.* Washington, D.C.: Public Affairs Press, 1971.

Guimond, James. *American Photography and the American Dream.* Chapel Hill: University of North Carolina Press, 1991.

Gunther, John. *Inside U.S.A.* New York: Harper and Brothers, 1947.

Gurtler, Jack, and Corinne Hunt. *The Elitch Gardens Story.* Boulder, Colo.: Rocky Mountain Writers Guild, 1982.

Hafen, LeRoy R., ed. *Colorado and Its People.* 4 vols. New York: Lewis Historical Publishing, 1948.

Harrison, Henry, ed. *Colorado Poets.* New York: Henry Harrison, 1935.

Hendrickson, Paul. *Looking for the Light: The Hidden Life and Art of Marion Post Wolcott.* New York: Alfred A. Knopf, 1992.

Hoffman, Abraham. *Unwanted Mexican Americans in the Great Depression: Repatriation Pressures, 1929–1939.* Tucson: University of Arizona Press, 1974.

Hosokowa, Dill. *Thunder in the Rockies: The Incredible Denver Post.* New York: William Morrow, 1976. Hosokowa provides a first-rate newspaper history

Hurley, F. Jack. *Portrait of a Decade: Roy Stryker and the Development of Documentary Photography in the Thirties.* Baton Rouge: Louisiana State University Press, 1972. One of the best-written and most complete accounts of Stryker and the FSA.

———. *Russell Lee, Photographer.* Dobbs Ferry, N.Y.: Morgan and Morgan, 1978.

Hurt, R. Douglas. *The Dust Bowl: An Agricultural and Social History.* Chicago: Nelson-Hall, 1981.

Huthmacher, J. Joseph, and Warren I. Susman, eds. *Herbert Hoover and the Crisis of American Capitalism.* Cambridge, Mass.: Schenkman Publishing, 1973. This book provides thoughtful essays that plumb Hoover.

Jameson, Elizabeth. *Building Colorado: The United Brotherhood of Carpenters and Joiners of America in the Centennial State.* Denver: Egan Printing, 1984.

Johnson, J. Percy H., ed. *N. W. Ayer and Son's Directory of Newspapers and Periodicals . . . 1940.* Philadelphia, Pa.: N. W. Ayer and Son, 1940.

Johnson, Vance. *Heaven's Tableland: The Dust Bowl Story.* New York: Farrar, Straus, 1947. Well-written laudatory account of federal efforts to save land.

Knight, Harold V. *Working in Colorado: A Brief History of the Colorado Labor Movement.* Boulder: University of Colorado Center for Labor Education and Research, 1971.

Lamm, Richard D., and Duane A. Smith. *Pioneers and Politicians: 10 Colorado Governors in Profile.* Boulder, Colo.: Pruett Publishing, 1984. Among the biographies is one of Edwin C. Johnson.

Lee, Everett S., et al. *Population Redistribution and Economic Growth, United States 1870–1950: I, Methodological Considerations and Reference Tables.* Philadelphia, Pa.: The American Philosophical Society, 1957.

Leonard, Stephen J., and Thomas J. Noel. *Denver: Mining Camp to Metropolis.* Niwot: University Press of Colorado, 1990. Includes a chapter on the Depression.

Leuchtenburg, William E. *Franklin D. Roosevelt and the New Deal, 1932–1940.* New York: Harper and Row, 1963. Long the standard summary of the New Deal.

———. *The Perils of Prosperity, 1914–1932.* Chicago: University of Chicago Press, 1958. Gives a succinct account of the 1920s.

Levine, Rhonda F. *Class Struggle and the New Deal: Industrial Labor, Industrial Capital, and the State.* Lawrence: University Press of Kansas, 1988.

Limerick, Patricia N. *The Legacy of Conquest: The Unbroken Past of the American West.* New York: W. W. Norton, 1987.

Lowitt, Richard. *The New Deal and the West.* Bloomington: Indiana University Press, 1984. Presents a significant synthesis, drawing together previously scattered information. This is a "must" book for anyone studying the New Deal's regional impact.

Lowitt, Richard, and Maurine Beasley, eds. *One Third of a Nation: Lorena Hickok Reports on the Great Depression.* Urbana: University of Illinois Press, 1981. Hickok's breezy style and righteous indignation make this a joy to read.

Lyons, Thomas, ed. *1930 Employment 1980: Humanistic Perspectives on the Civilian Conservation Corps in Colorado.* Boulder: Colorado Humanities Program, ca. 1980. Includes interviews with former CCCers. A pamphlet derived from this work is available at DPLWHD.

Mangione, Jerre G. *The Dream and the Deal: The Federal Writer's Project, 1935–1943.* Philadelphia: University of Pennsylvania Press, 1983.

McAdow, Beryl. *From Crested Peaks: The Story of Adams State College of Colorado.* Denver: Big Mountain Press, 1961.

McDonald, William F. *Federal Relief Administration and the Arts*. Columbus: Ohio State University Press, 1969. In more than 850 pages, McDonald has probably written the most words, although not the last, on art in the New Deal.

McGiffert, Michael. *The Higher Learning in Colorado: An Historical Study, 1860–1940*. Denver: Sage Books, 1964.

Monnett, John H., and Michael McCarthy. *Colorado Profiles: Men and Women Who Shaped the Centennial State*. Evergreen, Colo.: Cordillera Press, 1987. Includes essays on Josephine Roche and Wayne Aspinall.

Moore, O. Otto. *Mile High Harbor*. Denver: Associated Publishers, 1947. Moore, a major force in the pension movement, remained a power in Colorado politics for many years.

Morgan, David P. *Diesels West! The Evolution of Power on the Burlington*. Milwaukee, Wis.: Kalmbach Publishing, 1963.

Naylor, Colin, ed. *Contemporary Photographers*. Chicago: St. James Press, 1988. A useful research tool for biographies of photographers.

Noel, Thomas J. *Colorado Catholicism and the Archdiocese of Denver, 1857–1989*. Niwot: University Press of Colorado, 1989.

———. *Growing Through History With Colorado: The Colorado National Banks, The First 125 Years, 1862–1987*. Denver: Colorado National Banks and the Colorado Studies Center, University of Colorado at Denver, 1987.

Nora Eccles Harrison Museum of Art. *Life and Land: The Farm Security Administration Photographers in Utah, 1936–1941*. Logan: Utah State University Press, 1988. Notes that Russell Lee's Utah photographs show prosperity.

Nye, Russell. *The Unembarassed Muse: The Popular Arts in America*. New York: The Dial Press, 1970.

Oehlerts, Donald E., comp. *Guide to Colorado Newspapers, 1859–1963*. Denver: Bibliographical Center for Research, Rocky Mountain Region, 1964. Lists thousands of Colorado newspapers and gives locations of extant copies. The updated version at CHS's Stephen Hart Library should be consulted.

Palmer, Frank. *Chameleon on Plaid: A Tale of Two Lives*. Holland, Mich.: n.p., 1973.

Park, Marlene, and Gerald E. Markowitz. *Post Offices and Public Art in the New Deal*. Philadelphia, Pa.: Temple University Press, 1984. Useful for information on such artists as Boardman Robinson, Frank Mechau, Ethel Magafan, and Jeanne Magafan.

Patterson, James T. *Congressional Conservatism and the New Deal: The Growth of the Conservative Coalition in Congress, 1933–1939*. Lexington: University of Kentucky Press, 1967.

———. *The New Deal and the States: Federalism in Transition*. Princeton, N.J.: Princeton University Press, 1969.

Pellet, Betty, and Alexander Kline. *That Pellet Woman*. New York: Stein and Day, 1965.

Perkin, Robert. *The First Hundred Years: An Informal History of Denver and the Rocky Mountain News*. Garden City, N.Y.: Doubleday, 1959. Remains among the best books on Denver.

Pulcipher, Robert S., ed. *The Pioneer Western Bank — First of Denver: 1860–1980*. Denver: First Interstate Bank, 1984.

Reid, J. Juan. *Colorado College: The First Century, 1874–1974*. Colorado Springs: The Colorado College, 1979.

Riesler, Mark. *By the Sweat of Their Brow: Mexican Immigrant Labor in the United States, 1900–1940*. Westport, Conn.: Greenwood Press, 1976.

Risley, James H. *How It Grew: A History of the Pueblo Public Schools*. Denver: University of Denver Press, 1953.

Robinson, Joyce E., and Dale Vivirito, comps. *Colorado Springs Fine Arts Center: A History and Selections for the Permanent Collections*. Colorado Springs, Colo.: Colorado Springs Fine Arts Center, 1986.

Rogerson, Robert B. *The Last of the Rogersons: 95 Years of Colorado Pioneer History — Horse, Cattle, and Sheep Lore.* No imprint. In CHS.

Rothstein, Arthur. *Arthur Rothstein: Words and Pictures.* New York: American Photographic Book Publishing, 1979.

Salmond, John A. *The Civilian Conservation Corps, 1933–1942: A New Deal Case Study.* Durham, N.C.: Duke University Press, 1967.

Scamehorn, H. Lee. *Mill and Mine: The CF&I in the Twentieth Century.* Lincoln: University of Nebraska Press, 1992.

Schlachter, Gail, ed. *The Great Depression: A Historical Bibliography.* Santa Barbara, Calif.: ABC–Clio Information Services, 1984. Provides information on nearly 1,000 scholarly articles published between 1973 and 1982.

Seligson, Harry, and George E. Bardwell. *Labor-Management Relations in Colorado.* Denver: Sage Books, 1961.

Sherow, James Earl. *Watering the Valley: Development Along the High Plains Arkansas River, 1870–1950.* Lawrence: University Press of Kansas, 1990. Important, well-researched analysis.

Sitkoff, Harvard. *Fifty Years Later: The New Deal Evaluated.* Philadelphia, Pa.: Temple University Press, 1985.

Smith, H. Allen. *The Life and Legend of Gene Fowler.* New York: William Morrow, 1977.

Smith, Phyllis. *Once a Coal Miner: The Story of Colorado's Northern Coal Field.* Boulder, Colo.: Pruett Publishing, 1989.

Sprague, Marshall. *Newport in the Rockies: The Life and Good Times of Colorado Springs.* Chicago: The Swallow Press, 1971.

Stansell, Harold. *Regis: On the Crest of the West.* Denver: Regis Educational Corporation, 1977.

Steinel, Alvin T. *History of Agriculture in Colorado.* Fort Collins, Colo.: Colorado State Board of Agriculture, 1926.

Stryker, Roy Emerson, and Nancy Wood. *In This Proud Land: America 1935–1943 as Seen in the FSA Photographs.* Greenwich, Conn.: New York Graphic Society, 1973.

Susman, Warren I. *Culture as History: The Transformation of American Society in the Twentieth Century.* New York: Pantheon Books, 1984. Contains an excellent chapter on culture in the 1930s.

Sykes, Hope Williams. *Second Hoeing.* New York: Putnam, 1935.

Taylor, Paul S. *Mexican Labor in the United States: Volume I.* Berkeley: University of California Press, 1930; reprint New York: Arno Press, 1970.

Taylor, Ralph. *A Guide to Historic Pueblo.* Pueblo, Colo.: Pueblo Metropolitan Museum, 1978.

Trumbo, Dalton. *Eclipse.* London: Lovat Dickson and Thompson, 1935. One story says that the original plates for the book were destroyed in a World War II German bombing raid on London, another that someone in Grand Junction bought them and destroyed them.

———. *The Remarkable Andrew: Being the Chronicle of a Literal Man.* Philadelphia, Pa.: J. B. Lippincott, 1941.

Turner, Wallace B. *Colorado Woman's College: The First Seventy-Five Years.* Boulder, Colo.: Johnson Publishing, 1962.

Tyler, Daniel. *The Last Water Hole in the West: The Colorado–Big Thompson Project and the Northern Colorado Water Conservancy District.* Niwot: University Press of Colorado, 1992. This massive work of careful research covers one of the West's most important water projects.

U.S. Department of Agriculture and Colorado State Planning Commission. *Colorado Agricultural Statistics, 1940.* Denver: Colorado State Planning Commission, ca. 1941.

U.S. Department of Agriculture, Weather Bureau. *Climatological Data.* Monthly bulletins organized by states cover weather in detail.

U.S. Department of Commerce, Census Bureau. *Fifteenth Census of the United States: 1930.* This multi-volume monster is crammed with data, as is the *Sixteenth Census of the United States: 1940.* It is often easier for researchers to use the excellent and well-indexed *Year Book of the State of Colorado.*

Vandenbusche, Duane, and Duane A. Smith. *A Land Alone: Colorado's Western Slope.* Boulder, Colo.: Pruett Publishing, 1981.

Wahlberg, Edgar M. *Voices in the Darkness: A Memoir.* Boulder, Colo.: Roberts Rinehart, 1983.

Wells, Dale. *The Logan County Ledger* [edited by Nell Brown Probst]. Logan County Historical Society, 1976. This, like many other county histories, helps provide the flavor of the 1930s.

Wickens, James F. *Colorado in the Great Depression.* New York: Garland Publishing, 1979. Wickens's Ph.D. dissertation turned into a book is a superb piece of historical research. Absolutely essential reading for anyone wishing to understand the 1930s in Colorado.

Wolle, Muriel Sibell. *Stampede to Timberline: The Ghost Towns and Mining Camps of Colorado.* Chicago: The Swallow Press, 1974.

Wood, Nancy C. *Heartland New Mexico: Photographs From the Farm Security Administration, 1935–1943.* Albuquerque: University of New Mexico Press, 1989.

Worster, Donald. *Dust Bowl: The Southern Plains in the 1930s.* New York: Oxford University Press, 1979. Worthy of the press that published it, Worster's study calls into question some of the facilely accepted "truths" about the New Deal's response to the drought.

Wynar, Bohdan S., and Roberta J. Depp, eds. *Colorado Bibliography.* Littleton, Colo.: Libraries Unlimited, 1980. Wynar provides a categorized list of 9,181 items on Colorado.

Articles

The following list includes only major articles. Others from magazines such as *Time* and *The Nation* are cited in the notes.

Arrington, Leonard J. "The Sagebrush Resurrection: New Deal Expenditures in Western States, 1933–1939." *Pacific Historical Review* 52 (February 1983): 1–16.

Bailey, James Michael. "Notes of Turmoil: Sixty Years of Denver's Symphony Orchestras." *Colorado Heritage* (Autumn 1992): 33–47.

Chapman, Edward N. "The Menace to Life and Health From Improper Sewage Disposal in Colorado." *Colorado Municipalities* 10 (February 1934): 99–105.

Hornbein, Marjorie. "For the Public Good: The Strange Case of Colorado's Eavesdroppers." *Colorado Heritage* 3 (1985): 33–38.

———. "Josephine Roche: Social Worker and Coal Mine Operator." *The Colorado Magazine* 53 (Summer 1976): 243–260.

Howe, B. V. "Progress in Sewage Treatment in Colorado." *Colorado Municipalities* 16 (November 1940): 82–87.

Kerbey, McFall. "Colorado, a Barrier That Became a Goal." *The National Geographic* 62 (July 1932): 1–63.

Mergen, Bernard. "Denver and the War on Unemployment." *The Colorado Magazine* 47 (Fall 1970): 326–337.

Motian-Meadows, Mary. "Western Visions: Colorado's New Deal Post Office Murals." *Colorado Heritage* (Autumn 1991): 15–35.

Reese, Joan. "Two Gentlemen of Note: George Morrison, Paul Whiteman, and Their Jazz." *Colorado Heritage* 2 (1986): 2–13.

Secrest, Clark. "The Day Clara May Morse Died: Pearl Harbor and One Mother's Heartbreak." *Colorado Heritage* (Autumn 1991): 36–44.

Stagner, Mayme. "Resettlement — A Story of Faith and Courage, a Tape Recording Made by Mrs. Mayme (Bert) Stagner, April 8, 1981." *San Luis Valley Historian* 21, no. 2 (1989): 5–15.

Wickens, James F. "Tightening the Colorado Purse Strings." *The Colorado Magazine* 46 (Fall 1969): 271–286.

Unpublished Works

Bisbing, Leonard J. "Family Relief in Denver, 1928–1939." Master's thesis, University of Denver, 1939.

Brockway, Ronald S. "Edward P. Costigan: A Study of a Progressive and the New Deal." Ph.D. diss., University of Colorado at Boulder, 1974.

Bruner, Ronald I. "New Deal Art Works in Colorado, Kansas and Nebraska." Master's thesis, University of Denver, 1980.

Chait, Manuel L. "The Development of American Communism With Particular Emphasis on Colorado." Master's thesis, University of Denver, 1959.

Girvan, Robert B. "Carle Whitehead and the Socialist Party in Colorado, 1930–1955." Master's thesis, University of Denver, 1967.

Grundman, Adolph. "Denver: The Basketball Capital of the United States." Paper delivered at the North American Society for Sport History, May 18, 1990, Banff, Canada.

Harper, Thomas. "The Development of a High Plains Community: A History of Baca County." Master's thesis, University of Denver, 1967.

Hutchinson, Dorothy D. "History of Colorado's Private Relief Agencies." Master's thesis, University of Denver, 1944.

Kline, Hebron C. "A History of the Denver Theater During the Depression Era." Ph.D. diss., University of Denver, 1963.

McCarthy, Patrick F. "Big Ed Johnson of Colorado — A Political Portrait." Master's thesis, University of Colorado at Boulder, 1958.

Mills, James E., "A History of Brush, Colorado." Master's thesis, University of Colorado at Boulder, 1964.

Parham, Robert B. "The Civilian Conservation Corps in Colorado." Master's thesis, University of Colorado at Boulder, 1981.

Reading, Donald C. "A Statistical Analysis of New Deal Economic Programs in the Forty-Eight States, 1933–1939." Ph.D. diss., Utah State University, 1972. This provides a most useful listing of scores of programs and what they spent in absolute and per capita terms.

Siert, Gordon M. "An Historical Study of the Great Western Sugar Company" Master's thesis, University of Denver, 1962.

Sims, Robert C. "Colorado and the Great Depression: Business Thought in a Time of Crisis." Ph.D. diss., University of Colorado at Boulder, 1970.

Slatkin, Ellen A. "A History of the Response of the Colorado State Federation of Labor to the Great Depression, 1929–1940." Master's thesis, University of Denver, 1984.

Wilson, Grace E. "The History and Development of the Denver Bureau of Public Welfare." Master's thesis, University of Denver, 1938.

Manuscript Collections

Papers of Individuals, Businesses, and Organizations

William H. Adams Papers, CSA.

Charles Boettcher Papers, CHS.

John A. Carroll Papers, Auraria Library (Denver).

Edward P. Costigan Papers, University of Colorado at Boulder.

Louise Hill Papers, CHS.

Roy Howard Papers, Library of Congress.

Edwin C. Johnson Papers, CSA.

Edward Keating Papers, University of Colorado at Boulder.

Lawrence Lewis Papers, CHS.

NAACP (National Association for the Advancement of Colored People) Papers, Library of Congress.

National Socialist Labor Party Papers, CHS.

Northern Colorado Coals, Inc., Papers, CHS.

Wallis Reef Papers, DPLWHD.

Morrison Shafroth Papers, DPLWHD.

Benjamin F. Stapleton Papers, CHS.

Roy E. Stryker Papers, microfilm copy, Library of Congress.

William Sweet Papers, CHS.

Charles Thomas Papers, CHS.

Edgar Wahlberg Papers, Auraria Library (Denver).

U.S. Government Agencies by Record Group

All in National Archives, Washington, D.C., unless indicated as being at the National Archives in Denver (NARS, Denver Branch).

RG35, Civilian Conservation Corps.

RG69, Civil Works Administration.

RG69, Federal Emergency Relief Administration.

RG69, Works Progess Administration.

RG75, Bureau of Indian Affairs, Consolidated Ute Agency, Decimal Files, 1932–1940, NARS, Denver Branch.

RG96, Farmers Home Administration, NARS, Denver Branch.

RG119, National Youth Administration.

RG121, Public Buildings Service, Construction Management Division, NARS, Denver Branch.

RG121, Records Concerning Federal Art Activities, commonly called the Embellishment File.

RG135, Public Works Administration.

Interviews

Wayne Aspinall with David McComb, June 11, 1974, CHS.

Fred M. Betz, Sr., with David McComb, November 1, 1974, CHS.

Rev. John F. Brady, S. J., with Stephen J. Leonard, July 5, 1992.

Anna Carlson with Stephen J. Leonard, November 30, 1991.

George Carlson with David McComb, March 20, 1975, CHS.

Farrington Carpenter with Vi Ward, May 21, 1959, CHS.

Hatfield Chilson with David McComb, April 4, 1975, CHS.

Phil Goodstein with Stephen J. Leonard, March 8, 1993.

Amer Lehman with David McComb, January 25, 1974, CHS.

Margaret Reef with Helen Christy, October 1, 1979, DPLWHD.

King Shwayder with David McComb, April 17 and May 10, 1974, CHS.

Rev. James Sunderland, S. J., with Stephen J. Leonard, July 5, 1992.

Charles Tribble with Helen Christy, September 24, 1979, DPLWHD.

William Thayer Tutt with David McComb, June 12, 1975, CHS.

Donald D. Wall with Stephen J. Leonard, October 15, 1992.

E. Warren Willard with David McComb, February 20 and February 27, 1975, CHS.

Newspapers

Most newspapers are available on microfilm from the Colorado Historical Society. Some have been clipped and reside in the DPLWHD.

Alma Mining Record

Arriba Record

Aspen Times

Bent County Democrat (Las Animas)

Boulder Daily Camera

Brighton Blade

Cañon City Daily Record

Chaffee County Republican (Buena Vista)

Cheyenne County News (Cheyenne Wells)

Chronicle-News (Trinidad)

Colorado Labor Advocate (Denver)

Colorado Springs Gazette

Colorado Statesman (Denver)

Colorado Transcript (Golden)

County Seat News-Tribune (Kiowa)

Creede Candle

Daily Courier (Alamosa)

Daily Democrat (La Junta)

Daily Sentinel (Grand Junction)

Del Norte Prospector

Democrat-Herald (Springfield)

Denver Catholic Register

The Denver Post

Durango Herald-Democrat

Eastern Colorado Plainsman (Hugo)

Elk Mountain Pilot (Crested Butte)

Florence Daily Citizen

Fort Collins Express-Courier

Fort Morgan County Herald

Fort Morgan Times

Glenwood Post

Greeley Daily Tribune

Gunnison News-Champion

Herald-Democrat (Leadville)

Holly Chieftain

Holyoke Enterprise

Independent (Walsenburg)

Intermountain Jewish News (Denver)

Julesburg Grit-Advocate

La Junta Tribune

Lamar Daily News

Las Animas Leader

Limon Leader

Middle Park Times (Kremmling)

Monte Vista Journal

Montrose Daily Press

New York Herald Tribune

New York Times

Pueblo Chieftain

Pueblo Star-Journal

Pueblo Star-Journal and The Sunday Chieftain

Rocky Ford Daily Gazette-Topic

Rocky Mountain Herald (Denver)

Rocky Mountain News (Denver)

Silverton Standard

South Side Monitor (Denver)

Steamboat Pilot

Sterling Farm Journal

Summit County Journal (Breckenridge)

Walsenburg World

Weld County News (Greeley)

Westerns Nyheter (Denver)

World-Independent (Walsenburg)

Wray Rattler

Acknowledgments

The poet Ezra Pound admonishes the writer to "tell us at least something about the width, depth, and kind of ignorance which is plaguing him and for which he is seeking a cure." My journey into the 1930s began in ignorance the day I was born, late in 1941. It might seem paradoxical — going backward as one goes forward — but it is useful. The past helps us make sense of the present and glimpse the future.

So my thanks begin with my parents and others who sparked my interest in the 1930s. It must include my paternal grandmother, Mary Leonard, who never threw away a rubber band; my maternal grandmother, Katherine Krakow, whose cheerful optimism proved that the Great Depression had not depressed everyone; my father, William K. Leonard, who kept old sales-tax tokens in a cigar box; my mother, Vi Leonard, who told me of Franklin Roosevelt's cruelty to little pigs. My great-aunt Josephine Halley Heimrich also taught me about bygone days, passing on her home remedy for a cough: a mixture of whiskey, lemon juice, and honey. If times were hard, as they sometimes were for her, the luxury of lemon juice could be omitted.

Teachers also kindled my curiosity: the Reverend Harold Stansell, S.J., and Bernard Sheehan at Regis College in Denver; Gene Gressley and Herbert Dieterich at the University of Wyoming; John Niven and Douglass Adair at Claremont Graduate School. To Claremont I owe gratitude for the conference on the 1930s it sponsored in 1968, during which I had the chance to open a door for Rexford Guy Tugwell, one of the architects of the New Deal.

Many others have helped since I began the research, some 17 years ago, that has led to this book. Thomas J. Noel of the University of Colorado at Denver took time from his own work to review and improve mine. So did David Fridtjof Halaas of the Colorado Historical Society and Phil Goodstein of Metropolitan State College. They have all made suggestions and corrections of such value that mere thanks are not sufficient. If I were not a parsimonious child of the Depression, I would take them to lunch.

I should also lay the table for a score or more of librarians, archivists, and historical society administrators. From the Auraria Library, Rutherford Witthus. From the Colorado Historical Society, Anne Wainstein Bond, Patrick Fraker, Robyn Jacobs, Katherine Kane, Rebecca Lintz, Mary Ann McNair, Andrew Masich, Eric Paddock, Stan Oliner, Clark Secrest, Margaret Walsh, David Wetzel, Ann Wyckoff. From the Denver Public Library Western History and other departments, Lisa Backman, Matt Byers, Nancy Chase, Mary Daze, Don Dilley, George DeLucca, Bruce Hanson, Britt Kaur, Augie Mastrogiuseppe, Philip Panum, Mary Ruhland, Kathey Swan, Rose

Ann Taht, Lynn Taylor, Barbara Walton, William Watts, and Kay Wisnia. From the Library of Congress, the staffs of the Manuscript and the Prints and Photographs divisions, particularly Beverly Brannan. From the National Archives in Denver, Joan Howard. From the National Archives in Washington, D. C., the staffs of the Civil Records Section and, in particular, Richard Fusick. The president of the State Historical Society, James E. Hartmann, has been most helpful, as has Eleanor Gehres, head of the Western History Department at the Denver Public Library.

Among the treasures of the Denver Public Library, few rival the massive General Index in the Western History Department. This product of more than a half-century's work, if recreated at current costs, would be worth $2 million or more. An index of an estimated four million entries to articles, books, newspapers, and other material, it is an outstanding contribution to scholarship — a college in itself. Without it scholars would be impaired and devotees of well-researched local history would be impoverished. Without it the Denver Public Library would be a far less splendid institution than it is. All hail to the generations of librarians and Denver taxpayers who have supported, built, and maintained such a superb research tool.

At the University of Colorado at Boulder, I have been well served by the staff of the Norlin Library's Western Historical Collections. In Colorado Springs I have benefited from excellent service at The Colorado College and the Pike's Peak Regional Library. Thanks for similar favors go to Joanne Dodds and Noreen Riffe of the Pueblo Library District and to Richard Ellis of Fort Lewis College. Duane Smith, also of Fort Lewis, must perforce be thanked by everyone studying Colorado's past. Unfortunately the high cost of research at the Colorado State Archives, an interdict on knowledge not of the Archives's making, somewhat limited my use of that important repository. My thanks and good wishes, however, go to the beleaguered staff.

At Metropolitan State College of Denver, I have enjoyed, over the years, the encouragement of many people, including presidents Thomas Brewer and James Palmer, Provost David Williams, vice presidents Stanley Sunderwirth and Curtis Wright, and deans Phillip Boxer, Larry Johnson, and Joan Foster. My friends in the History Department have also contributed: Thomas Altherr has shared his research on baseball, Adolph Grundman has enlightened me on basketball, Donald Wall has told me about 1930s Brighton, Jeremiah Ring is always full of fresh insights, and George Archuleta and Paul Ton have enlightened me. My thanks also to Charles Angeletti, Vincent C. de Baca, Shirley Fredricks, Monys Hagen, Laura McCall, Thomas McInerney, Brooks VanEveren, Peggy Walsh, and Jodi Wetzel.

My colleague Frank Nation deserves a special word because he has patiently listened to me ramble about my research. Mary Nation has also proved a sympathetic auditor, has dug up old court cases, and has shared memories of the 1930s passed on to her by her father, Don Carver. By keeping the History Department running smoothly, Gloria Kennison has relieved me of burdens I imagine only in my nightmares.

Luther Wilson and the staff at the University Press of Colorado merit praise for patience, efficiency, dedication, and good taste in the manuscripts they publish. Thanks to Jody Berman, Terri Eyden, Peter Hammond, Carol Humphrey, Judy Wilson, Deborah Korte, Sarah Whalen, Brooke Graves. The Colorado Endowment for the Humanities provided publication support which, among other things, allowed the reproduction of large numbers of FSA photographs.

The bibliography and notes cite scholars whose work undergirds mine. I thank them all. One stands out: James F. Wickens, author of *Colorado in the Great Depression* (1979). His exhaustive treatment is bedrock reading for anyone wishing to more fully explore the Depression in Colorado. The errors that lurk herein are mine, or my computer's. As I can blame the computer, I will not mind if readers call mistakes to my attention.

This morning as I walked along Montview Boulevard in Denver, I came upon a sculpture of an eagle carved from the remains of a tree. Its creator could have hewn many things from that stump: a gorilla, a toad, a bust of Uncle Sam. By design and perhaps by accident the eagle emerged. So it is with history. The grain and texture of the past, my interests and the questions that nagged me, sheer accident — all conspired to make this book.

My thanks to those people, commonly thought of as "little," who have given substance to this account: Louie Bunelen, a relief recipient; Margaret Reincke, inventor of an improved soup spoon; Eddie Ives, a murderer hanged twice for his crime. My apologies to those, many prominent in their time, I have left out: Denver attorneys Clarence Ireland and William W. Grant; Palisade legislator Wayne Aspinall; Pagosa Springs artist Fred Harman; historians Ann and LeRoy Hafen; paleontologists Conrad Bilgery, S.J., and Jesse D. Figgins; seismologist Armand Forstall, S.J.; welfare director Earl Kouns; poet Clyde Robertson, who, despite the name, was a woman — the list is long. Still others, although briefly mentioned — Charles Armstrong, Homer Bedford, Anne Evans, Helen Fischer, Benjamin Hilliard, Earl Mosley, Margaret Reef, Byron Rogers, J. Foster Sims, Ray Talbot, Alice van Diest — deserve far more attention.

Fortunately history is a more durable medium in which to work than wood. The eagle will probably be the only thing carved from the tree. The story of the 1930s will continually be reborn and reshaped, likely with a different cast of characters each time, as other historians seek to cure their ignorance and mine.

S. J. L.
Denver, Colorado
March 24, 1993
Year 60 of the New Deal
Sunny, 70 degrees

Index